· JUDGMENT, DECISION, AND CHOICE ·

JUDGMENT, DECISION, AND CHOICE

A COGNITIVE / BEHAVIORAL SYNTHESIS

HOWARD RACHLIN

W. H. FREEMAN AND COMPANY / NEW YORK

Cover image: Picasso, Pablo. *The Studio*. 1927–1928. Oil on canvas, 59″ x 7′7″.
Collection, The Museum of Modern Art, New York. Gift of Walter P. Chrysler, Jr.
Photograph © 1989 The Museum of Modern Art, New York.

Library of Congress Cataloging-in-Publication Data:
Rachlin, Howard, 1935—
    Judgment, decision, and choice: a cognitive/behavioral
    synthesis/Howard Rachlin
        p.   cm.——(A Series of books in psychology)
    Bibliography: p.
    Includes index.
    ISBN 0-7167-1990-8
    1. Decision-making.   2 Choice (Psychology)   3. Psychology,
Comparative.   I. Title.   II. Series.
BF448.R33 1988   88-16329
153.8′3——dc19   CIP

701 2 4785

Printed in the United States of America

1 2 3 4 5 6 7 8 9 0 VB 7 6 5 4 3 2 1 0 8 9

To
NAHID AND LEILA

CONTENTS

PREFACE

ATTEMPTS TO RECONCILE cognitive research on human judgment and decision making with behavioral research on animal (including human) choice are not new. Tolman (1938) and Brunzwik (1943, 1952), as members of the logical positivist, unity-of-science movement, assumed that cognitivism and behaviorism would develop together. Tolman argued that the explanation of the behavior of a rat at a choice point in a maze would lead to the explanation of thought in general. Brunzwik did not hesitate to intermingle reports of results of animal and human choice experiments. Of course, a lot has happened in psychology in the last half century, especially the development of research methodology. This book attempts to recast Tolman's and Brunzwik's project of reconciliation in the light of intervening developments.

However, the present approach differs from that of Tolman and Brunzwik in that it is not positivistic; it does not start from a single, unchallengeable set of facts from which everything else can be derived. To use a currently fashionable term, the present approach is *hermeneutic*. It takes an historical, contextual view of method and theory in two apparently opposed areas, juxtaposes them and tries to construct a coherent framework for them in which each research program can be seen as background to the other.

There are several reasons why this is a textbook rather than a monograph. First, because cognitive and behavioral psychology are currently at loggerheads, researchers in one area are often completely unfamiliar with the methodology, theory, and even vocabulary of the other. Material that one reader may skim another will have to learn. Second, by presenting the material in a form that undergraduates can understand (following Jerome Bruner's dictum that no area of human knowledge is too complicated to be understood at some level by even the youngest child), I hoped to avoid pointless disputation. A person has to be convinced that both sides of an argument are worth knowing before he or she will spend the time and effort required to learn them. This cannot be done when one side is held to be trivial or pointless or vacuous. The temptation to apply such labels, so hard to resist and so rarely resisted in modern psychology, is less in a text than in a monograph. I hope that the balance as well as the clarity and coherence required by the textbook format will make up for lack of exhaustive detail.

TO TEACHERS AND STUDENTS

Both undergraduate and graduate courses on human learning, animal learning, and cognition do not adequately cover the fields of judgment, decision, and choice. Although theoretical and experimental studies of judgment, decision, and choice are currently at the forefront of their respective fields, these areas are covered only peripherally and at the very end of textbooks on learning and cognition. Studies of decision and choice, when included at all in these texts, are poorly integrated with other material.

It is not entirely clear how judgment, decision, and choice studies became isolated from other material in the fields of human and animal learning and cognition, but the following points may have something to do with the problem:

1. Understanding of current work in both human decision making and animal choice seems to require mathematical sophistica-

tion beyond the capacity of many undergraduate psychology majors.

2. Human judgment and decision and animal choice seem unrelated to each other (as well as to other areas in their respective domains).

3. It is not clear how the findings in judgment, decision, and choice pertain to the more general concerns of psychologists. Human decision making seems to be directed at business and economics; animal choice may explain foraging behavior of animals but hardly seems applicable to human behavior at all.

4. Traditionally, decision and choice in psychology have been subsumed under the apparently more general areas of cognition and learning. As studies of decision and choice have broken away from their traditional roots in psychology, they have not found a home elsewhere. Human decision making is often claimed to be part of modern cognitive psychology but seems unrelated to the work on memory, perception, imagery, and problem solving that dominates this field. Theories developed from laboratory studies of animal choice have been applied to foraging behavior of animals in the wild, but psychologists and ethologists studying such behavior are more concerned with the physiological and biological substrates of the animals observed than with theories of behavior as such. Thus, textbooks on animal behavior written from an ethological viewpoint barely cover the psychological work on choice.

This book attempts to deal with these problems as follows:

1. Mathematical aspects of the various theories are presented and analyzed graphically. The book contains many illustrations, most of them graphs. No mathematics beyond algebra is required.

2. The relationship between human and animal (cognitive and behavioral) studies is clarified for the undergraduate student and emphasized again and again.

3. Potential applications in everyday life are stressed. In addition, both human decision theory and animal choice theory are shown to be relevant to economics and business on the one hand and animal foraging on the other.

4. The historical origins of human decision theory and animal choice are traced back to common roots in philosophy and in psychology. Lateral relations of human decision and animal choice to human cognition and animal cognition are also discussed.

In addition, choice itself is defined from a philosophical viewpoint as it relates to questions of freedom, determinism, the applicability of science to human behavior, and the relation between the laboratory and the real world.

The book is intended primarily as a supplement for middle-level undergraduate courses in animal learning, human learning, and cognition. For such courses it could be assigned at the end of the course to give students a broader perspective on the material they have just learned. It could also be assigned at the beginning of upper-level undergraduate and lower-level graduate courses in learning and cognition to give students a broad base for the narrower material they would be investigating. Although the book is intended for psychology students, it can be read and understood by students in economics, business, and the biological sciences. Finally, although the book is intended primarily as a supplement, it can serve as the main text for a course. Such a course might substitute for a course in animal learning in the typical undergraduate psychology curriculum.

A NOTE ON COGNITIVISM AND BEHAVIORISM

I hope to convince readers that cognitivism and behaviorism are entirely compatible ways to view the human mind — compatible not only in the passive sense that nothing seen from one of these viewpoints can constitute evidence against the other, but also in the more active sense that what is learned from one viewpoint may enhance and enrich what is learned from the other.

To see what I mean, imagine that you and I go to the movies together and see Lawrence Olivier in *Richard III*. Let us assume (probably contrary to fact) that Shakespeare's play is historically accurate, especially in portraying the psychological aspects of the protagonist; thus the resentment (say) so powerfully expressed by Olivier was an emotion actually felt by Richard III. Suppose we further agree that however great an actor is (even if he were a "method" actor, which Olivier is not), there must be some difference between the thoughts and emotions of a real person (Richard III) living through a series of events and an actor (Olivier) behaving as though he were living through those events. What is the nature of that difference?

To a cognitivist, the difference between resentment as precisely portrayed by Olivier and as actually felt by Richard III is a difference between their internal states. Richard III's thoughts and emotions must have been more spontaneous and more deeply felt; Olivier's, more thought out and less deep. Cognitive psychology as a science aims to discover the mechanisms underlying spontaneity and depth (among other qualities) of emotions and thoughts. The difference between Olivier's resentment and Richard III's resentment must lie in the operation of those mechanisms; they form the *cognitive context* of the movie. Olivier and Richard III may have behaved identically during the events portrayed in the movie, but the cognitive contexts of their acts must have differed.

To a behaviorist, resentment as portrayed by Olivier resembles that actually felt by Richard III by virtue of common behavior during a brief period (the duration of the events portrayed in the movie). The emotions felt by the two men differ, however, by virtue of their differing behavior at other times and places. Richard III's resentment was genuine, from a behavioral viewpoint, not because it had one internal origin rather than another, but because it was (presumably) consistently exhibited from morning to night for weeks, months, years. Olivier's resentment (presumably) vanished once the cameras were turned off. Interactions with other people and things (with the environment) outside of a given setting constitute the *behavioral context* of that setting. It is to the behavioral context of the movie that the behaviorist would look for spontaneity and depth of resentment as actually felt by Olivier and Richard III.

It should be obvious that the cognitive and behavioral viewpoints are each incomplete. On the one hand, no difference in cognitive context would be meaningful unless it resulted in behavioral differences. On the other hand, it is impossible for most of us to conceive of differences in the behavioral context of two (perhaps identical) actions unaccompanied by differences in cognitive context. Surely the study of one sort of context must throw light on the other.

In this book, which includes many other illustrations of the above sort, I have attempted to give equal weight to both viewpoints. However, I have assumed that the folk psychology of everyday life is much closer to the cognitive than to the behavioral viewpoint. It was therefore necessary to spend more time explaining behavioral versions of events ordinarily thought to be cognitive than the reverse. If I went too far in this direction (perhaps because of my own behavioral background), it was not intentional.

ACKNOWLEDGMENTS

I am grateful to David Cross, Marvin Frankel, Carlos Rodriguiz, Monica Rodriguiz, and Jay Russo who read and criticized various sections of the book. Special thanks to Paulette Gerber who typed the manuscript with care and intelligence.

Finally, because this is a textbook and not a reference work, many psychologists who contributed much to the study of judgment, decision, and choice are not mentioned by name. To them I extend apology as well as gratitude.

Howard Rachlin
Stony Brook, N.Y.

· JUDGMENT, DECISION, AND CHOICE ·

BACKGROUND

Both methods and theories in modern studies of judgment, decision, and choice are highly diverse. Philosophers, psychologists, economists, mathematicians — all have different ideas about just what judgment, decision, and choice are and about how they are to be understood, studied, and incorporated within a larger theoretical context. What does it mean, for instance, to think rationally? Rationality, you might say, is obedience to the laws of logic or mathematics. But what about people who obey the laws of logic or mathematics in their language but not, as so often happens, in their behavior? Are they rational because what they say is logical or irrational because what they do is illogical? And how do we know when something said or done is rational, irrational, or arational? These questions and more like them that are relevant to judgment, decision, and choice cannot be understood (let alone answered) without first considering their historical and philosophical context.

DESCARTES

Modern conceptions of decision and choice are rooted in the philosophy of René Descartes (1596–1650). In Descartes's time, the physicists Johannes Kepler (1571–1630), Nicolaus Copernicus (1473–1543), and Galileo (1564–1642) asserted that the sun, not the earth, is the center of the physical world. This assertion seemed to contradict religious dogma, both Catholic and Protestant, which placed the earth at the center of the universe. A still more fundamental threat to religious teachings was the fact that anatomical discoveries were suggesting that a person's body is like a machine. Kepler himself discovered that the eye works like a camera, casting an inverted image on the retina. William Harvey (1578–1657) discovered that the heart works like a pump, circulating blood through the body.

Just as a person, by a stretch of the imagination, could be seen as a kind of machine, a machine could be seen as a kind of person. A surprising number and variety of machines were being built in those days. There were elaborate clockwork mechanisms by which movable statues enacted scenes such as St. George killing a dragon. There also existed gardens with elaborate hydraulic mechanisms by which, for instance, a person stepping on a treadle would cause a statue of a naked maiden to emerge from the shrubbery. When the person stepped further on the statue would withdraw and another statue, of a grinning Saracen with a sword, would emerge.

What particularly impressed Descartes about these Disneyland-like mechanisms was the fact that they were actually operated by the viewer, thus establishing a sort of communication between a person and a machine. If, as these discoveries and inventions seemed to imply, a person is like a machine, then "lower" animals must be even more machinelike. Where, then, is a person's soul? And what is the difference between people and animals? Descartes claimed that a person's body is indeed a machine except that deep inside the machine and interacting with it is an immortal soul. Other animals, without immortal souls, are thus just machines.

People, according to Descartes, are capable of two sorts of motion, voluntary motion, which is controlled by the soul, and involuntary, machinelike motion; other animals are capable only of involuntary motion. In voluntary motion, Descartes imagined, the soul directs the release of a substance, called animal spirits, through (hollow) nerves. The animal spirits blow up the muscles like balloons and thereby contract them. The contracting muscles, in turn, move the body. Although the transmission of animal spirits throughout the body is mechanical, the soul, by opening and closing valves in the center of the brain, controls the animal spirits — which nerves these spirits go into and how much goes into each nerve. Voluntary motion thus originates in the soul and therefore inside the person. The soul can receive information from the outside world through sense organs, Descartes said, but it need not react directly to that information. It has innate knowledge and innate reasoning power. It may use that knowledge and reason to originate motion independent of the immediate environment.

Involuntary motion, on the other hand, originates in the outside world as a stimulus — say, a fire touching a boy's hand. The fire transmits energy through the boy's skin to his nerve. The nerve then transmits the energy to the boy's brain, much as pulling a rope at the bottom of a church tower transmits energy to ring the bell. Instead of ringing a bell, the nerve pulls open a valve. Animal spirits, released into the nerve, rush back through it and, as they do with voluntary movement, blow up the boy's muscle like a balloon. The swelling muscle contracts and the boy's hand is pulled out of the fire.

Modern physiology has become more sophisticated about how and why boys pull their hands away from fires. The important point, as Descartes conceived it, is that the whole process originates in the outside world — in the fire. The boy himself when moving involuntarily is analogous to a mirror. He reflects the action of an object in the world back onto itself. The internal neural mechanism that accomplishes this "reflection" has come to be called a *reflex*. Figure 1-1 diagrams Descartes's conception of voluntary and involuntary motion in humans.

The main difference between Descartes's conception and the then-dominant religious conception lies in the issue of causation. For Aristotle, writing almost 2000 years prior to Descartes, a movement in the physical world could be caused by a goal or an aim — a "final cause." Aristotle believed that a stone falls to earth because the earth is the stone's natural place to be. Animal *passions*, for Aristotle, are also movements, not essentially different from the movements of stones except that passions require the senses. *Actions* further require the power to reason. Since all animals can sense (have sensible souls), all animals, Aristotle believed, are capable of passions. Since only humans can reason (have rational souls), only humans are capable of actions. For humans, other animals, and physical objects alike,

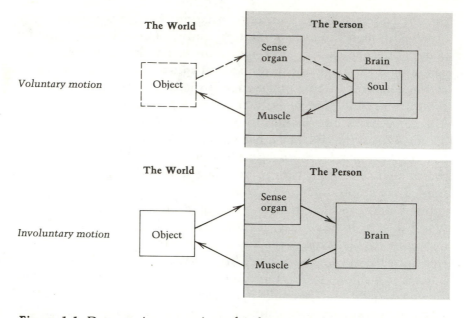

Figure 1-1 Descartes's conception of voluntary and involuntary motion. The dashed lines in the upper figure indicate events that may have happened in the past.

Aristotle held that the cause of a movement may be a final cause — the place or state of being that the human, animal, or object is headed towards, that is, its natural place or natural state. By the time of Descartes, physics had rejected the notion that the movement of an object in the physical world could be caused by the place or state toward which it was headed. The movement of a cannonball had to be caused by the explosion of the gunpowder (efficient cause), not by the target (final cause).

The rejection of final causes was a giant step in the development of physics and was recognized as such by Descartes. His contribution was to extend this notion to the bodies of animals, including people. There, too, the rationale of final causes would be banned. Only within the human soul would final causes operate. Because both of Aristotle's categories of movement, actions and passions, involve final causes, Descartes located both in the human soul. For Descartes, voluntary behavior encompasses actions and passions, both of which are properties of the soul; according to Descartes (and contrary to Aristotle), nonhuman animals, soulless machines, are capable of neither actions nor passions.

After Descartes, the study of internal sources of movement (voluntary movement encompassing actions and passions) became the province of religion and philosophy, while externally caused, involuntary, reflexive, machinelike bodily movements became the province of medicine and physiology. The study of human decision was to grow out of the former branch of Descartes's dualistic concept of man while the study of animal choice was to grow out of the latter. It was not until Darwin's time, 200 years later, that attempts would be made to unite the two branches. However, before discussing this unification (a process that is still under way now, and of which this book is a part), we need to sketch the histories of the two branches.

REFLEXES

No sooner had Descartes decreed that a gaseous substance called animal spirits traveled through the nerves and swelled the muscles than two independent investigators, the Englishman Francis Glisson (1597–1677) and the Dutchman Jan Swammerdam (1637–1680), independently proved that muscles could contract even though no substance entered into them through the nerves. If a man immerses his arm in water and contracts his biceps, no water is displaced. Glisson reasoned that an introduced substance (animal spirits) would have increased the volume of the biceps and displaced water. More conclusively, Swammerdam isolated a frog's nerve and muscle and found that the muscle would contract when the nerve was mechanically stimulated. No substance was required.

The question of whether a substance goes from the brain to the nerves was more philosophically important in those days than it may seem to us now. If each part of a person has its own principle of movement (its own specific "irritability," to use the term of the day), then the centrally located soul cannot be responsible for all of its movement. It was not long until some thinkers began to draw the conclusion that what Descartes (and the Church) called the soul was nothing but the natural organization of the specific irritabilities of the various bodily parts (as Aristotle had implied).

One such thinker was Julien Offroy de La Mettrie (1709–1751). In his book *L'Homme Machine*, ([1748] 1927), he cited evidence, systematic and anecdotal, that parts of the body may function without the brain (including "the case of a man convicted of treason who was opened alive, and whose heart thrown into hot water leaped several times, each time less high, to the perpendicular height of two feet" [quoted in Herrnstein and Boring, p. 274]). The thesis of *L'Homme Machine* is that all movement is involuntary; people, like other animals, are just machines: "A few more wheels, a few more springs than in the most perfect [nonhuman] animals, the brain proportionally nearer the heart and for this reason receiving more blood — any one of a number of unknown causes might always produce this delicate [human] conscience so easily wounded" (Herrnstein and Boring, p. 273).

For these views, La Mettrie was roundly persecuted. Not only did they go against both Catholic and Protestant doctrine, they also implied that the parts of the governmental state (individual people), like parts of the body (individual organs), could manage themselves. As the body needed no centrally located soul, the state might need no king.

Further anatomical work on reflexes through the seventeenth and eighteenth centuries demonstrated that reflexes run through the spinal cord of vertebrates and that different sections of the spinal cord are necessary for different reflexes. Until the beginning of the nineteenth century, however, most work on reflexes was functional. That is, kinds of movement were classified according to their functional properties. It was noted that most reflexes (as with the boy pulling his hand away from the fire) are protective. Some serve to move the body (as when the zebra runs away from the lion), and some serve to keep the body in an optimum internal state (as when breathing is accelerated or decelerated depending on the need for oxygen).

An important figure of the eighteenth century was the English physician and philosopher David Hartley (1705–1757). Hartley was a thoroughgoing psychophysical parallelist. He rejected Descartes's concept of an actual interaction between a person's soul and body, yet he believed that for each event that occurs in a person's soul (or mind), there exists a corresponding event in the body. He assumed that God had created the parallel worlds.

Hartley's parallelism proved to be very healthy for his physiological speculations. Since a person's soul and body were not supposed to interact, Hartley could not, when he failed to understand why people behave as they do, attribute the behavior to their souls. Hartley conceived of people, as Descartes did, as composed of body and soul. But unlike Descartes, he could not attribute voluntary behavior to the soul and involuntary behavior to bodily reflexes. For him there had to be something in the body corresponding to voluntary as well as involuntary behavior. His philosophy forced him to postulate an efficient cause for all movement in the person's body itself. When he could not discover the cause of movement in the body (as was frequently the case), he was compelled to infer its existence. Thus, in Hartley's book *Observations on Man, His Frame, His Duty, and His Expectations*, we find the first physiological theory of learning. Hartley, borrowing from Newton's physics, supposed that mechanical vibrations travel through the nerves to the brain, where they spread out like waves created by a stone dropped into water; the further the vibrations spread, the smaller they get. He called the small vibrations "vibratiuncles." When two vibrations occur at the same time frequently enough, one alone gives rise to the vibratiuncle, corresponding to the other. While learning is occurring in the mind, vibrations and vibratiuncles are occurring in the brain. Primitive as this physiological learning theory is, there was no better one available until Pavlov's in the twentieth century.

On a functional level, Hartley was the first to emphasize the interaction of voluntary and involuntary movements; involuntary movements can be brought under voluntary control, as when we control our breathing. Correspondingly, voluntary movements can become involuntary, as in addictions.

At the beginning of the nineteenth century, another pair of independent discoveries, this time by the Frenchman François Magendie (1783–1855) and the Scot Charles Bell (1774–1842), gave anatomical support to the theoretical conception of the reflex. At each level of the spinal cord, which was then known to be a central locus for reflexes, there are four clearly identifiable groups of entering nerves (roots), two at the rear (dorsal) and two at the front (ventral). Bell and Magendie discovered that when they cut the dorsal roots of spinal nerves in an experimental animal, the animal could still move the innervated limb but did not react to a pinprick on the limb. In contrast, when a ventral branch of nerves was cut, the animal responded to a pinprick but was not able to move the limb. Thus, the stimulus of a reflex must enter the spinal cord through the dorsal roots and leave through the ventral roots. (This discovery is known as the Bell–Magendie law in English-speaking countries and the Magendie–Bell law in French-speaking countries.)

The theory and practice of neurophysiological work on the reflex from Descartes to Darwin carries with it the implication that animal choice is nothing but the relative strength of reflexes. For instance, a bee confronted with two flowers has reflexive tendencies to fly to both of them and actually does fly to the one that stimulates the stronger response. The study of animal choice is, in this view, nothing but the study of reflex conflict. To the extent that human behavior is seen as mechanical or involuntary (La Mettrie included all human behavior in this category), human decisions are also nothing but conflicts of reflexes and may be studied as such. Both actions and passions, which together comprise Descartes's conception of voluntary behavior, could be reduced to reflexes.

Perhaps the strongest expression of this view is that of the Russian physiologist Ivan Michailovich Sechenov (1829–1905). In his book *Reflexes of the Brain* (published in 1863, four years after Darwin's *Origin of Species* but apparently uninfluenced by it), Sechenov discussed his research on inhibition. Many reflexes are controlled by signals from the brain, much as radio signals control the flow of electrons through a transistor or, less anachronistically, as a faucet controls the flow of water. The leg withdrawal reflex of a frog, for instance, is stronger when the upper part of the frog's brain is removed than when it is intact, showing that signals from the brain may inhibit, hence control, the reflex. The initial controlling stimuli, from the environment to the brain, may be very weak (just as the radio signals in the atmosphere are weak), but the response (the radio's sound energy, which comes from an electric outlet or battery) may be relatively strong. Figure 1-2 diagrams Sechenov's conception. In such a case, according to Sechenov, we do not notice (we do not react directly to) the weak stimulus and, seeing no corresponding variation in the strong stimulus, suppose that the response is controlled voluntarily (by the soul). Thus, all human activity, no matter how complex, "be it a child laughing at the sight of toys, or Garibaldi smiling when he is persecuted for his excessive love for his fatherland; a girl trembling at the first thought of love, or Newton enunciating universal laws and writing them on paper" (quoted in Herrnstein and Boring, p. 309), can be conceived as being composed solely of reflexes.

THE RATIONAL SOUL

According to Aristotle, the souls of all organisms — plants, animals, and humans — are capable of nutrition and growth; those of animals

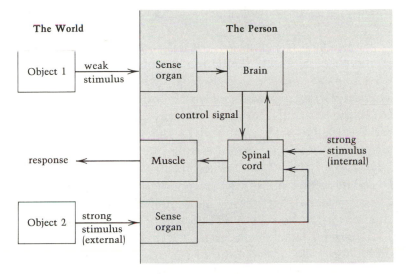

Figure 1-2 Sechenov's view of how the brain controls spinal reflexes.

and humans are capable of sensation; but only human souls are capable of reasoning. By *soul* Aristotle meant something like "principle of life." However, in late medieval times Aristotle's philosophy was reconciled with Catholic doctrine, most notably by St. Thomas Aquinas (1225–1274); the rational soul was abstracted and identified as an incorporeal, immortal substance.

St. Augustine (354–430), in premedieval times (much before Aquinas), had conceived of the soul as the actual presence of God in a person. Augustine had said that the soul's essential function is faith rather than rationality, and since God is present in the soul, faith is achieved primarily through self-reflection or introspection. This view of the soul complemented the medieval view of the good (holy) life as achievable only by retiring from the world and devoting oneself to contemplation.

However, in late medieval times and more especially during the Renaissance, powerful forces in the Church began to rebel against a life devoted solely to internal reflection. Aquinas's neo-Aristotelian position (that God could be known through reason about the external world as well as through faith about the internal world) provided justification for worldly interaction. According to Aquinas, it is possible to know God in two equally valid ways, indirectly by reason and directly by faith. This double-facing soul is diagrammed in Figure 1-3.

Descartes placed this soul (capable of reason and faith as well as action and passion) inside the bodily machine. Descartes, however, altered Aquinas's concept of knowledge; what Aquinas had seen (in religious terms) as two ways in which the soul could know God, Descartes saw (in secular terms) as two ways in which the mind could acquire knowledge — of itself and of the world. The direct way, internal reflection, is the most certain. By internal reflection the mind can know itself. "I think, therefore I am" was to Descartes the most fundamental certainty (corresponding to faith in God). The other way of knowledge, reasoning about information coming into the mind through the senses, is how we come to know the world. From Descartes's time to the present day, philosophers have been concerned about these two sorts of knowledge — how they are acquired, how certain they are, their content, their use. The issue concerns us because human decisions, as distinct from choices, are mental acts. In Descartes's view, each person's decisions can be directly known only by the person himself. A theory of decision must then be part of a theory of this sort of knowledge.

The first serious and influential modification of Descartes's view of the mind came from the Englishman, John Locke (1632–1704). Locke was concerned specifically with the question, Where does knowledge come from? Consider the idea of a rose. How does this idea arise in our minds? Descartes had assumed that a rose could be known in two ways: through internal reflection (corresponding to faith) and through external observation (corresponding to reason). The former idea is innate, and the latter due to experience. The correspondence of the innate image of our internal reflections to the

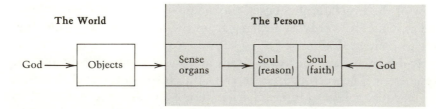
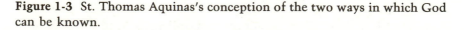

Figure 1-3 St. Thomas Aquinas's conception of the two ways in which God can be known.

object in the world was assumed to be due to the action of God, who had created them both.

Locke, in *An Essay Concerning Human Understanding*, asserted that knowledge could arise in only one way, through experience with the external world. As Locke conceived the mind, it was like a "white paper" upon which experience writes or an "empty cabinet" that experience fills. Locke argued that there are no innate ideas. The idea of the rose, as we internally reflect upon it, corresponds to the object in the world as we see it, not because God created both to correspond but because the former is caused by the latter.

This is perhaps best illustrated by a famous allegory of the French philosopher and follower of Locke, Etienne Bonnot de Condillac (1715 – 1780). Imagine a statue incapable of movement but possessed of a mind. If the statue has no sense organs, its mind, even though capable of reasoning, will have nothing to reason about—it will have no content whatsoever. It will not be able to say to itself "I think, therefore I am," as Descartes supposed, because, having nothing to think about (no "I think"), it will have no sense of self (no "I am").

Now suppose we endow this statue with a sense of smell and present to it only one smell—that of a rose. The statue, regardless of its ability to reason, will have no way of knowing about the rose as such. The statue's mind will simply be suffused with one smell. The statue will still be incapable of a sense of self. Now suppose the smell of the rose is taken away. Finally, the statue's mind will be capable of an action, memory of the smell, and a passion, desire for the smell's return. If another smell were then presented, say that of an onion, the statue could exercise *judgment* by preferring one to the other. However, only after other senses were added—sight and touch— could the statue come to conceive of objects as such (the smell of the rose associated with the sight and feel of the rose would be required for perception of the rose), and only after conceiving of other objects could the statue conceive of itself as an object (have a sense of self, or an ego).

Locke and Condillac were arguing against Descartes's concept of innate ideas, but they did conceive of innate capacities of the human mind. They did not consider memory, desire, judgment, and, most important, the mind's ability to reflect on itself as in any way derived from experience. A decision for these philosophers was still a mental act, accessible only to the person in whose mind it occurred.

Later British empiricist philosophers George Berkeley (1685–1753), David Hume (1711–1776), and John Stuart Mill (1806–1873) were concerned with how complex ideas could arise in the mind from elementary sensations. The culmination of their thinking was a view of the mind as capable of only two simple actions. The first capacity of the mind is the association of ideas: If two or more ideas arise in the mind at the same time frequently enough, then one alone is capable of giving rise to the other. So if the smell of the rose (a sensation and its corresponding idea) and the sight and touch of the rose (other sensations and their corresponding ideas) occur together frequently enough, then the smell alone gives rise to the idea of the sight and touch, hence perception, of the rose. (Hartley said that while this process occurs in the mind, a parallel process occurs in the brain.) The associationists argued that many complex mental processes are nothing but association. Berkeley saw visual space as the association of movement of the eyes with movement of the body; Hume conceived of cause and effect as frequent, invariable sequential associations; Hartley said that decision was the association of desire and object; John Stuart Mill stated that meaning was the association of word and object, and that reason was merely an extension of meaning.

A second capacity of the mind, according to the empiricists, is reflection on its own contents. Different empiricist philosophers differed on how complex this process is. Early ones like Locke tended to minimize the function of the more peripheral associative process and to emphasize the importance of the more internal reflective process. Later ones like Mill tended to emphasize the importance of the associative process and minimize the function of the reflective process.

Figure 1-4 diagrams the mind as seen by these British empiricist philosophers. This view contains a remnant of the earlier religious concept of St. Thomas Aquinas, which also distinguishes between a peripheral process (reason) and a central process (faith). At the same time, it presages the modern cognitive view of a peripheral process (representation) and a central process (decision).

While the British empiricists were claiming that much of what seems like innate mental capacity actually arises from the world, other philosophers, mostly on the European continent, were claiming that much of what seems to be aspects of the world actually arises from our innate mental capacities. The most influential of these philosophers was Immanuel Kant (1724–1804). For Kant the sense

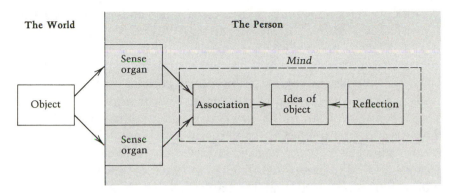

Figure 1-4 The British empiricist philosophers' view of the mind.

organs and everything else we can possibly conceive of are all derived from our phenomenal experience. Our phenomenal experience, in turn, arises from a sort of collision between us and the world. By "us" is meant a set of innate categories, basic concepts such as time, space, cause-and-effect, which determine how the world is organized. Figure 1-5 diagrams Kant's view of the mind. Phenomenal experience can be analyzed into its subjective components (psychology) and objective components (physics); neither can ever be wholly independent of the other. The starting point is always experience itself.

Kant agreed with Hume that a category such as cause-and-effect could be analyzed into a series of associations of sensations, but, he

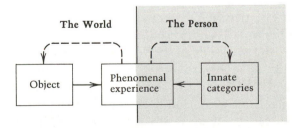

Figure 1-5 Kant's conception of phenomenal experience as arising from an interaction of a person with the world. The dashed arrows represent a person's construction of the world and the person's own mind out of phenomenal experience.

pointed out, no one actually experiences cause-and-effect as a series of associations. Hume's analysis is artificial (like the physicist's analysis of objects into atoms). The experience of cause-and-effect (like the perception of objects) still has to be explained.

Modern phenomenological philosophy is derived from Kant. In the modern view, each person constructs a view of himself and of the world around him out of his own experience with the world (which contains other people). This construction includes folk wisdom of various kinds as well as scientific knowledge. The debate nowadays is about criteria to determine which of several possible constructions is best: immediate utility, global utility, aesthetics, intuitive plausibility, conformance to a still higher reality, and so forth. Once criteria are agreed upon, the issue becomes how to determine which among several competing constructions actually conforms best to the criteria and, finally, whether there is such a thing as a better and a worse construction—perhaps they are all equally good or equally bad. This debate need not concern us here except to note that theories of cognitive decision and of behavioral choice may be viewed as two constructions from the observation of the choices of others, influenced more or less by the phenomenal experience of our decisions. To a strict Kantian, phenomenal experience would have priority. In modern philosophy, observations of someone else's choices may be considered no less fundamental than observations of one's own decisions, and the two constructions could (in agreement with the outlook of this book) be perfectly compatible.

FUNCTIONALISM

We turn now to Charles Darwin's (1809–1882) theory of evolution. Before Darwin, psychology was seen as part of philosophy and distinct from biology. Even for parallelists like David Hartley, the study of the mind and the study of the body were considered to be independent intellectual enterprises, the mind being approached through introspection, the body through observation. Darwin changed all that. His theory of evolution by survival of the fittest made discussion of final causes scientifically respectable once again. The theory of evolution reconciles final causes with efficient causes in biology. It was possible for Darwin to talk about the giraffe's long neck, for instance, in terms of its survival value—its final cause—leaving for later the discovery of the efficient cause (the genes passed along from generation to generation, which carry information controlling growth of the neck and the mechanism by which that information is translated into actual growth).

After Darwin, it became possible to say (without reference to God's intervention) that the cause of a giraffe's long neck is the height of the tree leaves on which it feeds or the necessity of spotting lions from far off on the African plains (the giraffe's long neck being a sort of self-contained crow's nest). Even modern biologists, knowing a great deal about the efficient (genetic) causes underlying evolution, may explain the existence of inherited features (such as the giraffe's neck, the color of its coat, the sensitivity of its hearing and sight, or its digestive system) in terms of aspects of the giraffe's environment that contribute to the survival and reproduction of giraffes. (From current knowledge of the giraffe and its environment, we may infer how the giraffe's genes must function. Biologists do not yet know enough to infer from the genes of an unknown animal what its structure and environment must be.)

The theory of evolution had two very important implications for psychology. The first was explored by Darwin himself. If particular features of animals' bodies can be explained by their survival value, perhaps particular features of their minds could be explained in a corresponding way. As an animal's body evolves, its mind must evolve too. Just as a fox is born with a brown coat (which serves as camouflage and thus contributes to its survival), so it is born with a set of tricks that help it get into and out of the chicken yard (thus also contributing to its survival). Certain tricks are common to all foxes of a given species and constitute a set of instincts possessed by the fox.

You may believe that the mind and the body are separate (as Descartes did) or that the mind is nothing but a set of reflexes (as Sechenov did) and still agree that foxes and people are born with a set of mental "tricks." Darwin, in his book *The Expression of the Emotions in Man and Animals*, was concerned to show the survival value of various forms of emotional expression common to people and other animals. The psychologist Carl Jung (1875–1961), initially a follower of Freud, believed that people inherit minds filled with complicated images and even stories that had served useful purposes in the past (but that now could cause neuroses).

The philosopher Herbert Spencer (1820–1903) used the concept of the evolution of the mind to explain the apparent correspondence between the mind and the world. Just as in the world snakes signal danger, so in the mind the idea of a snake tends to cause fear. People may have an innate tendency to fear snakes, but no one seems to be born with an innate tendency to fear rabbits. The difference corresponds to and is explicable in terms of the environment—snakes are dangerous and rabbits are harmless, hence the enhanced survival of people born with a tendency to fear snakes and the nonenhanced survival of people born with a tendency to fear rabbits.

The concept of evolution of the mind supports Descartes's concept of innate mental properties—instincts. But it also implies, contrary to Descartes, that other animals have minds as humans do. After Darwin, scientists began to study animal minds in a functional sense. While Sechenov may have been said to be studying the anatomy of the animal mind, psychologists began to study the function of the animal (and human) mind—its relation to the environment or its survival value. Modern ethology and comparative psychology are direct outgrowths of the concept of mental evolution. For us the important feature of mental evolution is its explanation of innate mental capacities of people and of other animals in terms of how they function in their environments—in terms of final causes.

A second important implication of Darwin's theory for psychology is much more a subject of dispute than the first—its extension to mental changes within the lifetime of an animal, that is, to learning. The American philosopher William James (1842–1910) argued that the mental property most useful to animals is the ability to learn, or to evolve over the course of a single animal's lifetime. The fox is born not only with an innate set of tricks but also with the capacity to alter those tricks when it proves useful to do so. (As the farmer changes the fence, the fox changes its way of getting into the barnyard.) Whereas for the evolution of foxes, usefulness is measured by differential ability to survive, for learning, usefulness is measured by differential ability to produce pleasure and pain (and this capacity, in turn, is seen as a product of biological evolution). James's student, the psychologist E. L. Thorndike (1874–1949), showed that chickens and cats gradually alter their behavior to become more functional— to obtain food (increase pleasure) and escape discomfort (decrease pain).

Once you accept the idea that learning within the lifetime of an animal (the tricks the fox acquires) works like inherited instincts over the lifetimes of a species of animals (the tricks the fox is born with), it becomes reasonable to explain much of the fox's behavior in terms of final causes, that is, in terms of its environment. The tendency of foxes to tunnel under fences, for instance, may be explained as a function of the success they achieve by that behavior. To what extent, if any, the behavior itself is subject to alteration over the lifetime of a fox may be determined by experiment.[1]

SUMMARY

Consider the following three categories of movement:

1. of objects in the world, including animals and humans as objects,

2. of animals, including humans as animals but distinct from objects, and

3. of humans as distinct from other animals and objects.

Aristotle explained all three categories of movement in terms of final causes, the thing that the movement was heading towards — its purpose or its function.

After Descartes, following the trend of physics, category 1 became explicable (with scientific respectability) only in terms of efficient causes. Category 3 remained explicable in terms of final causes with the proviso that the final causes be reserved for the operation of the mind, an entity within the body capable of purposes and intentions. In other words, Descartes explained voluntary human movement as efficiently caused by the mind, but the mind itself could be explained only in terms of final causes. Thus, human choices are simple (efficiently caused) outcomes of decisions which, in turn, are explicable in terms of purposes and intentions. (Descartes's view of human decision and human choice underlies our intuitive belief system today. It has permeated the way we talk about decisions, choices, purposes, intentions, and the mind itself. It is part of our folk psychology.)

After Descartes category 2, the movement of animals, became ambiguous. People who agreed with Descartes that nonhuman animals have no purposes or intentions categorized these animals with physical objects and explained their movements by efficient causes — just as one would explain the movement of a mechanical statue. People who disagreed with Descartes (and many did) explained some movements of some animals in terms of the animal's purposes and intentions.

The general rule was as follows: We know that we ourselves have minds (hence consciousness) because our introspection tells us so. Other creatures have minds if their movements display purpose and intention, and those movements cannot be explained solely in terms of efficient causes, that is, reflexes. (Around 1850, just before Darwin, a great debate took place as to whether consciousness existed in the spinal cord of a frog because the frog seemed capable of purposive movement after its head was cut off.) The fact that this view remains part of our belief system today is evidenced by the trouble we have in deciding whether computers, because they have purposes and intentions, can think. One extreme resolution of this problem is to suppose that *only* a computer can think. Thus, because we humans can think, our minds must be nothing but computers.

This neat method of deciding whether something other than ourselves has a mind inside of it (presence or absence of purpose) was disrupted by Darwin's theory of evolution. That theory showed how final causes could be reconciled with efficient causes. Molar biologists were able to discuss structural characteristics of organisms in terms of final causes in the environment, while molecular biologists searched for efficient causes (genes). Correspondingly, ethologists and comparative psychologists have formulated final-cause explanations of animal instincts, and behavioral psychologists have formulated such explanations of animal learning. After Darwin, categories 2 and 3 could not be logically separated. Whatever methods had been developed to study human purposes (including the methods of human decision theory) could now be applied to other animals. Whatever methods had been developed to study animal purposes (including the methods of animal choice theory) could now be applied to humans.

N O T E

1. Final causes were banished from physics initially because they seemed arbitrary and not amenable to mathematical explanation, and hence not useful for prediction. Modern physics, however, does not shun final causes. The founder of quantum theory, Max Planck, has said

the *cause efficiens*, which operates from the present into the future and makes future situations appear as determined by earlier ones, is joined by the *cause finalis* for which, inversely, the future — namely a definite goal — serves as the premise from which there can be deduced the development of the processes which lead to this goal. (Quoted in Yourgrau and Mandelstam, 1968, p. 165)

In modern physics, the difference between an efficient cause and a final cause of a phenomenon may be viewed simply in terms of the sort of mathematics most appropriate to describe the phenomenon; differential mathematics implies efficient causes, and integral (variational principles) mathematics final causes. In psychology (not nearly so well reducible to mathematics) the difference between an efficient cause and a final cause may be viewed as a difference in direction of inference from behavioral observations: Inference towards internal mechanisms (cognitive psychology) implies efficient causes, while inference towards the environment (behavioral psychology) implies final causes.

C H A P T E R ▪ T W O ▪

PROBABILITY

PROBABILITIES POP UP everywhere. It is not even possible (note the word *possible*) to conceive of a judgment, decision, or choice without first considering what *probability* means. Even when you choose between cans of soup on a supermarket shelf, you have to take into account (albeit unconsciously) the probability of the labels being correct, of the marked prices being correct, of the soups being consistent in taste with your previous experience (if any), of your being of the same mind when you come to eat them as you are now, of the soups being safe to eat, and so on. Someone observing you and trying to construct a coherent theory of your mental state or behavior would then worry about the probability of your choosing the same way this time (and next time) as last time, not to mention the probability of your choosing neither can and making soup yourself at home or eating out in a restaurant. Thus it is essential to understand probability before analyzing judgment, decision, and choice.

DEFINITION OF PROBABILITY

The weatherman on the 6 P.M. news predicts rain tomorrow, saying there is a "75 percent chance of rain." The next morning it is cloudy, and you take your umbrella to work. However, the skies clear. It does not rain. You lugged your umbrella to work and back for nothing. If you were to call the station and complain, the weatherman might defend himself by saying, "My prediction was essentially correct. The chances *were* seventy-five percent that it would rain. On one hundred days like today, it would rain on seventy-five of them. This just happens to be one of the other twenty-five. I'm sorry if you were inconvenienced, but meteorology is not an exact science. We never guarantee anything. Goodbye." He hangs up.

Figure 2-1 diagrams your interaction with the weatherman. Included in the diagram is your hypothetical internal decision process and the conceivable effect of the outcome on that decision process as it handles future decisions. For instance, in the future you might place less trust in that weatherman's predictions. (Excluded from the diagram is your subsequent telephone call, and the effect it might have on the weatherman.)

There is great debate currently among philosophers, psychologists, and statisticians about what constitutes a probability. Since our behavior undoubtedly depends on or reflects probabilities (objective and subjective), our conception of probability will determine how we

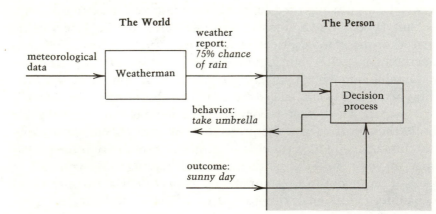

Figure 2-1 Probability as dialogue.

should behave and our evaluations of other people's behavior. Should we discount the weatherman's estimate of probability of rain by his accuracy? Should we additionally take into account the "base rate," the overall chance of rain (which we could assume to be in effect in the absence of the weather report)? And if so, how? The answer to these questions depends on our concept of probability in the first place. We cannot even begin to discuss the issue without taking some sort of stand.

It will be convenient for us to take a very broad view of probability and then, when necessary, consider more narrow views as subcategories of the broad view. We will therefore follow the lead of the philosopher J. R. Lucas (1970) and consider a probability as a guide to behavior, a graduated guide that ranges from "certainly go ahead and do it" (take your umbrella) to "certainly do not do it" (do not take your umbrella) and covering, as degrees of probability, all points in between.

To relate this concept of probability to cognitive and behavioral views of choice, consider Figure 2-2 where, still following Lucas, we consider the dialogue between you and the weatherman as a monologue. In this figure there is no weatherman. As is perhaps more frequent in everyday life, you have to make a decision, not with the aid of a neatly packaged probability statement, but in the face of the data themselves. In buying a house, for instance, it is rare to have before you statements like "the probability is 5 to 1 that this house will double in value in the next ten years" or "the odds are 1 in 100 that you will be fired from your job and fail to make the mortgage payments next year." Rather, like the weatherman himself, you have only your previous experience and current information (in his case, current weather conditions, in yours, bank accounts, economic conditions, etc.) to go on.

In Figure 2-2 the external weatherman is replaced by a sort of internal weatherman. Your decision mechanism, instead of watching a TV broadcast, watches a (metaphorical) internal representation of a TV broadcast. Instead of hearing about probabilities from a weatherman, you hear about probabilities from an internal representation. This is the cognitive view of probability. There are two important things to note about Figure 2-2. The first is that there is no way to bypass the box labeled "representation of data." Even when an actual weatherman exists, according to the cognitive viewpoint you treat his statement "The probability of rain is 75 percent" like data and convert it from an external statement of probability to an internal

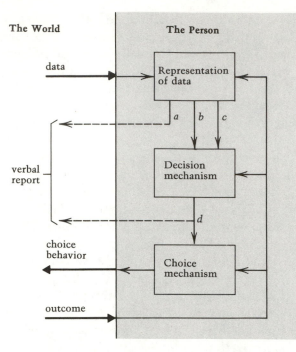

Figure 2-2 Probability as monologue (a = subjective probability; b = decision weight; c = other information; d = decision).

representation (a personal interpretation) of that probability. Some-times that internal representation is called a "subjective probability" (arrow *a* in Figure 2-2). It has also been called a "decision weight" (arrow *b*), because its job is to influence the decision mechanism. When a cognitive theory talks about probability, it refers to one of these (internal) probabilities because, consistent with our definition, these probabilities guide behavior most directly.

The second important thing to note about Figure 2-2 is the pair of dotted arrows leading from the person to the world, labeled "verbal report." Cognitive theories differ considerably over how **valid** verbal reports are as revelations of the workings of the various stages of the decision process. For instance, Daniel Kahneman and Amos Tversky (1979), two of the foremost cognitive decision theorists today, prefer the term "decision weight" (arrow *b*) to "subjective probability" (arrow *a*) as a label for internal probability because people's verbal reports of subjective probability seem unrelated to their actual deci-sions. At the same time these theorists believe that people's verbal reports of decisions do coincide with their actual choices. Thus, Kahneman and Tversky (1979) reject (as relevant to decisions) one kind of verbal report (arrow a) but accept another (arrow d).

The behavioral view is different. A behavioral theory relates inputs and outputs to and from the person as a whole. Therefore, in Figure 2-2, a behavioral theory must be about the relationships among the data, the choice behavior, and the outcome — the three heavy arrows. This three-way relationship is often referred to as a three-part contingency. The "data," "choice behavior," and "outcome" of Figure 2-2 are, in behavioral jargon, "discriminative stimulus," "response," and "reinforcement" (or "punishment"). Where, then, is probability?

Consistent with our definition of probability as a graduated guide to behavior, the behaviorist must view the data themselves as probabilities. It is true that outcomes also guide behavior. For instance, the outcome of your current experience with the weatherman will guide your future behavior regarding taking an umbrella to work. Remember, however, that included in the data are previous outcomes. The outcome of current behavior cannot guide that behavior since by definition it occurs afterwards. Just as previous outcomes are part of current data, so are previous choices — previous times that you took or did not take an umbrella (and it rained or did not rain).

For the behaviorist, then, the most direct guide to current behavior (current data) consists of *objective* probabilities in the form of objective relationships among data, choice behavior, and outcomes. For the cognitivist, on the other hand, the most direct guide to current behavior consists of *subjective* probabilities (or decision weights), that is, internal representations of objective probabilities. To see the difference in the two conceptions more clearly, consider again the dialogue pictured in Figure 2-1. When the weatherman says "75 percent chance of rain," the behaviorist sees this statement itself as an external representation of a set of complex contingencies that occurred in the past — relationships between previous conditions (like those prevailing today) and outcomes (rain or no rain). The weatherman's statement serves as an adequate guide to behavior only to the extent that it adequately represents those prior contingencies.

In general, to discover true probabilities (true guides to your current behavior) the behaviorist looks *backward* from current data to past events. The cognitivist, on the other hand, looks *forward* into the person. True probabilities (true guides to your current behavior) are to be found, according to the cognitivist, not in your past but in you. The cognitivist tends to argue that current internal states are the most direct guide to current behavior because a single subjective probability or decision weight (hence, a single behavioral guide) can arise from a bewildering variety of past events. The behaviorist tends to argue that past (external) events are the most direct guide to current behavior because a single objective probability (hence, a single behavioral guide) may be mediated by a bewildering variety of internal (neural) states.

If behaviorists see behavior as arising directly from objective probabilities, how do they view verbal reports of internal states? To be consistent, behaviorists must view all such reports as independent actions themselves — that is, as guided directly by objective probabilities ("by a history of reinforcement or punishment"), like other behavior. When reports of internal states and other behavior are correlated (as when a person says, "I think it's going to rain," and also takes an umbrella to work), the behaviorist attributes the correlation to common objective probabilities (common correlations with data and outcome) rather than to a common internal state.

In some cases, as with the above example, common *objective* relationships are easy to find. In other cases, as when a person says, "I am in pain," and at the same time cries, common objective probabilities are more difficult to find, and we are tempted to attribute both verbal and nonverbal behaviors to a common internal state (the pain itself). The behaviorist, to be consistent, must not succumb to this temptation and should keep looking for common environmental contingencies — common stimuli such as wounds and blows and common consequences such as help from other people, sympathy, and the availability of drugs.

To summarize, the behaviorist agrees with the cognitivist that the weatherman's statement of Figure 2-1 is a probability in the sense that it serves as a guide to the person's behavior and conforms to the mathematics of probability. The difference between the behaviorist and the cognitivist (illustrated in Figure 2-3) arises in their explanations of what happens when there is no weatherman. For the cognitivist, the probability itself moves into the person as the output of a sort of internal weatherman — a representation mechanism that converts data into probabilities. For the behaviorist, the weatherman just disappears and the person confronts the data directly. For the behaviorist, a mathematical probability is a construction of the theorist or the observer rather than of the person — a way the ob-

Dialogue

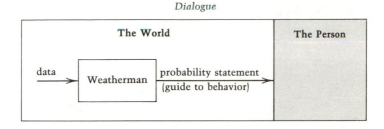

Monologue: Cognitive View   *Monologue: Behavioral View*

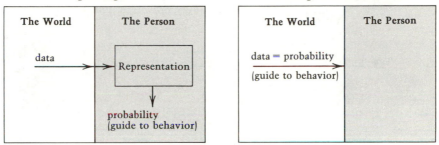

Figure 2-3 Cognitive and behavioral views of probability.

server has of organizing the data and making calculations so as to predict the person's behavior. We now briefly turn to how such calculations work.

CALCULATING PROBABILITIES

The mathematics of probability is the mathematics of fractions. The first question to ask about fractions is, fractions of what? In terms of pure mathematics, the answer is "fractions of the number 1," or fractions of a unit. In applying the mathematics of fractions to other spheres, it then becomes necessary to say what a unit is. Let us consider a few conceivable units, illustrated in Figure 2-4. The rule that must be followed is that the value of the fraction cannot go above 1 or below 0. If there is any danger of doing so, terms will have to be redefined; otherwise it will be impossible to apply the mathematics of fractions to the other spheres, where, after all, our interest lies. There is no collection of individuals greater than all, no proposition more certain than a true one, no object that occupies more space

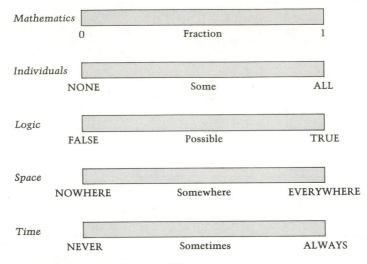

Figure 2-4 Conceptions of probability.

than everywhere, and no event that last longer than always. Correspondingly, there is no collection of individuals fewer than none, no proposition less certain than a false one, no object that occupies less space than nowhere, and no event more brief than one that never happens.

A case can be made to consider any of the nonmathematical dimensions in Figure 2-4 as a fundamental probability and to derive the rest of the probabilities from it. For instance, one person may argue that space and time can be broken up into individual elements on the all–none dimension. Logical propositions must be propositions about something; otherwise they could not be true or false. Thus logic, as well as space and time, can be reduced to individual elements ranging from none to all. Another person might argue that the words on this page, if they mean anything, can be reduced to logical propositions. That person might say that probabilities apply not to individual objects themselves nor to objects in space and time but to propositions—sentences—such as those the weatherman utters or those we may say to ourselves. A probability exists in our language, not in things; a chair cannot be probable, any more than it can be true or false. Thus, all probabilities reduce to logical propositions.

A third and fourth person, arguing together, could say that space and time define our concept of a *thing*. Nothing exists outside of both of these dimensions. For these two people, language is only a kind of action — writing or speaking — that exists in space and time. Individuals, logic, everything, must be expressible in space and time, hence probability is also so expressible. If these two people should carry the argument together, you can easily imagine one turning on the other and the subsequent debate over whether space or time was more fundamental.

For our part, we may safely leave such arguments to the philosophers. We will be ecumenical and apply the mathematics of fractions whenever convenient and consistent with our definition of probability as a guide to behavior. After all, a person's behavior may be guided by individual fractions (the fraction of students at a given college who go on to graduate or professional schools) ranging from none to all, by propositional statements ("If you cheat on your income tax, you'll get caught") ranging from false to true, and by spatiotemporal events (traffic jams on a given road) ranging from nowhere and never to everywhere and always.

As an example, consider all of the students at the hypothetical Acme School of Languages and their majors. The total of all the students (t) is represented as an empty bar at the top of Figure 2-5. Let us assume that $t = 100$. Now suppose that twenty of the students are French majors ($F = 20$). Thus the fraction of students who are French majors is F/t, or $^{20}/_{100}$. If you were to select a student at random from all of the students, the odds of selecting a French major would be $^{20}/_{100}$.

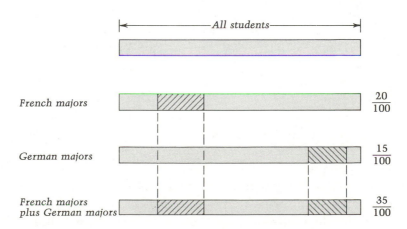

Figure 2-5 Simple addition of nonoverlapping probabilities.

RANDOMNESS

What does it mean to select something at random? A reasonable way to do it might be to put each student's major on a piece of paper, thoroughly shuffle the papers, and then pick one blindly. In doing this, note that we deliberately ignore everything about the students except their majors. Randomness requires ignorance. Sometimes the ignorance is deliberate, as when, in selecting a student randomly, we ignore the student's dormitory (because French majors might be concentrated in certain dormitories), the student's sex (because there might be a preponderance of male or female French majors), economic status, age, class, grades, appearance, extracurricular activities, and so on. any of these factors might tell us something more about whether a student is a French major than we want to know. Once we determine to select a student randomly, we deliberately ignore all of this information.

Sometimes our ignorance is not deliberate. It may be that somewhere in the brain of every French major is a common neural structure, or neural mechanism — the neural structure or mechanism that, when fed the string of words "Are you a French major?" (or its equivalent) as an input, produces the word "Yes" (or its equivalent) as an output. This mechanism, if it exists, may well be only an adjunct to much more important mechanisms (as a fuel gauge is an adjunct to a car's fuel system). And (like a fuel gauge) it would not be infallible. Still, if we knew about such a mechanism, we would have to ignore it when selecting randomly. Correspondingly, many French majors may have had a common incident in their previous experience — say, encouragement from a French teacher in high school — that we do not, perhaps cannot, ever know about. If we did know about such incidents, however, we would have to ignore such information when selecting randomly among students.

As soon as we have all the relevant information about something, it cannot be random. For instance, once it is dealt, there is no such thing as a random poker hand. A royal flush is no more or less random than a worthless hand. (In the game of low ball, normally worthless hands are transformed into winning ones and vice versa, but the hands themselves are no more or less random than in ordinary poker.) What may be random is the *process* by which the hand was dealt—the shuffling of the deck—which insures ignorance before play commences.

A problem arises with randomness when we know only the results of some process but have no access to the process itself. For philosophical or religious reasons we might want to assume that everything is in principle knowable.[1] If the day ever came when everything was in fact known, there could be no random process and no probabilities. However, one thing we do know is that, for the foreseeable future, everything is not known.

Consider the fabled monkey who, if put in a room with a typewriter for an infinite time, will eventually type out the complete works of Shakespeare. Suppose the monkey is in one room and you are in another and the monkey (unseen by you) passes papers through a slot as they are finished. You get, let us say, the first ten pages of *Hamlet*. How many pages will you need in order to be certain that the process generating those papers was not random? People will differ on this point. Could we settle a bet on the basis of twenty or thirty pages? No? Then forty of fifty? There must be some number that would satisfy you. If all of *Hamlet*, *King Lear*, and *Othello* were typed out, then would you be sure? Yes? But sure of what? The papers could have been typed by an illiterate person trained to copy a printed text, letter by letter. Even in that case there still must have been foreknowledge by man or beast or machine of what was to be passed to you. It is the absence of that foreknowledge, that ability to predict in some intelligible language what will happen, to which we refer when we say that a process is random.

Technically, random events satisfy two conditions: independence and similarity. To satisfy the condition of independence, each event in a set of random events must be uninfluenced by the others. In other words, in ten tosses of a coin, the outcomes of the first nine tosses must have absolutely no influence on the tenth for the coin tossing to be random. To satisfy the condition of similarity is really to satisfy two conditions. First, the things you know about the events must be identical from event to event within a given set: the coin used, the person doing the flipping, the rules under which the coin is flipped (whether it will be caught and placed on the back of the hand or allowed to fall to the floor). The probability of a coin falling heads is *usually* around .5, but some coins may vary; the condition of similarity demands the same "universe of discourse," or the same conditions of knowledge for each toss. Second, there must be equivalence of ignorance. The things you are ignorant of on any given toss (how the coin is held, how far off the floor, which side is up when the coin is tossed, the force of the flips, etc.) must be the same for all tosses.

OVERLAPPING

Figure 2-5 represents the probability of $^{20}/_{100}$ that a student is a French major by filling in $^{20}/_{100}$ of the bar representing all students. All of the French majors are grouped together in one clump that is placed randomly (unpredictably) on the bar. On the bar below is another clump representing the hypothetical $^{15}/_{100}$ of the students who are German majors. On the third bar all the students who are French or German majors are represented by adding the fraction of the students who are French majors to the fraction who are German majors and getting the total ($^{20}/_{100} + {}^{15}/_{100} = {}^{35}/_{100}$). In order to do this addition in a straightforward way, however, it is necessary to assume that no student is a double major in French and German. Otherwise that student would be counted twice, once among the French majors and once among the German majors. Then, the sum of all the fractions, representing all the majors (French, plus German, plus all the other languages taught at Acme), would be a number greater than 1 (because all double majors would be counted twice). This result would violate the initial rule that no collection of things can be greater than the sum of all of them. In a college where double majors are not allowed, simply adding the fractions suffices. However, where double majors are allowed, the number of double majors would have to be subtracted from the sum of all the individual majors (that is, the fractions of students majoring in French, German, Italian, Japanese, etc.). If there were any (highly ambitious) triple majors, their number would have to be subtracted twice because they would be counted three times. The general rule is that probabilities are simply added together only if the individual instances do not overlap. If they do overlap, the amount of overlap has to be subtracted from the total.

That is about as far as we can go with anything approximating a real language school with real students. Let us now imagine another, unreal, hypothetical school where ignorance (hence randomness) reigns supreme — the School of Arbitrary Decisions (SAD). At SAD, students are assigned majors randomly by the chairpersons of the various departments in ignorance of the students' desires, their abilities, or any other personal traits. Furthermore, each chairperson picks majors from the student body in total ignorance of the choices made by the other chairpersons. After being given a quota by the dean, each chairperson takes the entire roster of incoming students and randomly (by shuffling slips of paper, throwing darts at a list, or some other such means based wholly on ignorance) chooses the students to major in his or her department. At SAD, some students might end up majoring in nothing and others in everything. (It is hard to say who would be more unlucky.) Figure 2-6 shows the French majors, the German majors, and their overlap.

At a normal school you might predict students' majors by their interests or their abilities. At SAD you could make predictions based only on the randomness, that is, on the (in this case deliberate) ignorance with which the chairpersons made their selections. Let us assume that the French department gets the list first and randomly chooses twenty majors from a hundred incoming students. Then the German department randomly chooses fifteen from this same list of one hundred. When throwing darts, the German chairperson is just as likely to choose a student already chosen by the French chairper-

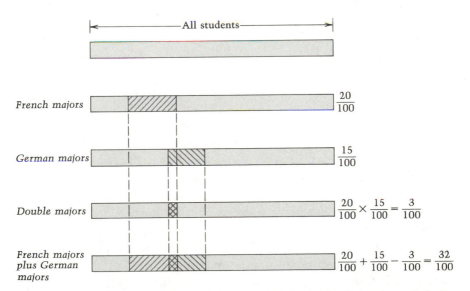

Figure 2-6 Addition of independent probabilities and subtraction of their product.

son as to choose an unassigned student. In other words, each of the twenty students previously chosen by the French chairperson has just as much chance of being chosen by the German chairperson as any of the other students. On the average, $^{15}/_{100}$ of the twenty students already chosen by the French chairman ($^{15}/_{100} \times 20 = 3$ unlucky students) will be chosen by the German chairperson too.

Predictions from this ignorance-based process are, of course, average predictions. In any particular year, it is theoretically possible that all of the German chairperson's darts will pinion the names of French majors. The general rule here is that when probabilities are independent (when one random process is ignorant of the others) and when each probability ranges randomly over the same set of individuals (or possibilities or places or times), their product indicates the expected degree of overlap. That product must be subtracted from the sum of individual probabilities (if we want the total to remain within the original range).

BAYES' RULE

At SAD, the chairperson of the French department is a megalomaniac. To him the universe consists only of French majors. His annual report to the dean bemoans the fact that $^3/_{20}$ of the French majors are distracted from their studies by their German studies. As far as he is concerned, there are only three German majors — those among *his* students. Likewise, the chairperson of the German department, of similar temperament to the French department head, reports that an average of $^3/_{15}$ of the German majors are distracted from their German studies by their French studies. As far as she is concerned, there are only three French majors — those among her students.

The two chairpersons have each essentially *normalized* the original group of students by considering only their own majors as the base on which to calculate the reported fraction. More technically, the chairpersons have reported not fundamental probabilities (the fractions of all the students) but *conditional probabilities* (the fractions of their own students). However, the dean is not interested in these subgroups but in the whole class. He wants to know what fraction of all students are double majors. To get this fraction, the dean must *renormalize* the fractions from the French and German chairperson's reports back to the whole class. He can do this by

considering the original allocation of majors to the two chairpersons
(twenty to the French, fifteen to the German) and calculating the
overlap of each allocation with that chairperson's reported fraction

To express this mathematically, let F, G, and D stand for the
number of French, German, and double majors, respectively, and t
for the total number of students). We then get

$$\frac{D}{t} = \frac{D}{F} \times \frac{F}{t} = \frac{3}{20} \times \frac{20}{100} = \frac{3}{100}$$

or

$$\frac{D}{t} = \frac{D}{G} \times \frac{G}{t} = \frac{3}{15} \times \frac{15}{100} = \frac{3}{100}$$

All this is fairly obvious and may even seem trivial and pointless.
However, the above calculations, in which a single fundamental
probability is obtained from either of two conditional probabilities,
lead to a very useful rule called *Bayes' rule*.

Since the fundamental probability of double majors in French and
German is the same whichever way it is obtained, we can set the two
expressions equal to each other:

$$\frac{D}{F} \times \frac{F}{t} = \frac{D}{G} \times \frac{G}{t}$$

Dividing both sides by F/t we get

$$\frac{D}{F} = \frac{D}{G} \times \frac{G/t}{F/t}$$

This equation, interpreted generally, says that one conditional probability (here, D/F) equals the inverse conditional probability (D/G)
times the ratio of their two fundamental probabilities (called the base
rate).

Bayes' rule is a formula for calculating one conditional probability
from another. In real life (as opposed to at SAD) this rule may be very
useful. We often know or can easily obtain one conditional probability but are really interested in the other. Let us abandon SAD and
consider another, sadder example. Suppose you are tested for a disease and the test is positive. What is the probability that you have the
disease? Here you may be able to find out one conditional probabil-

ity, the probability that a person like you tests positively given that the person has the disease, but you are really interested in the other, the probability that a person like you has the disease given that the person tests positively. You need the latter probability in order to guide your behavior (to decide whether to begin treatment).

Applying Bayes' rule we get

$$\frac{PD}{P} = \frac{PD}{D} \times \frac{D/t}{P/t}$$

where PD stands for the number of people who test positive and have the disease, P is the number of people that test positive, D is the number of people who have the disease, and t stands for the population of people like you. The conditional probability term (PD/D) reflects the reliability of the test, while the base rate reflects the disease's prevalence in the population (relative to the positive test rate). If the test were unreliable but the disease were prevalent in the population of people like you, you might well undergo treatment. If the test were highly reliable, you might undergo treatment even though the disease might be rare among people like you. However, if the test were unreliable and the disease were rare, you might not want to undergo treatment, especially if the treatment was expensive or dangerous.

When applying Bayes's rule it is very important that the variables (people like you with the disease and people like you tested) be randomly distributed across the population, with ignorance of everything about the population except the one characteristic of concern. Thus it is important that you be administered the test randomly (with ignorance of everything about you except that you are a member of the population of people like you), not because you had any particular symptoms. Otherwise the fundamental probabilities (the base rates) of "people like you" would have to be changed from those incorporating the general population to those incorporating only people like you with your particular symptoms. For instance, people like you (say, Americans of your sex and age with eating habits like yours) would have one base rate of stomach cancer, while people like you with severe stomach pain and blood in their stool would have another. In applying Bayes' rule to particular cases, it is often a matter of dispute what the base rate should be. We will pursue this issue further in the next chapter; now we shall turn to some statistical considerations.

INDIVIDUAL CASES

Probabilities depend on the *universe of discourse* to which they refer (the variable we have been labeling *t*). The probability of having twins has one value for a human and another for a mouse. There is no relation between the two probabilities because their baselines — their universes of discourse — are different; what we know and what we do not know about the two cases do not match up.

Imagine a sect that believes the world will end one year from today, but only if it rains on that day anywhere in New York City. Imagine their interest in the weather in New York on that day. The best they can do right now is to determine the overall probability of rain on this day next year: the number of times it has rained on this date in the past divided by the number of times it has rained plus the number of times it has not. However, as the critical day draws near, they can get a better probability. They can narrow their universe of discourse to days preceded by cloud formations, temperature gradients, and characteristics of the jet stream that are just as they are now. Because the universe of discourse changes, the probability will change. As the day draws still nearer, the universe of discourse becomes still narrower and narrower with probabilities changing correspondingly until, finally the probability of rain becomes meaningless. It either rains or (one hopes) it does not.

Consider another case. You work for a restaurant and are sent to count how many patrons enter a competitor's restaurant in a given month. You could make your job easier by counting the number of patrons in a day and then multiplying by 30. However, business could very across days randomly (no one knows why) or nonrandomly (because people tend to eat out more on weekends, for instance). You could do better if you counted the patrons for a week and multiplied by 4.2 (the number of weeks in a month). If you observed for a whole month, you would no longer be estimating what your boss told you to observe — you would be absolutely certain about how many customers came in during the month.

Let us say we randomly select over a universe of discourse (that is, the conditions of independence and similarity are satisfied) and we begin to accumulate a series of independent and similar cases. For simplicity, suppose we are flipping a coin and recording the number of heads (*H*) and tails (*T*). A theorem of Daniel Bernoulli says that as we go on and on, accumulating more and more cases, the fraction $H/(H + T)$ will approach a single constant fraction. The probability that the fraction reached in your necessarily limited number of tosses equals the fraction that you would obtain in an infinite number of tosses approaches 1.0 (certainty) as the number of your tosses approaches infinity. In the case of an unbiased coin, this fraction is ½ (or .5; that is what we mean by an unbiased coin).

Bernoulli's theorem provides a method by which an ignorant person can become less ignorant — a method for learning. For instance, suppose two people are betting on the tosses of a coin. The coin is actually biased to come up heads 70 percent of the time, but neither of the two bettors knows this. Their bets are thus fair because their ignorance is balanced. (A third person not involved in the betting may know about the biased coin, but such knowledge would be irrelevant as long as that third person does not interfere in the betting).2

Now suppose that the coin is tossed over and over again. Both bettors have opportunities to see the strings of heads and tails. Even though the fraction $H/(H + T)$ begins to approach .7 instead of .5, it will always be possible to assume that the preponderance of heads is a coincidence. However, Bernoulli's theorem allows us to specify a criterion — say one chance in a hundred — beyond which we will refuse to accept the preponderance of heads as a coincidence. For just a few cases, preponderances of heads are not unlikely. If the bettors have some reason to believe that the coin is not biased (say, it was found on the street or just given in change for a purchase), their criterion for abandoning their belief that the coin was unbiased might be very stiff (one in a hundred or even one in a thousand). But if either of the bettors has some reason to suspect that the coin might be biased (say its edges are unusually rough or it seems to weigh more than usual or it was bought in a magic store), then the bettor's criterion for changing her mind might be fairly loose and (assuming the coin really is biased) the bettor with the looser criterion would be able to win a great deal of money by betting on heads.

However, regardless of a person's criterion, Bernoulli's theroem tells us that if enough cases are accumulated, there is some point at which the person will be convinced that the coin is biased. Eventually everyone will be convinced. The knowledge obtained by the bettors that the coin is biased is in every way as good as the knowledge of the third person who "knows" the coin is biased — say it was that third person who manufactured it. The manufacturer could be wrong too. (The coin could have been switched or the biasing process could have been faulty.) You might wonder what the third person's criterion would be (how many tosses with $H/(H + T) \approx .5$) for changing his mind. Using this method, we can never know the value of any probability with absolute certainty, but if we have more and more opportunities to observe relevant events, we can become as sure as we want to be.

Look again at Figure 2-4. As the number of cases increases, we observe the following:

1. Generally, an observed probability (anywhere between zero and unity) is itself more and more certain (the probability of the probability approaches unity).

2. In particular, the proportion of individuals we observe that have a certain trait becomes the proportion of all individuals who actually have the trait.

3. A statement of possibility (a proposition) derived from the data becomes a true statement.

4. The spatial distribution that we have repeatedly observed in limited areas applies everywhere.

5. The temporal distribution (the rate or frequency) of some event that we have repeatedly observed for limited periods of time will continue to be observed as time goes on.

In other words, we can be certain about probabilities even though we are uncertain about the individual events that comprise them; we can be certain about frequencies (spatial and temporal) even though we are uncertain about the individual events that comprise them. (What does it mean to be certain of such things? The extent of our certainty is the extent to which we allow them to guide our behavior.) When we are uncertain of a probability, rate, or frequency, we may become more certain by examining more cases. Are you uncertain that a coin is biased after a thousand tosses with $H/(H + T) = .7$? Then perhaps you will be certain after another thousand tosses or another thousand. At some point, even the most stubborn skeptic will have to succumb.

COGNITIVE AND BEHAVIORAL EXPERIMENTS

In the example at the very beginning of the chapter (Figure 2-1), the weatherman's statement "The probability of rain is 75 percent" is a representation of the data available to him. When the weatherman is absent, the behaviorist views behavior as guided by the data (the events) themselves while the cognitivist views behavior as guided by an internal representation of them (Figure 2-3).

The weatherman's representation of the data is propositional — a sentence containing a number standing for a probability. Correspondingly, cognitive decision theorists have tended to study probabilities in propositional form. In their experiments, stimuli are often verbal propositions, subjects' internal representations of probabilities are assumed to be propositional, and frequently subjects are asked to respond by stating a proposition or choosing from a group of propositions. Since propositions are by definition linguistic entities and since only humans are capable of using language to guide their behavior, only humans have been used as subjects in cognitive decision experiments.

Behaviorists, on the other hand, have tended to use nonhuman animals as subjects in their experiments because rates of events (rates of food delivery, for instance) guide the behavior of all animals. Since the calculus of probabilities applies to rates of events (the time bar of Figure 2-4) as well as propositional statements (the logic bar of Figure 2-4), it will provide us with a means of relating the two (now quite separate) areas of psychological investigation. However, before comparing the two areas, we must explore them separately. The next two chapters will focus on cognitive studies of judgment and decision, the following two on behavioral studies of responding and choice, and the remaining chapters on comparing these two types of studies and developing a comprehensive viewpoint.

N O T E S

1. One of the reasons that quantum mechanics is so difficult to understand and even then to accept is that it rejects this assumption.

2. Daniel Ellsberg performed an interesting experiment regarding ignorance of probability (described by Slovic and Tversky, 1974). Ellsberg presented subjects with a pair of urns, one containing 50 red

balls and 50 black balls, the other containing a total of 100 red and black balls but in an unknown proportion. The subjects were told that a prize would be awarded if they drew a red ball. Which urn would they choose? A majority of subjects chose the 50:50 urn. In Chapter 6 we shall see that people prefer outcomes that are certain to outcomes that are uncertain. Ellsberg's experiment shows that people also prefer probabilities that are certain to probabilities that are uncertain. In this case the subjects' preference for the certain over the uncertain probability could not be attributed to mistrust of Ellsberg (who might have known how many red balls were in the second urn and was presumably paying for the prize), because subjects maintained their preference for the 50:50 urn even when they were told that the prize would now be awarded for drawing a black ball. It would be interesting to determine whether preference for certainty of probability would remain if the subjects were to lose something rather than win a prize. Chapter 6 will show that people's choices often reverse when losses are substituted for gains.

JUDGMENT

THE WEATHERMAN'S STATEMENT that the probability of rain tomorrow is 75 percent is a judgment. The input to the weatherman consists of data and, of course, the context in which the data are set. The output — what the weatherman says — is the result of some process inside the weatherman, a judgment about the weather. However, unlike a decision, a judgment is never the end of a process. The weatherman's judgment provides him with no direct reward. A judgment is always a guide for making a decision (such as your decision to take an umbrella to work), which leads to a choice, which then produces an outcome.

In the case of the weatherman, the outcome does not directly affect the weatherman himself, but it does affect the listener — the person who takes his advice and carries or does not carry an umbrella to work. The effect of the weatherman's judgment on himself is indirect. If there are enough negative outcomes for enough listeners, the weatherman will soon lose his job. Our social system rewards and punishes judgments indirectly through choices based on them.[1]

A probability is a kind of judgment, and judgments, like probabilities, are guides to behavior (in behavioristic terms, "discriminative stimuli"). However, judgments are often stated as certainties (probabilities of 1.0). For instance, if you were lost in a strange city, you might ask a passerby for directions to your hotel. The passerby's response, "Your hotel is three blocks south," is a judgment, a guide to behavior expressed in this case as a certainty. A judgment need not be verbal. The passerby might just point or draw you a map.

JUDGMENT AND DECISION

According to cognitive decision theory, even a decision made all by yourself — without weathermen or passersby — involves judgment, except in this case the judgment is an internal process. You might not verbally express the output of that process or even be conscious of it. Nevertheless, it is assumed to be part of your cognitive decision mechanism. The study of people's judgments, therefore, is the study of part of the decision process, not the complete process. (This is so even when the process encompasses a social unit of two or more people, as in the case of the weatherman and the listener.)

In studying cognitive processes, often some artificial means have to be devised to bring the internal event out into the open (much as an oil pressure gauge indicates something about the internal state of an automobile). In the case of judgments, however, an artificial device is not necessary because everyone expresses judgments as part of their social interaction with other people. That is, judgments are part of our normal conversational repertoire; we make explicit judgments about our environments all the time. However, a judgment is always a stage in a wider decision process in which a choice is eventually made and an outcome is experienced. A judgment all by itself is incomplete as it normally functions in the world. Judgments need decisions, choices, and outcomes to form a complete process.[2]

ERRORS OF JUDGMENT

In what sense can a judgment be wrong? If a judgment is a guide to behavior, then it is wrong when it guides behavior badly. For instance, you would consider a movie reviewer wrong if you hated a movie that she said was highly entertaining.

When one person makes a judgment and another makes choices based on it, there exists a good criterion by which to determine errors in judgment—the satisfaction of the person making the choices. If you take your umbrella to work on the basis of the weather report, if you go to a movie on the basis of a review, if you walk three blocks south on the basis of directions from a stranger, you will be able to tell by the outcome if the judgment was in error.

Studies of judgment in the psychology laboratory typically put the subject in the place of the weatherman, the movie reviewer, or the stranger on the street; they put the experimenter in the place of the listener to the weather report, the moviegoer, or the asker of directions. That is, the experimenter asks the subject a question that requires the subject to make a judgment. However, the experimenter need not take the trouble of waiting to see what the weather will be tomorrow, going to the movie, or walking down the street. Instead, the experimenter phrases questions so that they fit into some normative theory, usually the mathematics of probability or statistics, which predicts what the outcomes will be. These normative theories have been well tested. For instance, it is not necessary for the experimenter to go to a casino and play roulette in order to discover whether he will win or lose in the long run. The expected value of roulette is negative, and a judgment that you can win in the long run is a wrong judgment, an error.

As you will see, people make plenty of wrong judgments. This chapter is about why they do so. As an example, consider the following question:

A roulette wheel has thirty-two holes numbered 1 to 32. Half of them are red, half black. In addition, the wheel has two green holes labeled 0 and 00. Betting on red or black pays off at even money. Is there any way, in the long run, for a person to win at roulette betting on red or black?

Consider why a person might tell you (without deliberately lying) that you can win at roulette in the long run. First, the person might be very good at calculating odds but might not understand the game of roulette as you described it (an error of perception). In particular, your question by no means makes it clear that the outcome of each spin of the wheel is independent of the outcomes of all other spins. Second, the person might understand the game of roulette and attempt to calculate the odds, but he might calculate them incorrectly (a cognitive error). Third, the person might understand the game but not try to calculate the odds, relying instead on his recollection of his own experience or the second-hand recollections of others. However, his experience might not be extensive, or his recollection might not be accurate. (He might forget losses.) This too is a cognitive error. Lastly, the person might understand the game perfectly well, calculate the odds perfectly, and have excellent memory of his own extensive experience with the game, but he might understand your question differently from how you intended; the person might have considered "winnings" in terms other than total money won or lost in the long run.

The normative theory, by which the judgment is wrong, considers the long run to be an infinite time containing an infinite number of gambles. A person might be less patient than the normative theory demands. It is certainly possible to win big at roulette in the short run, walk away with the winnings, and never gamble again — thus coming out ahead in the long run (as far as a human life is concerned) and letting infinity take care of itself. This is a perfectly reasonable interpretation of your question, however irrelevant it might be from a normative point of view. Alternatively, the person might consider winning in terms of rewards entirely different from monetary gain, such as the excitement of casino gambling or social interaction with other players. The error in such cases would not be due to cognitive malfunctioning but rather to a misunderstanding of your definition of "winning in the long run." More generally, a subject's error might be due to a difference between the subject's and experimenter's conceptions of *value*.

The cognitive psychologist is usually interested in errors of cognition (like those illustrated above) and tries to eliminate errors of perception and misunderstandings of value from the experiment. Whether a specific error is attributable to cognition, perception, or misunderstanding of value depends to a large extent on how the problem is phrased — how the experimenter puts the question to the subject. If the roulette question is rephrased in a more abstract way, say in terms of red and black balls in an urn, the subject is less likely to factor in the excitement of playing in a casino when making a judgment. However, removing a specific background of a problem does not remove all background. The subject might perceive the balls and urn in some idiosyncratic context (as a lottery, for instance). Furthermore, rephrasing the problem in purely mathematical terms (Is $16/32$ grater than $16/34$?) takes away much of the element of judgment that is presumably the object of study.

The usual experimental tactic in the face of misperception and misunderstanding is to vary the context (the frame) of the problem. If various subjects make the same error no matter how the problem is couched, experimenters can be more certain that subjects' errors are due to the internal structure of the problem itself (and therefore cognitive errors) than to misperception or misunderstanding of value.

The next section presents some examples of the sorts of errors of judgment that people commonly make. The sections after that discuss theories about why people make errors.

LOGIC ERRORS

Perhaps the most vivid example of a common logic error is the four-card problem studied by Wason (1966). In the standard version of this problem, the experimenter places four cards in front of the subject. The cards have an A, a T, a 4, and a 7 on their faces. The experimenter states the rule "If a card has a vowel on one side, it has an even number on the other" and then asks, "Which cards have to be turned over in order to test the rule?" Most subjects correctly turn over the A card, but many incorrectly turn over the 4 card and very few turn over the 7 card (as they should). Turning over the 4 card is wrong because, regardless of whether there was a vowel or a consonant on the other side of the 4 card, the rule would not be violated. However, turning over the 7 card is necessary because a vowel on the other side of the 7 card would violate the rule. To test the rule, therefore, you have to turn over the 7 card.

Subjects make this error (failing to turn over the 7 card) under many conditions: when the wording of the problem is varied, when the nature of the problem is explained to them in detail, when they are rewarded for the correct answers, and when subjects' attention is called to their inconsistencies. However, there exists one version of the problem that does reduce errors considerably. In the easy version (Johnson-Laird, Legrenzi, and Sonino-Legrenzi, 1972) envelopes are substituted for cards and the rule is "If a letter is sealed, it has a five-cent stamp." In this version the subject sees two envelopes from the back, one sealed and one unsealed, and two envelopes from the front, one with a stamp and one without. The subject should turn over the sealed envelope and the one without the stamp. Most subjects do.

Several explanations have been offered for why people generally fail to solve the four-card problem in its abstract version. One explanation is that people misunderstand the logical consequences of if – then statements. In logic, the statement "If p then q" is not equivalent to the statement "If q then p." For instance, if an animal is a collie it is necessarily a dog, but if it is a dog it is not necessarily a collie. However, in the four-card problem, subjects may understand "If a card has a vowel on one side, it has an even number on the other" as implying "If a card has an even number of one side, it has a vowel on the other."

In ordinary conversation, we do make if – then statements and expect their converses to be understood also. In conversation, the order of our if – then statements is often determined by the order of stimuli and responses in the actions those statements are intended to guide rather than by logical inclusion. For instance, in normal conversation the statement "If the light at the crossing flashes, a train is coming" is meant to imply "If a train is coming, the light will flash." (Fail-safe design would insure that when the signal mechanism failed, the light would flash continuously. Assuming such design is in fact used, the latter statement would be correct.) However, the person who approaches the crossroads sees the light flashing first, so behavior is better guided by referring first to the signal and then to the consequences.

In the case of the four-card problem, we behave as if the problem were "If you turn over the A card, you will find an even number on the other side, *and* if you turn over the 4 card, you will find a vowel on the other side." If the problem is understood this way, it makes perfect sense to turn over the A card and 4 card and to leave the now irrelevant T card and 7 card untouched. It is possible that the abstract nature plus the logical complexity (involving contrapositives of conditionals) of the four-card problem invites stereotypical reinterpretation, hence misinterpretation, while the concrete nature of the envelope-and-stamps problem, being unambiguous, prevents stereotypical reinterpretation and, somewhat paradoxically, forces subjects to focus on its abstract, logical aspects.

In cognitive psychology (as opposed to behaviorism), tracing a logical error to a conceivable function (in the above example, to only one of several conceivable functions) in ordinary conversation does not directly answer the question, Why do people make the logical error? To answer this question cognitive psychologists need to trace the logical error to its internal source in the person's cognitive processing mechanism. We will consider possible internal sources (mistakes of perception, of cognition, and of value) later in the chapter. First it is necessary to discuss several other kinds of errors in judgment to which people are susceptible.

RANDOMNESS ERRORS

It is difficult to grasp the nature of randomness. As the last chapter indicted, a random process is one where we are ignorant, sometimes deliberately so, of what causes each particular outcome. Thus, given that the cards have been thoroughly shuffled, a royal flush in poker is no less random than a junk hand. If you toss a coin six times, the sequence *H-H-H-T-T-T* is just as likely to occur as the sequence *H-T-H-T-T-H*. Yet most people regard the former sequence as less likely than the latter (Kahneman and Tversky, 1972). Perhaps people have these misconceptions because when a poker player gets a royal flush in real life, there is some possibility, however low it may be, that the player has cheated (a violation of randomness, or of the social agreement of deliberate ignorance about the order of cards in a hand). Cheating, hence a violation of randomness, is much less likely to have occurred when a player has a junk hand. Similarly, in real life, a license plate saying O-U-KID is much less likely to be the result of a random process of issuing licenses (and more likely to be a vanity plate) then U-A-OJZ. Laboratory subjects, therefore, may be somewhat suspicious (consciously or unconsciously) when they see symmetrical or familiar patterns in the results of a random process. This suspiciousness may persist (especially if it is unconscious) when the experimenter assures the subject that the process is random. When subjects say that *H-H-H-T-T-T* is less likely than *H-T-H-T-T-H* to be the result of random process, they may really mean that is more likely to be the result of a nonrandom process.

Consider another example. Psychologists who study the behavior of rats in mazes often try to "randomize" events. For instance, an experimenter studying pigeon behavior might want to put food in one of two hoppers randomly for ten trials. To select a random sequence, the experimenter might toss a coin ten times or look up a sequence in a random-number table. It is just as possible, of course, to get *L-L-L-L-L-L-L-L-L-L* as any other particular sequence. Even with the restriction (on randomness) that five elements must be L's and the other five R's, it is just as possible to get L-L-L-L-L-R-R-R-R-R as any other particular sequence. When these patterns occur, experimenters commonly (and quite correctly) throw out the sequence and try again until they get one that seems subjectively random to them. The experimenter's object is to prevent the pigeon from predicting which hopper the food is in, and sometimes this objective cannot be satisfied with a process that generates a truly random sequence of numbers. True randomness refers to a process whose results are unpredictable "in the long run." Even a truly random process will occasionally produce sequences that not only seem predictable (in the short run) but also *are* predictable, as in the cases of L-L-L-L-L-R-R-R-R-R and L-R-L-R-L-R-L-R-L-R.

Suppose that instead of flipping a coin or consulting a random-number table, the pigeon experimenter asked you to produce a random series of five L's and five R's. What would you do? When people as subjects in experiments are asked to produce random strings of L's and R's (or H's and T's), they tend to do exactly what the psychologist does with the pigeon—they avoid familiar patterns having long strings of a single letter. However, with extensive training, people can come to produce long strings of letters indistinguishable, in all tested ways, from a truly random process (Neuringer, 1986). When Neuringer rewarded pigeons for producing random sequences of pecks on two illuminated buttons (keys), the pigeons initially made the same sorts of errors as people do, avoiding long repetitions of pecks on a single key; however, with extended training, the pigeons eventually came to peck randomly on the two keys.

One consequence of people's difficulty in understanding randomness is the famous gambler's fallacy. If the ball of a roulette wheel lands on red ten times in a row, it somehow seems more likely that the eleventh outcome will be black. Fairness seems to demand compensation for the previous string of reds. What we forget is that (unless someone is cheating) each spin of the wheel is independent of all other spins. For all the effect they will have on the eleventh spin, the first ten spins might as well have occurred in Timbuktu as in the gambling casino that night. We mistake the gambling casino (and the psychology laboratory), where each event is independent of events that have gone before it, for situations more common in everyday life where events are interdependent, such as being at bat against a pitcher with a good fastball who has just thrown five curves in a row.

SAMPLE-SIZE ERRORS

Here is a problem:

> A certain town is served by two hospitals. About forty-five babies are born each day in the larger hospital, and about fifteen in the smaller hospital. As you know, about 50 percent of all babies are boys. However, the exact percentage varies from day to day. Sometimes it is higher than 50 percent, sometimes lower.
>
> For a period of one year, each hospital recorded the days on which more than 60 percent of the babies born were boys. Which hospital do you think recorded more such days?

This problem, along with others, was put to ninety-five undergraduate subjects by Tversky and Kahneman (1974). Twenty-one said the larger hospital, twenty-one said the smaller, and fifty-three said both hospitals had the same number (within 5 percent of each other).

The correct answer is the smaller hospital. If you take repeated samples from a population, the smaller the sample you take, the more variable it is. Thus it is less reliable as an indicator of the characteristics of the population. Consider what the answer to the hospital question would be if the smaller hospital had only two births each day. With two births there would often be days with 100 percent boys (thus more than 60 percent) and often days with 100 percent girls. As the sample grew larger and larger, the fewer extreme values there would be in either direction. If the sample were the entirety of births in the United States on a given day, there would virtually never be a day with more than 60 percent boys (or girls). As discussed in the last chapter, in a random process, the larger the sample, the less deviation there is from the true probability.

Like errors in logic and randomness, errors in sample size are very common. Kahneman and Tversky (1972) found that people believe (given a true probability of .5 of the birth of a boy) that the odds of 6 boys being born in a sample of 10 births equals the odds of 60 boys in 100 births equals the odds of 600 boys in a 1000 births (whereas the odds are much higher of finding 6 boys in 10 births than 600 in 1000). Sample-size errors occur in many settings. They occur in abstract problems (often formulated as drawing balls from urns) as well as other concretely phrased problems (finding various heartbeat types in samples of people, finding various heights in samples of men, etc.). However, with extreme values of sample size (e.g., two-bed hospitals) or extreme deviations from true probability, subjects tend to make fewer sample-size errors. Bar-Hillel (1979) found that in the hospital problem, more subjects correctly answered the smaller hospital when the proportion of boys exceeded 70 percent instead of 60. With 100 percent boys, the number of correct answers obtained was greater than with the other two formulations combined.

Is there some way to frame a sampling problem to reduce sample-size errors? Possibly. Notice that in the hospital problem, no indication is given of the *use* to which this information will be put. In other words, the hospital problem asks for a judgment (as it is intended to do), not a decision. Now consider this problem (for readers familiar with baseball) that does indicate a use — that is, it asks for a decision. You are a manager of a major league team and need to bring up an outfielder from your minor league team. Two are available. The first has a batting average of .325 accumulated over a whole season of play. The second has been playing in the minors for only three weeks. Assuming that the two players are equivalent in every other way (age, fielding, scouting reports, etc.), what average would the second player have to have (over those three weeks) for you to pick him?

For readers unfamiliar with baseball, an equivalent problem is this: You have inherited a million dollars and are about to invest some of it in a local department store. You have calculated that if the store averages 1000 customers per day it will make a big profit and therefore be an excellent investment. You hire someone to stand at the door and count the customers for sixty days. You find that the store indeed averages 1000 customers per day. You are about to invest, when a second store suddenly becomes available for investment. However, there are only five days to count customers at the second store before the offer will be withdrawn. You hire someone to count the customers at this second store. Assuming it is equivalent to the first in every way other than how many days you count customers, what would the daily average have to be for you to invest in the second store?

If your answer to the baseball question is greater than .325 and your answer to the department store question is greater than 1000, you have understood that averages taken from small samples are less reliable than averages taken form large samples. In that sense, your answer is right. Let us assume that most people get the baseball or department store decision problems right but get the hospital problem wrong. (Several people, in a very nonrandom and small sample of my own, got the baseball problem right, explaining quite cogently why they did, and then proceeded to get the hospital problem wrong.)

One possible reason for errors in judgment is that the additional information that must be supplied to a subject so that he or she can make a decision could influence the answer either way. Perhaps subjects implicitly convert (presumably incomplete) judgment problems to (complete) decision problems. If the experimenter provides no decision frame, subjects may provide stereotypical ones of their own. In making a choice, it is not always a good idea to choose the alternative about which you have the most information. When the alternative you know is bad, you might be better off taking a chance on the alternative you do not know. In the baseball example, if the first player had a season's batting average of .175 you might be better off picking one who was batting .175 averaged over three weeks. The second player may prove to be not that bad a hitter in the long run. Similarly, if the first department store averaged 500 customers a day for sixty days, it would more likely be truly below the threshold of profitability than one that averaged 500 customers a day for only five days.

However, these examples do no more than emphasize the fact that all judgments, as such, are in a sense incomplete — without a frame that asks for a decision. We have not yet answered in cognitive terms why errors in judgment are made.

BASE RATE ERRORS

In the last chapter we briefly considered a hypothetical decision (which we hope will never be a real one): Suppose you go to the doctor for a general checkup. You have no particular symptoms. However, you test positively for a certain disease. Should you begin a course of expensive, possibly dangerous treatments?

Let us consider this example further. One question you will immediately ask is "Given that I test positively, what is the probability that I have the disease?" Determining this probability is not as easy as it may seem. Suppose doctors check the medical records of all people with the disease. They find that a certain fraction of those patients had tested positively but, like you, had no symptoms at the time. As indicated in the last chapter

$$\frac{PD}{P} = \frac{PD}{D} \times \frac{D/t}{P/t} \qquad (3\text{-}1)$$

PD/P is the probability that you want to know — the probability that you have the disease given that you test positive. PD/D is the probability that the doctors can measure — the probability that a person will test positive given that the person has the disease. D/t and P/t are base rates — fractions of the population of people like you (t) who, respectively, have the disease and test positive.

In many real-life situations, it is impossible to discover all relevant base rates. The usual practice in such situations is to assume that all base rates are equal. In Equation 3-1 the assumption that the base rates are equal is equivalent to setting the base rate term to 1.0. Respected statisticians, in making decisions, are often ignorant of base rates. They, too, are often forced to use the conditional probability that they can observe rather than the one they cannot, the one that would be the best guide to their behavior.

For medical decisions, the threshold of what is considered a positive test is often made very low in order to catch as many people as possible with the disease. The price of lowering the threshold of a medical test is that a lot of people without the disease will test positive. Physicians frequently assume that is better to treat someone without the disease than to fail to treat someone with the disease. (Of course, this assumption may not always be in the patient's interest.) Even when physicians do not have base rate information (in the form of their own estimates prior to a test), they tend to discount it and assume that the probability that a patient has the disease given that the patient tests positively is about equal to the probability that a patient tests positively given the patient has the disease (Eddy, 1982). The consequence of ignoring base rates and relying strongly on tests with low thresholds is that the probability of a patient having the disease is overestimated.

The point of running through this example again is to illustrate how difficult base rates are to grasp intuitively. There is no question that subjects in psychology experiments tend to ignore base rates (just as physicians do) even when the base rates are clearly indicated. Let us consider an illustrative example. The following problem was put to subjects by Tversky and Kahneman (1982, p. 156):

A cab was involved in a hit and run accident at night. Two cab compa-
nies, the Green and the Blue, operate in the city. You are given the
following data:

(a) 85% of the cabs in the city are Green and 15% are Blue.

(b) a witness identified the cab as Blue. The court tested the reliability
of the witness under the same circumstances that existed on the night of
the accident and concluded that the witness correctly identified each
one of the two colors 80% of the time and failed 20% of the time.

What is the probability that the cab involved in the accident was Blue
rather than Green?

Here is how to make the appropriate calculations. Let B equal the
number of Blue cabs, I equal the number of cabs identified as Blue,
and BI equal the number of cabs correctly identified as Blue. According to Bayes' rule,

$$\frac{BI}{I} = \frac{BI}{B} \times \frac{B/t}{I/t} \qquad (3\text{-}2)$$

Here BI/B is .8, B/t is .15, and I/t is equal to the fraction of correct
blue identifications $(.8 \times .15 = .12)$ plus the fraction of incorrect
blue identifications $(.2 \times .85 = .17)$, or .29.
Thus

$$\frac{BI}{I} = .8 \times \frac{.15}{.29} = .41 \qquad (3\text{-}3)$$

Taking base rates into account, the probability that the cab was
actually blue is less than .5. As Tversky and Kahneman (1982, p. 157)
put it: "In spite of the witness's report . . . the hit-and-run cab is
more likely to be Green than Blue, because the base rate is more
extreme than the witness is credible."

However, Tversky and Kahneman (1982) report that a large number of subjects with various versions of this problem ignored the base
rate entirely and equated the probability that the cab was Blue, given
that the witness said so, with the probability that the witness identified the cab as Blue, given that it was Blue. In other words, the
median and modal answer is typically .8, a value which coincides
with the credibility of the witness and is apparently unaffected by
the relative frequency of Blue and Green cabs.

As with logic errors, randomness errors, and sample-size errors,
base rate errors are common over a very wide range of problems.
Here is another example (from Kahneman and Tversky, 1973). Two

groups of subjects were given descriptions of people, including their interests and their hobbies. One group of subjects was told that the descriptions were drawn randomly from a group of seventy engineers and thirty lawyers. For convenience, we shall refer to this group as group 1. The other group of subjects, group 2, was told that the descriptions were drawn randomly from a group of seventy lawyers and thirty engineers. All subjects were asked to estimate the probability that each person described was a lawyer or an engineer. The subjects were told that a group of experts was also doing this task and that they would receive a bonus if their evaluations approached those of the experts.

Some of the descriptions were extremely vague, giving hardly any information one way or another. Nevertheless, subjects in both groups assigned probabilities to descriptions almost identically — purely on the basis of the descriptions. Subjects seemed to use only the descriptions (which were common across groups, however vague they were) rather than the base rate information (70 : 30 or 30 : 70), which differed across groups.

Here is one particularly ambiguous description:

> Dick is a 30-year-old man. He is married with no children. A man of high ability and high motivation, he promises to be quite successful in his field. He is well liked by his colleagues.

On the average, subjects in both groups said that the probability was .5 that this person was an engineer. The subjects were clearly wrong to guess in this way. What they should have done, given such an ambiguous description, was to fall back on the base rates. The subjects in group 2 should have guessed that the probability was .7 that the description was that of a lawyer, and the subjects in the other group should have guessed that the probability was .7 that the description was that of an engineer. The only case where the two groups actually separated in this way was with the following description:

> Suppose now that you are given no information whatsoever about an individual chosen at random from the sample.
>
> The probability that this man is one of the 30 [70 for the other group of subjects] engineers in the sample of 100 is _____%.

Unlike some of the other kinds of errors people make, base rate errors appear in abstract as well as concretely phrased problems and persist even when problems are framed as decisions instead of judgments. However, if you are like me, you will feel a certain affinity for the subjects in these experiments and harbor an intuitive resistance to base rates. Where could that resistance come from?

First, base rates are, in general, prior probabilities or background probabilities — the forest as opposed to the trees. When we are faced with a problem of any kind, our training leads us to cope with it on its own terms. To account for base rates is, in a sense, to give up on the problem itself. Second, accounting for base rates is often frowned upon in our society. To account for base rates is to be prejudiced about the particular case being judged. In a courtroom, for instance, jurors are specifically told to disregard base rate information such as the defendant's prior record, economic status, social class, race, religion, age, and sex and to make judgments solely on the basis of the immediate evidence, however vague and uncertain it may be. Similarly, in hiring, acceptance to schools, renting apartments, and choosing friend, prejudice is socially condemned. A subject in a psychology experiment, given evidence on the point in question, however vague, might well find it difficult to adopt biases that in everyday life might be considered unfair.

Third, it is often not clear what the relevant base rates are. In the medical example, how do you select a population of "people like you"? All human beings? All Americans? All Americans of your sex and age? Where do you draw the line? The base rate question becomes still more ticklish if you are of Jewish ancestry and the test is for Tay–Sachs disease, if you are black and the test is for sickle cell anemia, or if you are homosexual and the test is for AIDS.

In the Blue–Green cab problem, should the base rate be cabs in the city, as given, or cabs in that neighborhood or cabs involved in accidents? (When the cab problem is phrased in terms of cabs involved in accidents, subjects do indeed take base rates more into account.) It is also possible that subjects given the cab problem assume (consciously or unconsciously) that the witness's perception has already taken base rates into account, perhaps more relevant base rates than those supplied by the experimenter.

In the engineer–lawyer problem, the base rates are clear. However, it is not clear whether the experts whose judgments the subjects are instructed to match took base rates into account themselves. Subjects might assume that an expert would be exactly the person who is so good at making judgments on the basis of specific descriptions that base rates would not be necessary. A subject seriously trying to match the experts might see taking base rates into account, even on highly ambiguous descriptions, as a form of cheating.

As with the other types of errors, it is worthwhile to ask, "When is a base rate error not made?" As with the other errors, base rate errors can be reduced and even eliminated by changing the frame of the problem. According to Tversky and Kahneman (1982, p. 156), base rate errors tend to diminish when problems are rephrased so that subjects view a base rate as causing the outcome rather than as a statistical biasing factor. In the case of the Blue – Green cab problem, base rate errors are diminished when subjects are told that 85 percent of the cabs *in accidents* are Green. When the problem is framed this way, subjects presumably imagine some scenario — perhaps the Green cab company pays drivers less or fails to maintain its cabs. Then the base rates emerge from the statistical background and become part of the problem itself.

In a recent extensive study of both the Blue – Green cab problem and the lawyer – engineer problem, Ginossar and Trope (1987) found that people took base rates into account more frequently: (1) when they were experienced with using base rates in other judgment problems, (2) when the base rates in the current problem were more salient (more vivid), (3) when use of base rates was rewarded, and (4) when the specific information (other than base rates) was apparently random or unreliable. For Ginossar and Trope, people use base rates just like they use a rule in solving a problem. If the rule is well learned and demonstrably applicable in a given situation, it is used.

So far we have considered only a few of the kinds of judgment errors that people make. In an informal way we have discussed some explanations for those errors. Now we will discuss a comprehensive theory that views judgment errors in a cognitive context. Then we will briefly indicate how the same errors can be viewed in perceptual terms and finally as misunderstandings of value.

COGNITIVE ERRORS: HEURISTICS

The Nobel Prize – winning economist and psychologist Herbert Simon (1978) claims that animals (including people) do not always solve each particular problem in life in the best possible way — they do not optimize — because optimizing is too difficult. Instead, according to Simon, over the course of evolution or over the course of experience during our lifetimes, we have developed convenient, easy problem-solving methods that pretty much get us what we want. When confronted with a given problem, we bring to bear our limited information and our limited cognitive mechanisms and arrive at the best solution we can under the circumstances. Simon calls this process "satisficing."

We will discuss satisficing further in the chapters on decision and choice. For now it is important to note that if we have developed cognitive mechanisms that satisfice (rather than optimize), we will in certain situations make errors. Those situations, perhaps unusual or extreme, test the limits of our cognitive mechanisms — mechanisms that usually work well enough. Through analysis of errors, it may be possible to discover the nature of our cognitive mechanisms. We have just discussed a few of the many errors in judgment uncovered by psychologists. What do these errors tell us about the cognitive mechanisms involved?

Lest the reader jump to hasty conclusions, it must be said that cognitive psychology is far from being able to describe specific functional cognitive mechanisms. It is not now possible to build a computer containing a set of cognitive mechanisms that, given a wide range of problems as input, will produce an output consisting of both correct solutions and errors that are characteristic of those by a normal human being — although this is a goal of many cognitive psychologists, including Simon.

At present it is possible to specify those mechanisms only in terms of a set of *heuristics*. Let us consider a few of the heuristics that the psychologists Daniel Kahneman and Amos Tversky have proposed.

REPRESENTATIVENESS

In many situations in life we are called upon to make judgments about events on the basis of limited information. For instance, we may buy a car on the basis of a test drive, we elect officials on the basis of their ability to campaign, and we get married on the basis of our experience during a brief courtship. Our implicit assumption in these cases is that the experience we have under one set of circumstances is representative of what our experience will be under another, often much wider set of circumstances. The heuristic we use is that of representativeness — the resemblance between one situation and another.

Several of the errors discussed in previous sections may arise when the heuristic of representativeness goes awry. For instance, you will commit a randomness error if you assume that a brief sequence of events (left–right sequences or head–tail outcomes) cannot be the result of a random process because it resembles (is representative of) the output of a nonrandom process. You will commit a sample-size error if you assume that any sample, no matter how small, has the same statistical properties as the population from which it is drawn (of which it is representative). Finally, you will commit a base rate error if you ignore base rates and judge a person's occupation wholly on the basis of the degree to which that person's description resembles (is representative of) a typical person engaged in that occupation. (If you meet a man on the beach whose outfit and behavior perfectly resembles your image of a U.S. Navy frogman, he is still more likely to be an accountant than a frogman simply because there are so many accountants and so few frogmen.)

Choosing a spouse is a decision that seems particularly susceptible to malfunctions of the representativeness heuristic. We tend to go by the resemblence of our prospective mate to our ideal, while our relatives and friends supply us (often to no avail) with base rate data.

Perhaps the reason that base rate errors tend to diminish when base rates are seen as causal rather than statistical is that perception of causality acts through representativeness. For instance, if you have just read an article about accountants who compensate for their staid image by dressing up in strange costumes, you might alter your image of accountants to include people in wetsuits and flippers. Similarly, if you want to convince a friend not to marry a particular person, a better tactic than citing statistics on divorce (statistical base rates) might be to cite evidence that as people get older they grow more and more to resemble their parents.

AVAILABILITY

You are driving along the highway and see the flashing lights of police cars and ambulances on the other side indicating an accident. You drive a little slower for the next hour or so. You hear that Betty Ford has breast cancer or that President Reagan has rectal cancer and you make an appointment with your own doctor for an examination. In making judgments as well as decisions, we tend to use the information that is most available to us. In so doing we often fail to compensate for the tendency to remember most strongly the events that are most salient or most recent — like accidents on the road or illnesses of famous people.

It is of course easiest and fastest to make judgments on the basis of what is easiest to call to mind — the heuristic of availability. Nevertheless, this heuristic can also lead to errors. For instance, which are more frequent, English words beginning with *re-* or English words ending with *-re*? Most people say words beginning with *re-* are more frequent, presumably because it is easier to recall words that begin with certain letters than those that end with certain letters. (It is easier to recite the Pledge of Allegiance forward than backward — but that does not mean that the words at the beginning are more common in English than the words at the end.) Actually, words ending with *-re* are more frequent in English.

ADJUSTMENT AND ANCHORING

One group of subjects was given five seconds to estimate the product $8 \times 7 \times 6 \times 5 \times 4 \times 3 \times 2 \times 1$; another was given five seconds to estimate the product $1 \times 2 \times 3 \times 4 \times 5 \times 6 \times 7 \times 8$. The median estimate for the descending sequence was 2250; the median estimate for the ascending sequence was 512. The correct answer is 40,320. When given a problem where time is of the essence, people tend to apply a familiar heuristic — they make an initial estimate on the basis of the information as it begins to arrive or as they scan it, and then they adjust upwards or downwards on the basis of subsequent information. However, because of time pressure, the adjustment is often insufficient. With the multiplication problem, subjects who began with small numbers had to adjust more than those who began with large numbers. Neither group adjusted enough, but the one beginning with small numbers evidently had a great deal more trouble.

In making judgments about other people, our initial impressions are notoriously resistant to revision. Perhaps part of our tendency to ignore base rates stems from the heuristic of adjustment and anchoring. Even though we may be aware of base rates before meeting someone, we form initial impressions of an individual on the basis of immediate evidence and often do not adjust that impression sufficiently by considering base rates or, once we have made a judgment, by considering later-arriving facts.

BIASES

Normative rules of judgment are derived from logic, mathematics, or statistics. If followed, normative rules lead to decisions and choices with optimal outcomes in the long run. Heuristics are rules of thumb, easier to learn and remember than normative rules. If followed, heuristics lead to decisions and choices with satisfactory outcomes in the short run (satisficing). We have seen how some heuristics work and how, if a person uses them in certain situations, there may be outcomes that are far from optimal in the long run. In that case we say that the person has made an error of judgment.

It is important to remember that *error* is a relative term. Here, "error of judgment" means any judgment that deviates excessively from the optimal judgment given by normative rules. Defined in this way, errors may arise from sources other than the application of heuristics. One such source is a *bias*. Biases are expectations we have about problems in judgment. Instead of solving the problem as it is stated or in its actual context in the real world, we impose a context of our own — usually the context of ordinary conversation or ordinary experience. In logic, "If *p* then not *q*" does not imply "If not *p* then *q*." But in everyday life, I obey the rule "If you see a no-parking sign, hydrant, or driveway in a space, do not park there," and I also assume "If you do not see a no-parking sign, hydrant, or driveway in a space, you may park." Although my assumption has not led to absolute optimization (I occasionally get parking tickets), it has served me well enough in parking in New York City. My (illogical) assumptions bias my judgment in all problems I face, whether in real life as a student taking a test or in a psychology experiment as a subject. People's difficulties with the four-card problem may, as we have indicated, arise from logical biases of this kind.

Consider another sort of expectation (bias) most of us have about problems in judgment. When we make guesses in a series of problems, we expect that there will be some chance, however small, of getting them all right. Suppose you are taking a multiple-choice test and you do not have the faintest clue to any of the answers (another example that we hope will never happen). However (perhaps instead of studying the course material) you have studied the previous examinations given by this teacher and have noted a tendency for correct answers to be choice *a*. In fact, 60 percent of the correct answers in tests given by this teacher over the years have been *a*'s. In an exam of

100 questions, you can virtually guarantee yourself a score of 60 percent (passing with a D) if you answer *a* to all questions. (The exams are graded by machine, so no one will notice the nonrandom pattern.) Because there is absolutely no chance that *all* answers are *a*'s you cannot do better than getting a D. Yet this is the optimal solution. It is what you should do.

However, you can go for broke and guess *a* on 60 percent of the questions and spread answers *b*, *c*, and *d* among the rest, thereby possibly getting an A on the exam. Given that you really have no clue at all about the answers, the latter tactic is very risky. On the average, each guess of *b*, *c*, or *d* will tend to lower your grade. Yet if you are like me, you will at least be tempted to guess in a pattern and go for broke. Perhaps this tendency arises from situations in everyday life where getting part of a sequence right is of no use at all. (For instance, in guessing the sequence of numbers to open a push-button combination lock, there would be no point in guessing all 7's even though that might be the most common number. No one would set a combination at all 7's).

It is not easy to distinguish between a bias and a heuristic (they are rarely distinguished in the literature on judgment). For convenience, let us say that a heuristic is a nonnormative rule while a bias is a tendency to violate a normative rule. This makes a rather fuzzy distinction, but to paraphrase the philosopher Wittgenstein, a clear picture of a fuzzy scene would be an inaccurate picture.

ERRORS OF PERCEPTION

The Gestalt psychologist Kurt Koffka (1931) cited an experiment with spiders by H. Volkelt. A spider normally attacks and kills flies caught in its web but, when Volkelt inserted a dead fly in its nest, the spider ran away from it. A spider that runs away from a fly, like a hungry man who runs away from a bowl of soup, is making an error. Koffka says "the spider's stupidity consists, not in running away from a frail victim, but in mistaking its victim for a formidable foe" (p. 117).

Certain errors in judgment are clearly errors of perception. The weatherman may give a perfectly rational report based on the data available, but his report will be in error if he mistakes a cumulus cloud for a cirrus cloud. A radiologist may make a perfect diagnosis based on the X ray she sees, but her perception may be wrong in the first place. In the psychology laboratory a person might misperceive a number or a sign in a problem, otherwise solving the problem perfectly. In the days before copying machines, teachers frequently wrote examinations on the blackboard. "I copied it wrong" was my favorite excuse. I hoped the teacher would agree with me that a perceptual error was not as bad as a cognitive one.

A more difficult case to analyze arises when we consider a person's perception of a problem in terms of the relation of the problem to its context. In perception, context is crucial. A single gray spot may seem almost white against a black background and almost black against a white background. Any problem that can be rephrased in terms of the relation of the problem to its context may be thought of as a perceptual problem. For instance, in the Blue – Green taxi problem, the subject in the experiment *perceives* the witness's testimony in the context of the base rates. Recall Equation 3-3. The fraction .15/.29 is the correct base rate ratio. Yet the modal answer to the question was .8. This result may be said to reveal that, whatever the experimenter may have intended, the problem was framed so that the subjects *perceived* the base rate ratio to be 1.0.

Thus, psychologists may see people's responses in the Blue – Green cab problem in at least two ways: errors of cognition (people do not take base rates into account) or errors of perception (people do take base rates into account but the base rates are subjective ones, not those specified by the experimenter).[3] These two points of view (themselves subject to cognitive or perceptual analysis) differ in how they explain changes in judgment as the context is varied. For instance, when the base rates are phrased in terms of cabs in accidents rather than cabs in the city, the cognitive explanation says that now base rates are taken into account (perhaps explaining this change in terms of the influence of causality on cognition). The perceptual explanation says that base rates are now perceived differently (perhaps explaining this change in terms of the influence of causality on perception).

There is some debate today between cognitive and perceptual views of judgment errors (see Cohen, 1981, and the accompanying commentary). In general, the perceptual view supports the rationality of people and ascribes errors to the perceptual mechanism ("cognitive illusions"), while the cognitive view supports the veridicality of perception and ascribes errors to the cognitive mechanism. Until there is agreement on the line between internal perceptual and internal cognitive processes, the debate has no chance of being settled.

Most likely people make errors of perception and errors of cognition. Given our current state of knowledge, we have no way of assigning behavioral variation to one internal mechanism or another.[4]

MISUNDERSTANDINGS OF VALUE

In the course of describing various judgment errors and providing cognitive explanations for them (in terms of heuristics and biases), we have implied that at least some errors might be due to misunderstanding of value. Until the behavioral viewpoint is fully explained, we cannot add either much detail or much consistency to this outlook. At this point no more can be done than to give the reader some idea of a behaviorist's approach to judgment and judgment errors.

In behavioral theory, judgments are choices of a sort. They are not abstract or disinterested reports of the state of an internal process but choice behavior — learned, maintained, and extinguished just as other choice behavior is — by contingencies of reinforcement. (We shall discuss later exactly how this process works.)

The difference between judgments and other choices is that the latter are reinforced directly while the former, serving as guides to other behavior, are usually reinforced indirectly. For instance, taking your umbrella to work (a choice) is directly reinforced, while predicting rain (a judgment) is indirectly reinforced. Correctly predicting rain is not primarily reinforced by the appearance of rain. Rather, it is reinforced by the consequences of preparing for rain when it actually does rain and not having to prepare for rain when rain is not predicted. Similarly, the dentist who correctly predicts when it's going to hurt you not only prepares you for pain but allows you to relax at other times. Otherwise, her predictions would be valueless (and you would be thrown back on base rates.)

The difference between judgment and choice (in behavioristic terms) is a social one. The very same topography of behavior may be a judgment in one social context and a choice in another. For instance, a choreographer performing a certain step may be directly rewarded by applause for himself and indirectly rewarded by applause for the dancer who learns the step by imitating him. Teachers are sometimes directly rewarded by students for being good teachers and sometimes indirectly rewarded when their students go on to use what they have learned. Students are directly rewarded for making good judgments, but those rewards are intended to be mere substitutes for the most substantial and direct rewards that accrue from the actions inherent in being an educated person.

The behavioral theory agrees with the cognitive theory that the use of heuristics is often reinforced. In the course of describing heuristics, we have speculated on possible sources of that reinforcement in everyday life (for instance, assuming a good fastball pitcher who has just thrown five curves in a row is likely now to come in with a fastball) and the errors it leads to in certain situations (for instance, betting on red in roulette after five blacks in a row). The difference is really one of attitude. Although the cognitive psychologist is interested in the heuristics themselves, the behavioral psychologist is interested in the rewards and punishments that are obtained by using them.

The cognitive psychologist traces people's failure to use base rates to a heuristic (in the case of base rate errors, this is usually the representativeness heuristic). The behavioral theorist traces the same behavior to the short-term, direct benefits that people get from ignoring base rates (quicker and easier computations, being considered unprejudiced by your peers, being more precise if not more accurate) and the long-term benefits and penalties of ignoring base rates (for instance, the relative value of treating a patient without a disease versus failing to treat a patient with a disease). The behaviorist assumes that the behavior of people (both judgments and choices) reflects their values. Humans, as animals capable of making choices, by definition cannot choose alternatives they value less over alternatives they value more. However, people can choose in the short run what they would reject in the long run (as a smoker chooses short-term pleasure over long-term health). Lack of self-control in behavioral theory corresponds to error in cognitive theory. We will have a lot more to say later about the dynamics of this sort of error.

JUDGMENT IN A SOCIAL CONTEXT

Examples throughout this chapter illustrate that errors of judgment abound in everyday life, but the most significant area of everyday-life judgments has barely been discussed — the ethical judgments we make about people, both ourselves and others. In this area, too, our judgments are subject to errors, sometimes with serious social consequences; judgments often incorporate praise or blame and consequent social action. Wrong judgments, by definition, lead to wrong actions. The psychologists Nisbett, Borgida, Crandall, and Reed (1976) have collected an extensive list of examples and experiments showing errors in "popular induction." Let us consider one of them.

In a classic study of obedience, Milgram (1963) found that most people as subjects in experiments administer high amounts of shock to other people if an experimenter tells them to do so. In a further experiment (Miller et al., 1973) cited by Nisbett and colleagues (1976), one group of subjects was told about the Milgram experiment and its results. These subjects had originally expected, as most of us do, that Milgram's subjects would have refused to administer (what they believed to be) high intensities of shock to other people. The second group of subjects in the Miller experiment was not told about Milgram's results. "They were left," as Nisbett and colleagues say, "with their naive expectations that such behavior would be rare" (p. 103). In terms of the present chapter, the two groups of subjects were given differing base rate data. One group now believed that people generally do administer high-intensity shock to other people; the other group believed that people generally do not.

After this, all subjects in both groups of the study by Miller and others (1973) were asked to rate two individuals who they were told went "all the way" in the Milgram study and administered high-intensity shock. Note how similar this is to the lawyer–engineer study; in both studies two groups of subjects were given different base rate information and identical specific information about individuals. In both studies the outcome was the same. The subjects in the study by Miller and others rated the two shock administrators virtually the same (and pretty negatively) whether or not they knew that most people behaved the same way in the same situation. This experiment and many others indicate that people judge other people negatively on the basis of the actions of those other people in specific situations and ignore whether their actions in those situations are typical or atypical. That is, we tend to attribute a person's bad qualities to the person's *character* rather than to the *situation* the person is in even when evidence indicates that most people behave the same way in that situation. The fact that anyone would have done the same in the same situation (the base rate) seems not to be relevant.[5]

As Nisbett and colleagues (1976) point out, base rate information is abstract, and particular information is concrete. To anticipate an analogy elaborated in later chapters between concepts of thought (concrete versus abstract) and duration of events (short term versus long term), a concrete concept corresponds to a short-term (or immediate) event, while an abstract concept corresponds to a long-term (or delayed) event. The cigarette smoked today is concrete, while the resulting poor health is abstract; the ice cream sundae is concrete, while the consequent weight gain is abstract; today's bottle of scotch is concrete, while alcoholism is abstract. By this analogy, people's reluctance to consider (abstract) base rates in making a judgment is, like their reluctance to give up smoking, a problem of motivation as well as of cognition — of will power as well as of thought.

JUDGMENT AND OUTCOME

As illustrated over and over again in this chapter, people's judgments are often wrong. Let us assume that you made an error in judgment. From a cognitive viewpoint, this means that you did not correctly use a normative process. From a behavioral viewpoint, it means that your judgment did not guide your behavior to optimize reward. What did you do? From a cognitive viewpoint, you used a heuristic that, in this context, did not correspond to the normative rule. From a behavioral viewpoint, your judgment guided behavior to provide reward in the short run which, in this context, did not work in the long run.

To take a simple example, suppose you are driving in a city that you had visited ten years before and are trying to find the hotel you stayed at then. You could buy a map and consult it (the normative process), you could ask directions of a stranger, or you could rely on your memory and instinct (the heuristic of availability). Let us assume that buying a map is the most difficult but the most error-free of the three methods; relying on your memory and instinct is easiest but most prone to error.

If you are lazy, as I am, you will avoid the immediate costs involved in buying a map or asking directions and accept the possibility that you might not find your hotel on the first try. (My rule is "Go by instinct until frustrated, then ask directions until frustrated, then consult map.") In some people's opinion (my wife's, for instance), the cost of asking directions or of buying a map is well worth the higher probability of finding the hotel and, in general, spending less time driving aimlessly around strange cities. Perhaps I should change my rule.

In order to decide whether my rule is good or even adequate, I would need to know the probabilities of success (and failure) using each of the three methods. As pointed out by Einhorn (1980), a single outcome is woefully insufficient in this sort of situation. Using my instincts, I could be lucky in the first try and drive straight to the right hotel even though the probability of success in the long run (the "true" probability of success) is only one out of ten. Even having experienced several outcomes that reflect the true success ratio, I doubt whether my memory of the outcomes would be accurate. I would be no more accurate at remembering my success rate than I am at remembering the location of the hotel. Like everyone else, I tend to remember my successes and forget my failures. What I need to do is to systematically try all three methods an equal number of times under roughly equivalent conditions and keep a box score of successes and failures. Obviously this would be more trouble than buying a map in the first place. In other words, the cost of obtaining sufficient data to evaluate my rule is far greater than any benefit I could get by changing it. Therefore I am truly better off just going along with my rule or altering it as a matter of immediate convenience (if I happen to be stopping for gas anyway I might ask directions or pick up a map) than by behaving in a systematic way.

There are many situations in everyday life where it does not pay to go by the normative rule. The above example illustrates that in addition there are many situations where it may pay to go by a normative rule but not to spend the effort to discover what the normative rule is. Einhorn calls such situations "outcome-irrelevant learning situations." Such situations are paradoxical in that the best policy is not to worry about what the best policy is.

Many situations in everyday life, perhaps even most situations, are outcome-irrelevant in the sense illustrated above. In some cases, obtaining the data necessary to test a rule is not just difficult or costly but virtually impossible. To test a doctor's ability to diagnose a given disease or a mechanic's ability to repair a given make of car or the taste of a given breakfast food relative to others would involve setting up controlled experiments where diseases, makes of car, and foods eaten for breakfast are varied systematically and outcomes recorded. Since we cannot set up such experiments, our usual procedure is to stick with doctors, mechanics, and breakfast foods that we find satisfactory — that satisfice — even though better ones may be available.

As common as outcome-irrelevant learning situations are in the everyday lives of individual people, they are even more common in decisions made by institutions. Einhorn (1980) cites the examples of colleges selecting students or firms hiring employees. Colleges and firms set up criteria for admission or hiring. They then can observe the performance of the people they admit or hire. If those people perform in a generally satisfactory way, the college or firm tends to maintain its criteria. The data evaluated describe people who pass the criteria by being admitted or hired and perform well and people who pass the same criteria but perform poorly. However, as Einhorn points out, a complete box score requires additional data: People who fail the criteria — are not normally admitted or hired — who would have performed well or poorly. It may be that the ratio of successes to people admitted or hired would be no greater than the ratio of potential successes to people not admitted or not hired.

Even if they kept strict track of the outcomes of their judgments (the performances of their students or employees), colleges and firms (unless they deliberately admit a sample of below-criteria applicants) will never know what proportion of the people rejected *would have* succeeded. If a high proportion of acceptees actually do succeed, a school or firm is unlikely to change its admission rule (even if an equally high proportion of rejectees would have succeeded). As long as a high proportion of acceptees do succeed, it may not pay to experiment with a change of rules ("If it ain't broke, don't fix it"). However, it is easy to see how such situations can lead to prejudice. For instance, until recently the New York City Fire Department had set a criterion of upper body strength for employment that most women could not meet. Because of pressure from external sources the criterion was changed, and only now will its meaningfulness be tested.

In studies of animal learning, limited exposure to a narrow sample of the full range of contingencies of reinforcement (only a part of the box score) results in what has been labeled "superstitious" behavior. A pigeon will continue pecking a key for long periods of time if food is delivered at a rate completely independent of the pigeon's pecking. It is as if the pigeon learns the rule "If you peck the key, food will come" on the basis of a few successful (i.e., lucky) pecks and does not abandon that rule as long as food comes, regardless of whether the rule is still valid. Similarly, people like me may learn the rule "Go by your instinct when driving in a strange city" on the basis of a few successful (i.e., lucky) experiences and not abandon that rule as long as we eventually get where we are going. However, I would change my driving rule, pigeons would change their pecking rule, colleges would change their admission criteria, and firms would change their hiring policies if our success rates were low instead of high.

In summary, we may learn judgment rules "superstitiously" on the basis of a few positive outcomes, and those rules may be maintained inappropriately if a full range of outcomes is not experienced. Rules are more likely to be maintained if the outcomes are positive and more likely to be changed if the outcomes are negative. We will return to the question of the learning of rules in later chapters.

N O T E S

1.   The National Weather Service does keep tabs on weather predictions, and a poor performer would be fired on that ground alone. However, the weather bureau's main concern, like that of the weatherman, is ultimately the outcome of behavior. Taking an umbrella to work is a trivial example. Outcomes of decisions by pilots and farmers, of course, carry more weight.

2.   Because judgments constitute an early stage of a process that ultimately leads to a choice and an outcome, they are by no means secondary phenomena. The length of this chapter attests to the amount of interesting and important work that has been done on the topic of human judgment. To say that judgments are functionally incomplete is not to say that they are unimportant. The foundation of a building is functionally incomplete but not any the less fundamental.

3.   For instance, subjects might use odds (like $2:1$) rather than probabilities (like .67) in making judgments. In that case computation would be required to translate the stated base rates to prior odds.

4.   Modern work has blurred the distinction between perception and cognition considerably. In many respects perceptions work like cognitions and cognitions work like perceptions. Much of what was studied as perception by the Gestalt psychologists would now be called cognition. To be consistent with modern usage, *perception* should be understood as "early stage" or "peripheral" processing (or "editing" or "problem structuring") and *cognition* as "late stage" or "central" processing.

5.   Another example of the same forces at work: Social psychologists have discovered a pervasive pattern of human judgment (of

which the Miller et al., 1973, study forms a part) which Pettigrew (1979) calls the "ultimate attribution error." People tend to attribute their successes to their own character and their failures to their situation. On the other hand, people tend to attribute the successes of others to their situation and their failures (as in the Miller et al. study) to their character. Assuming that society tends to reward or punish people when success or failure is perceived to be due to character but to withhold reward or punishment when success or failure is perceived to be due to situation (because reward and punishment are thought to be capable of altering people's characters but not their situations), the "fundamental attribution error" can be explained as an attempt to seek reward and avoid punishment — not an error at all. Assuming, furthermore, that rewards and punishers are economic goods (in limited supply) so that one person's gain is to some extent another's loss, the fundamental attribution error can be explained in terms of economic maximization (see Chapter 8). This, of course, does not preclude a cognitive explanation of the same facts.

DECISION

In the dialogue illustrated in Figure 2-1, the distinction between judgment and decision is clear. On the basis of meteorological data, the weatherman expresses a judgment as a probability. Then, on the basis of the weatherman's judgment, "the person" makes a decision (to take an umbrella to work). As indicated at the beginning of the previous chapter, studies of *judgment* typically put the subject in the place of the weatherman, where the input to the subject corresponds to meteorological data and the subject's output corresponds to a weather report. In studies of judgment the actual use to which the judgment is put is not of *direct* concern (although, as we saw, judgments may be strongly influenced by their function whether that function is stated or assumed).

In studies of *decision*, on the other hand, the experimenter usually makes a judgment for the subject. Typically, in studies of decision, subjects are presented with *alternatives*, already packaged in a certain standard form. For instance, each alternative may be expressed as a set of outcomes and probabilities; the probabilities of all the alternatives sum to 1.0 (or 100 percent).

A set of alternatives may be presented in outline form, as the following problem is:

I. Which of the following would you prefer?
   1. 50% chance to win $200,   2. $100 for sure
      50% chance to win nothing

A set of alternatives can also be couched in an everyday problem such as the following:

II. Suppose you inherited $100,000, which you could either put in the bank for a year or invest in a small business with a 50% chance of failing and a 50% chance of doubling your investment. Which would you choose?

Note that in the everyday problem a judgment has already been made (implicitly) about the business and is presented to the subject as such.

At the present stage of development of cognitive theory and practice, judgments and decisions are studied separately. Theories of judgment are not necessarily applicable to studies of decision, and vice versa. (A striking example of the apparent inconsistency of judgment and decision is the so-called preference reversal effect discussed later in this chapter.)

The clear distinction that can be made between the processes of judgment and decision in two people (as in the dialogue in Figure 2-1) becomes fuzzier when the two processes are conceived as distinct and yet occur in a single person (as in the monologue of Figure 2-2). If it were possible to bypass the judgment mechanism, the decision mechanism could be studied in isolation (as when judgment and decision are conceived as a dialogue). However, as Figure 2-2 shows, it is not possible to bypass the judgment mechanism. Even when the simplest alternatives are presented as already-formed judgments, it is still necessary (according to Figure 2-2) for the subject to represent them internally before entering them in the decision mechanism. An internal representation may well differ from the experimenter's external representation. Thus, even in studies of decision alone, the cognitive model of Figure 2-2 demands at least a two-stage analysis: first, internal representation (consisting of perception and evaluation) and, second, the decision itself.

Figure 4-1 illustrates the decision process as it will be discussed in this chapter. Two vertical arrows (two alternatives) run downward through the representation mechanism and are then fed to a decision mechanism. The output of the decision mechanism — the datum that decision theories attempt to explain — is the subject's report of a decision in choosing between the alternatives. In an experiment, decision report (often in the form of circling a stated alternative on a questionnaire) is assumed to indicate what a subject's choice would be if the stated alternatives were actually available.

By varying the experimental situation and observing subjects' reports of decisions, the experimenter infers (1) how the alternatives

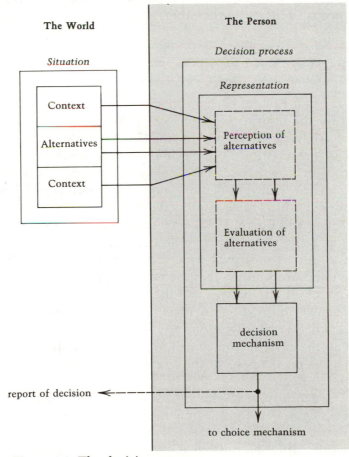

Figure 4-1 The decision process.

are internally represented and (2) how the decision mechanism works. It is important to note that the decision theorist's inference of how the alternatives are represented (based on the subject's decision) may or may not correspond to the subject's introspective report of those representations. In other words, people may not have introspective access to their own representations. This should not be surprising to the reader. After all, any stimulus that ultimately affects behavior must be represented over and over at various stages of the nervous system. For instance, the world is represented upside down on our retinas, yet we are not conscious of this representation. The cognitive decision theorist merely identifies critical stages (or "nodes") of a very complicated process. Those stages need not correspond to critical physiological stages (such as retinal representations of visual scenes) on the one hand, and they need not correspond to introspective reports on the other.

SEARCH STRATEGIES

The very first item of concern in studying decisions is how people search for the information upon which to base their decisions. One way of studying the search process (Payne, 1980) is by concealing items of information (usually amounts and probabilities) behind windows in a matrix (or on a computer screen where individual items can be revealed by pressing appropriate buttons) and observing the order in which subjects press the buttons. Another, more subtle way (Russo and Rosen, 1975) is by measuring a subject's eye movements as he or she searches an array of information.

If a person is presented with several alternatives, each with an amount and probability, does the person observe (and compare) the amounts of all alternatives and then their probabilities and finally combine the information somehow; or does the person first observe the amount and probability of each alternative one at a time, then combine the information somehow, and finally decide among the alternatives on the basis of the combinations? Figure 4-2 illustrates the two strategies.

The evidence from several studies indicates that people can make decisions based on either search strategy. However, when there are few alternatives and the decision process is simple (as with two alternatives differing on two dimensions), people tend to use the

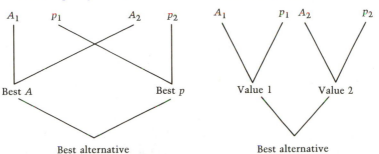

Figure 4-2 Two strategies of searching for information and comparing two alternatives ($i = 1$ and 2) differing in amount (A_i) and probability (p_i).

second search strategy illustrated in Figure 4-2 — that is, they find out all they can about each alternative individually before going on to the next. When there are many alternatives with many dimensions, thus making the decision process difficult, people tend to use the first strategy illustrated in Figure 4-2 — they search across alternatives on a single dimension and then go on to search across alternatives on the other dimensions.

Theorists assume that the search strategy a person uses must correspond to his or her decision strategy. For instance, when faced with a complicated decision, a person's decision mechanism might begin to compare alternatives on a single dimension. However, in order to do this the person needs to create a representation of each alternative on the particular dimension of concern. Working further backwards, in order to create a representation of several alternatives on a given dimension, the person has to search across the various alternatives on that dimension. Thus a search strategy (the direction of eye movements) must reflect a decision strategy (a comparison of particular dimensions of prospects).

In behavioral theories of choice, search behavior may be conceived as a form of choice behavior itself (and must obey the same laws as choice behavior does). In this chapter, however, the search process is conceived in cognitive terms as a preliminary stage in a series of events leading from an external situation through an internal process to an ultimate decision.

MEASURING DECISIONS

Although choice is usually ignored in studies of decision, the subject must still somehow indicate the results of the decision process. Otherwise the experimenter would never know what the subject's decision was. Suppose you are a subject in a decision experiment and that the decision process is complete. You have searched the input, represented the alternatives internally, evaluated them, and are about to report your decision. Let us say you like alternative 1 twice as much as alternative 2. There are several ways in which you might be asked to report this decision. First, you could be asked merely to indicate which you prefer. There is no problem for you in this case. You would just say alternative 1. However, there is a problem for the experimenter. Information about the *degree* of your preference is lost.

A frequent solution is to ask the same question to many people (say, 100 people); if a large percentage of them (say, 90 percent) prefer alternative 1, the experimenter infers that the average person strongly prefers alternative 1, whereas if a smaller percentage of them (say, 55 percent) prefer 1, the experimenter infers that the average person weakly prefers alternative 1. The problem with this method is that it is possible for 90 percent or even 100 percent of the subjects in an experiment to weakly prefer alternative 1 and so indicate. For instance, a large fraction of people would prefer a bicycle with a bell to the same bicycle without a bell (creating a strong measured preference), but that preference would in fact be a weak one.

Another frequently used method of reporting decisions is for the subject to indicate degree of preference by drawing a line, giving a number, expressing a probability, or squeezing a hand spring. The problem with this method is that it introduces another mechanism into the decision process. It cannot be assumed that a person's *internal* degree of preference corresponds exactly to that person's *expressed* degree of preference. The arrow in Figure 4-1 leading from the "decision mechanism" to the "report of decision" would have to go through still another (internal) mechanism, by which a preference is transformed to a line, a number, or a squeeze. The theorist would then have to explain the operation of the new mechanism in addition to the others.

A third commonly used method of measuring degree of preference among alternatives is for a single subject to indicate preference for a particular alternative repeatedly. The subject's degree of preference is then assumed to correspond to the percentage of times the alternative is indicated. For instance, if a boy buys one brand of soda twice as much as another, he is assumed to like it twice as much. Unfortunately, there are two main problems with this method. First, each choice may not be independent of the others. For instance, people might remember their earlier choices and, in striving for consistency, always choose the same way even though their preference may be slight. (Again, the bicycle-with-bell example is relevant. Even though you may prefer a bicycle with a bell to one without a bell only slightly, in a thousand choices you would pick the one with the bell a thousand times.) A slight preference may thus be measured as extreme.

Experimenters deal with this problem by varying alternatives on several dimensions and avoiding sharp, easy-to-discriminate increments in value (like bells on bicycles). Furthermore, instead of simply repeating a problem over and over, they imbed repetitions in a series of other very similar problems, so as to disguise them and discourage subjects from being consistent just for the sake of consistency. For instance, ginger ale and cherry soda differ on more than one dimension; neither equals the other plus something else (as does a bicycle with a bell versus one without a bell); thus their overall values are not clearly discriminable. A boy choosing between them several times over several days, with each pair of alternatives embedded among dozens of others (club soda versus ginger ale, Coke versus Pepsi, Sprite versus Seven-Up, Seven-Up versus cherry soda, and so forth), would find it difficult to be intentionally consistent. Across repetitions of choices like the sodas above, individuals often choose in a graded fashion ranging from an even split (for indifferent alternatives) to all-or-none (for strong preferences).

Bruner, Goodnow, and Austin (1956), in their classic studies of decision, pointed out a second, more serious problem that may arise when measuring degree of preference by repeatedly presenting a subject with a single problem. In repeated trials with a given problem, subjects tend to adapt various *strategies* of behavior strongly depending upon the framing or context of the problem. When a repeated problem is framed so as to imply that it has a determinate solution, subjects will try to guess at this solution and to get the problem right 100 percent of the time. For instance, suppose you were given 100 cards with complicated designs on them and were told that 70 designs were drawn by artist X and 30 by artist Y. (Suppose, unknown to you, that the cards actually were randomly drawn by a computer.) You are asked to sort the cards by artist. Most likely you would put 70 in one pile and 30 in the other. Only by doing this could you hope to get the problem right. (Here is a case where you have only base rate information.)

When, on the other hand, a problem clearly has no determinate solution but only a probabilistic one, people tend to behave in an all-or-none fashion, thus maximizing correct answers. Suppose in the artist identification problem you are now told the truth — that all of the cards were drawn by a computer but nevertheless 70 were randomly labeled on the back with the name of artist X and 30 with the name of artist Y. Furthermore, you will be given $10 for each card sorted correctly. Now you are likely to put all the cards in the artist X pile, ensuring yourself $70. Here is a case where the frame of the problem determines your strategy of indicating decisions. We will have a lot more to say about this sort of behavior in the chapter on choice. Meanwhile, notice that if the experimenter had been measuring the strength of your decision that the cards were drawn by artist X, the measure would have been 70 percent with one frame and 100 percent with the other.

A perhaps simpler example is the case of two slot machines, one paying off at a slightly higher rate than the other. Even though your preference might be slight (compared with two machines where one pays off at a *much* higher rate), there would be no reason at all for you to choose the lower-paying slot machine. You would choose the higher-paying machine 100 percent of the time (and thus frustrate the psychologist observer who is looking for a continuous measure of preference).

Frequently the experimenter's object is to obtain a graded response from an individual subject over a series of similar or identical decision problems. In practice, a graded response is achieved by avoiding contingencies (relations between reported decisions and outcome) that reward all-or-none decisions and by framing the problem so as to focus the subject's attention on immediate relationships rather than base rates. (In the two-artist problem, the immediate relationship is that of artist to drawing. The base rate is the number of designs by each artist in the set to be sorted.) Perhaps the most common way of preventing base rates from influencing decisions is to equalize the base rates (in the two-artists problem, to equalize the number of designs by each artist).

Despite much effort by experimenters, considerable problems of measurement remain in the laboratory testing of various decision theories. In particular, data obtained with the three methods described here (single all-or-none decisions of many subjects, single graded decisions of a single subject, and many all-or-none decisions of a single subject) have generally not agreed. This may partly explain why so many theories (several of them mutually incompatible) flourish in the area of human decision. When a theory cannot be adequately tested, it cannot be eliminated from consideration. Because we cannot consider all proposed decision theories here, the remainder of this chapter will focus on a few examples.

NONPROBABILISTIC ALTERNATIVES DIFFERING ONLY IN AMOUNT

The simplest alternatives among which to decide are those available with certainty ($p = 1.0$). Of these, the simplest are those that differ only in amount. For instance, which do you prefer, $20 or $10 ($A_1 = \$20$ and $p_1 = 1.0$, or $A_2 = \$10$ and $p_2 = 1.0$, where A_i is the amount of alternative i and p_i is the probability of that amount). Almost everyone agrees that more is better than less.

Much more interesting questions are by how much do you prefer $20 to $10, and by how much do you prefer $100 to $90? Here a graded measure is required. The strength of most people's preference for $20 over $10 is greater than the strength of their preference for $100 over $90. In other words, people tend to be more indifferent between $100 and $90 than they are between $20 and $10. The mathematician Daniel Bernoulli (1700–1782) and the economist Jeremy Bentham (1748–1832) knew about this difference in degree of preference. They noted that the value of most goods increases with amount but at a decreasing rate as more and more of that good is accumulated. Since money is used in exchange for goods (in behavioristic terms, it is a "secondary reinforcer" rather than a "primary reinforcer"), the value of money also increases with amount and, as with primary goods, the rate of increase tapers off as more and more is accumulated. This tapering can be expressed by the equation

$$v = kA^s \tag{4-1}$$

where v stands for value, A for amount, and k and s for constants (described below). Figure 4-3 illustrates the function of Equation 4-1, called a *power* function.

In Equation 4-1 the exponent s stands for the *subjective sensitivity* of value to amount. When $s = 1.0$ as in the left graph of Figure 4-3, value is directly proportional to amount (k being the constant of proportionality). As s decreases from 1.0, the function tapers off more and more. The right graph of Figure 4-3 illustrates the function for $s = 0.5$ (square root). On the right graph the differences between $10 and $20 and between $90 and $100 are shaded in. Note that the curvature of the function makes the difference in value between $10 and $20 greater than the difference in value between $90 and $100. Bernoulli speculated that the subjective sensitivity of value to amount of money is 0.5, in other words, that subjective value grows as amount of money to the 0.5 power (square root). Theorists today are not so certain that this particular sensitivity to amount of money is universally applicable.

Stevens (1957) has shown that a power function describes the subjective change (in loudness or brightness, for instance) as any stimulus is varied in intensity. In Equation 4-1 and Figure 4-3, the subjective change is a change in subjective value and the stimulus is the amount (of money or of some primary good). According to Ste-

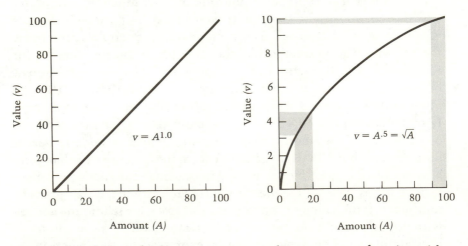

Figure 4-3 Relation of value to amount according to a power function with different values for sensitivity.

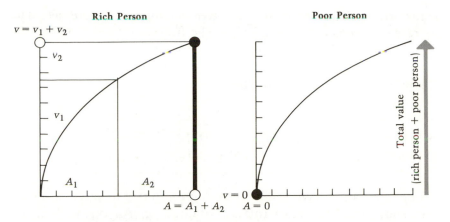

Rich person has all his money; poor person has none.

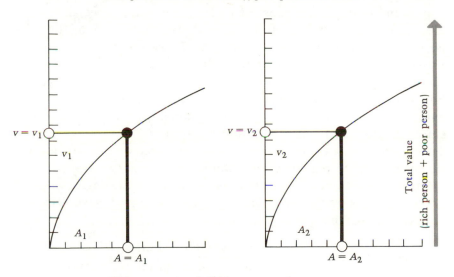

Rich person gives half his money to the poor person.

Figure 4-4 How the principle of "the greatest good for the greatest number" is satisfied when a rich person gives half of his money to someone who has none.

vens, each separate modality (sound, light, etc.) has its own subjective sensitivity.

The economist Jeremy Bentham based his moral precept "the greatest good for the greatest number" on the tapering off of the value function. As Figure 4-4 shows (with $s = 0.5$), if a person gives half of his money to someone who has no money, the total subjective value (the greatest good for the greatest number) increases. The increase depends on the bending of the function. In economics, the tapering off of the value function is called the law of diminishing marginal utility. We will discuss further consequences of this law in Chapter 8, "Economics and Choice."

NONPROBABILISTIC ALTERNATIVES DIFFERING IN AMOUNT AND QUALITY

Would you rather have $5000 or a one-month trip to Paris? Not only quiz show contestants face this sort of question. Anyone with $5000 in the bank faces a form of it. They say that you cannot compare apples and oranges, but most of us frequently do, especially when making purchases at fruit stores. How do we choose among dissimilar alternatives? According to Luce (1959), we do so in two stages. First, we convert the amount of each good (dollars, days in Paris, number of oranges, or number of apples) to its respective value. Equation 4-1 provides a means of converting amount of a good to a value. The sensitivities (s's) may differ among goods; and the constants of proportionality (k's) almost certainly differ. However, according to Luce, all alternatives, can be compared on a single universal scale of value regardless of differences in quality.

Once the value of an alternative is determined, the degree of preference (as measured by the probability that an individual subject will choose that alternative) is given by

$$\text{Degree of preference} = \frac{\text{value of alternative}}{\text{sum of values of all alternatives}} \quad (4\text{-}2)$$

According to Luce's model, Equation 4-2 holds not only when alternatives 1 and 2 are the only alternatives but also when they are accompanied by other alternatives. This property is called *independence from irrelevant alternatives*. Thus, your *relative* preference between alternative 1 ($5000) and alternative 2 (a trip to Paris) should be unaffected by the presence of another alternative (say a motorcycle). You might choose the motorcycle over one or both of the other two alternatives, but your preference between those other alternatives should remain constant.

To summarize, Luce's model implies that decisions are made in two stages: Each alternative is evaluated separately; then alternatives are compared with each other by calculating the degree of preference using Equation 4-2. Preference for any alternative relative to any other alternative is proportional to their respective values regardless of the remaining alternatives.

NONPROBABILISTIC ALTERNATIVES DIFFERING IN AMOUNT AND SIMILAR IN QUALITY

Let us now digress a bit about the concept of similarity. Figure 4-5 shows three degrees of similarity between a pair of alternatives according to a theory of "identical elements" (originally proposed by Thorndike and Woodworth, 1901). We have already considered the first two cases. In case I, alternatives differ only in the amount of some single kind of element (type *a*). We discussed the example of alternatives differing only in amount of money. In case II, alternatives differ in amount and also in quality (types *b* and *c*). The alternatives of $5000 and a trip to Paris approximate such qualitatively dissimilar alternatives. Experiments have tended to support Luce's model and its implication of independence from irrelevant alterna-

Case I: Complete similarity   *Case II: Complete dissimilarity*

   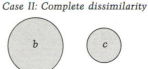

Case III: Partial similarity

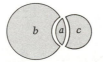

Figure 4-5 Illustrations of degrees of similarity according to a theory of identical elements. The sizes of the circles roughly represent the numbers of elements. Degree of similarity depends on degree of overlap between the two alternatives.

tives as it applies to case I and case II. However, Luce's model does not apply in a simple way to case III, when there is some overlap in similarity. In case III the two alternatives contain not only qualitatively different elements (types b and c) but also some identical elements (type a).

The simplest application of identical elements to the concept of similarity is to suppose that similarity between a pair of alternatives consists of the fraction of identical elements they contain (Tversky, 1977). Case I has 100 percent identical elements and therefore complete similarity; case II has 0 percent identical elements and therefore complete dissimilarity; case III has a fraction of identical elements equal to $a/(a + b + c)$. (Another conception of similarity of alternatives, in terms of their *substitutability* in use, will be discussed in Chapter 8.)

Let us now consider how independence from irrelevant alternatives may be violated when alternatives differ in degree of similarity. Again, you are offered a choice between \$5000 (alternative 1) and a trip to Paris (alternative 2). Suppose that the two alternatives are of equal value to you. For convenience, let us assume $v_1 = v_2 = 10$ units of value. According to Luce's model, your preference between them (Equation 4-2) should equal .5:

$$\frac{v_1}{v_1 + v_2} = \frac{10}{20} = .5$$

Now consider a third alternative, a trip to Rome (see Figure 4-6). Suppose this alternative, too, has a value of 10. If the trip to Paris is offered with the trip to Rome (approximating case I) or with the \$5000 (approximating case II) Equation 4-2 predicts a preference for the trip to Paris of .5. However, if the trip to Paris is offered in a three-way decision with *both* of the other alternatives, Equation 4-2 predicts a preference for the trip to Paris of .33:

$$\frac{v_1}{v_1 + v_2 + v_3} = \frac{10}{30} = .33$$

This does not seem right. It seems as if you would first decide whether to take a trip or the \$5000; only after choosing a trip would you attempt to decide between the trips to Paris and Rome. Figure 4-6 illustrates this hierarchical process. The conditional probability

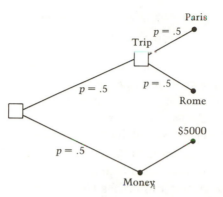

Figure 4-6 A hierarchy of decisions (□ = decision).

of your deciding to take the trip to Paris with the three alternatives should be .25 (.5 × .5 = .25) and not .33.

Similarly, your preference for the $5000 (in the three-alternative problem) is predicted by Equation 4-2 to be .33, as shown above. However, if you actually decided first between the money and a trip, your preference for the money would be .5, as Figure 4-6 shows (not .33), and if you opted for the money, you need never make the decision about which trip to take.

Case III is a mixture of cases I and II. In general, the principle of independence from irrelevant alternatives holds when all alternatives are either completely similar or completely dissimilar. The reason that the principle does not hold when alternatives are partially similar is because decisions are often made in a hierarchical fashion, as shown in Figure 4-6, rather than by comparing the values of all alternatives at once. When a third alternative is more similar to one of two original alternatives, the third alternative is likely to be lumped along with the one it resembles — both considered as one unit — when decisions are made. The two similar alternatives will be separated (unlumped) if and when other alternatives have been discarded and the time comes to decide between the two.

The hierarchal process of choice just described is an essential part of a choice heuristic proposed by Tversky (1972) called *elimination by aspects*. Like the judgment heuristics previously discussed, elimination by aspects facilitates the decision process. (However, as with judgment heuristics, ease of use is gained at the possible cost of optimal outcome.)

In elimination by aspects each alternative is viewed as a set of aspects. A trip to Paris, for instance, might consist of the aspects of plane travel, eating out in interesting restaurants, obtaining a passport, meeting new people, staying in a hotel, and so on. Most of those aspects are included in a trip to Rome, but none of them are included in $5000 in cash, which has its own set of aspects (liquidity, security, ability to earn interest, a degree of power).

An aspect of an alternative is like a dimension of the alternative except that an alternative either has the aspect or does not. Let us say, for instance, that on the dimension of height a person is 6 feet 1 inch. That means the person (as an alternative) has the aspect of being over 6 feet tall and not the aspect of being over 6 feet 10 inches tall. In using elimination by aspects you must first decide which aspects of the various alternatives are the most important to you in making your decision. If you were choosing a center for a professional basketball team, the aspect of being over 6 feet 10 inches tall might be the most important one. You then eliminate all the alternatives that do not contain that aspect — all candidates under 6 feet 10 inches. Then you might eliminate all the poor rebounders, then all the poor shot-blockers, then all the poor shooters, then all the poor dribblers, and so on. If you were fortunate enough to have more than one candidate still left you might eliminate the ones demanding high salaries. Eventually you would be left with one candidate. Similarly, in choosing a coat you might eliminate first those not your size, second those not warm, third those that cost too much, fourth those not in fashion, fifth those not immediately available, sixth those sold by obnoxious salesclerks, and so on.

One great advantage of elimination by aspects is that it takes into account the fact that among several alternatives, some may be identical (case I), some may be widely different (case II), and some may be similar but not identical (case III). Consider two alternatives with overlapping but not identical aspects (case III): a car with a stereo radio but no air conditioning and an identical car with air conditioning but no stereo radio. Assume that the value of the car is 100, the value of the stereo radio is 2, and the value of the air conditioning is 1. If you simply took ratios of the values of the alternatives as Equation 4-2 dictates, you would calculate the preference for the car with the stereo as about $.5 : 102/(102 + 101)$. However, since (by assumption) you value the stereo twice as much as the air condition-ing, this calculation underestimates the strength of your preference. Elimination by aspects says that before comparing the two cars, you first eliminate all common aspects (the bare car) and *then* calculate value on the basis of independent aspects. So, according to elimina-tion by aspects, your preference for the car with the stereo is .67: $2/(2 + 1)$. Elimination by aspects says that you choose among the options, the unique aspects of the alternatives, rather than among the alternatives themselves.[1]

Elimination by aspects is an easy heuristic to use for complicated decisions. Its disadvantage is that sometimes we may discard a better alternative and retain a worse one. For instance, one alternative might be slightly better than the others on all aspects and therefore retained, while another might be far better than the others on all aspects but one on which it may be slightly below the cutoff line (which defines the aspect on a dimension) and therefore rejected. So, using elimination by aspects, you could buy a mediocre coat, barely satisfactory in warmth, style, and price (and therefore never elimi-nated) and reject a much cheaper and warmer but less stylish coat.

Like other decision strategies, elimination by aspects may or may not be used consciously by the person making the choice. As a theoretical process, it is inferred by the observer from the decisions or choices of a person. The relevant question for a theorist is whether a person's choices are consistent with the elimination-by-aspects heuristic, not whether the person claims to be using this heuristic. The latter question is interesting in its own right but not a substitute for experimentation and theory in cognitive psychology.

As we said in the section on search strategies, when alternatives are numerous or complicated, people tend to compare alternatives on each dimension separately. Elimination by aspects is a decision heuristic that reflects this. However, when alternatives are few and differ on only one or two dimensions, people tend to evaluate each alternative by combining its dimensions. After they evaluate each alternative, they decide to choose the one with the highest overall value.

Some of the decisions considered in this section involved multidi-mensional alternatives, but all alternatives were alike on the dimen-sion of probability. In all cases $p = 1.0$. In the next few sections we will consider decisions among what Kahneman and Tversky (1979) call "prospects." Prospects are simple in the sense that they vary along only two dimensions, amount and probability, but complicated in the sense that the dimension of probability acts on decision in a complex way.

PROBABILISTIC ALTERNATIVES: AVERAGE AMOUNT

The *average amount* of an alternative is the average amount (per trial) that would be obtained if the alternative were chosen repeatedly over a series of trials.[2] Average amount is obtained by multiplying the probability of an alternative by the amount of the outcome. In problem I at the beginning of this chapter, the average amount of alternative 1, a 50 percent chance to win $200 ($p = .5$, $A = \$200$) and a 50 percent chance to win nothing ($q = .5$, $B = \$0$), would be $100 where q is the probability of not getting A ($q = 1 - p$) and B is the outcome if A is not gotten:

$$(.5 \times \$200) + (.5 \times \$0) = \$100$$

Of course, the average amount of alternative 2, $100 for sure, would also be $100. In problem II, expressed in everyday terms, the average amount of putting the money in the bank would be $100,000, and the average amount of investing in the small business would also be $100,000:

$$(.5 \times \$200,000) + (.5 \times \$0) = \$100,000$$

Since average amount is the average amount won or lost per trial, a person who chooses the alternative with the highest (or least negative) average amount would be maximizing the amount won (or minimizing the amount lost) per trial. The same principle operates here as in the case of any statistical sample. For instance, the more people in a sample, the more likely is the average height of the sample to equal the average height of the population; similarly, the more trials there are, the more likely the actual average amount won per trial will equal the product of probability and amount. This is why gambling casinos, where games are all of positive average amount for the casino, must eventually win and why individual gamblers must eventually lose.

However, as demonstrated by the number of people who gamble in casinos, people often do not choose the alternative with the highest average amount. To see intuitively why this might be so, consider the following hypothetical situation: A man stands outside a factory on payday and offers to flip a coin for each worker's paycheck. If the coin comes up heads, the man gives the worker an amount equal to the paycheck and the worker goes home with a double paycheck. If the coin comes up tails, the worker signs over the paycheck to the man and goes home with nothing. Most people would not accept a gamble of this kind, even if they were offered a bonus (say $10) to do so. A possible behavioral rationalization for rejecting the gamble with the bonus is that although acceptance pays more (the amount of the bonus) in the long run, there are also important short-run considerations (such as feeding and housing the worker's family) that make it unwise to accept the man's offer (hence, unwise to rely exclusively on maximization of average amount as a rule for guiding decisions).

In the example of the worker's paycheck, the amounts in question are positive. Now consider this negative scenario. Because a farmer has had a bad year, he has fallen behind in mortgage payments and owes the bank $5000. If the money is not raised immediately the farm will be lost. The man with the coin, tired of making futile offers to factory workers, offers the following gamble to the farmer. He will flip the coin. If it comes up heads, he will pay the bank; the farmer will then owe nothing and can keep the farm. If the coin comes up tails, however, the farmer will still owe the bank $5000 and will owe the man an additional $5000 plus a penalty of $100. Because the farmer would then have to sell the farm, he would have much more cash than $10,000 and so could easily pay the man. In such a situation, most farmers would take the bet, even with the penalty. Again, maximization of amount — long-term maximization — demands refusal of the bet, but here there is an overwhelming short-term consideration (retaining the farm) that makes acceptance wise. If the farmer refuses, the farm will surely be lost. If the farmer accepts, there is a 50:50 chance of saving it.

In the positive example of the factory worker, a higher average amount was attached to acceptance of the gamble than to refusal, yet short-term considerations dictated refusal. In the negative example of the farmer, the higher average amount was attached to refusal of the gamble yet short-term considerations dictated acceptance. This pervasive and strong difference between the positive and negative cases has been observed in people's everyday decisions and has been found in laboratory studies of gambling. *People avoid low-probability alternatives (risks) that involve gains and seek low-probability alternatives (risks) that involve losses,* even at the cost of sacrificing average amount.

PROBABILISTIC ALTERNATIVES: AVERAGE UTILITY

Just as average amount equals probability times amount, *average utility* equals probability times value. One relation of amount to utility (value) is given by Equation 4-1 and shown in Figure 4-3. Let us continue with the supposition that the exponent s in Equation 4-1 is 0.5 and the constant k is 1.0. That supposition is equivalent to saying that value is equal to the square root of amount, as depicted in the right graph of Figure 4-3.

Whereas average amount is an objective quantity that can be calculated according to statistical properties of events, average utility is a subjective quantity that depends on how people evaluate amounts —our tendency to value a given increment added to a small amount more than that same increment added to a large amount. Going back again to problem I, the average utility of alternative 1 ($p = .5$ and $A = \$200$; $q = .5$ and $B = \$0$) would be as follows:

$$(.5 \times \sqrt{200}) + (.5 \times \sqrt{0}) = 7.07$$

The average utility of alternative 2 ($p = 1.0$ and $A = \$100$; $q = 0$ and $B = \$0$) would be

$$(1.0 \times \sqrt{100}) + (0 \times \sqrt{0}) = 10$$

(Corresponding calculations can be made for problem II.)

Even though the average amounts are the same for alternatives 1 and 2, the average utility is higher for alternative 2 than alternative 1. Since people usually do prefer alternative 2 (the sure thing) to alternative 1 (the risky gamble), they may be said to be maximizing average utility (the subjective quantity) rather than average amount (the objective quantity).

When problem I is presented in terms of losses rather than gains —a 50:50 chance of losing $200 (alternative 1) versus a sure loss of $100 (alternative 2)—people usually choose the risky alternative (alternative 1). The shift from choice of the sure thing to choice of the risky alternative as the frame of the problem changes from gains to losses is called the *reflection effect* (Kahneman and Tversky,

1979). The reflection effect is explained by calculating gains and losses in terms of average utility (rather than average amount); if both alternatives were wins, you would want to win the one of higher utility (alternative 2), but if both alternatives were losses, you would want to lose the one of lower utility (alternative 1). This strategy maximizes subjective wins and minimizes subjective losses. In the factory worker example, the worker maximizes subjective gain (in average utility) by keeping the paycheck; in the farmer example, the farmer minimizes subjective loss (in average utility) by accepting the man's offer.

So far we have two noncompeting explanations of the farmer's and worker's choices (hence, of the reflection effect). The first is a behavioral speculation about immediate versus long-term gains and losses, and the second a cognitive recalculation in terms of subjective quantities (average utilities) rather than objective quantities (expected average amounts). Later chapters will be much more specific about short-term versus long-term gains and losses and will clarify how these two explanations differ.

Although average utility theory explains the reflection effect satisfactorily, it has not been accepted as a general model of decision making for two reasons. First, the theory does not account for people's behavior when the amount of gain or loss in gambles is very high and probabilities are very low. Second, it does not account for some aspects of people's behavior when the probability of gain or loss is very high (when it approaches certainty, regardless of amount). These shortcomings of expected average utility theory were cited by Kahneman and Tversky (1979) and Tversky and Kahneman (1981). They proposed another theory of choice, *prospect theory*, as a better model for how people make decisions. We will discuss the difficulties with average utility theory, and then we will explain prospect theory, which attempts to overcome them.

In everyday life, gambles with high amounts of gain are available in the form of lotteries. The average amount $(p \times A)$ of a lottery ticket is almost always less than the price of the ticket—otherwise the state could not raise any money. Yet we do buy lottery tickets. Say that the cost of a lottery ticket is $1, the prize is $1,000,000, and the probability of winning is $\frac{1}{1,200,000}$. The average amount of the win is thus $0.83 ($\frac{1}{1,200,000} \times$ $1,000,000). In other words, the $1 ticket is actually worth 83¢.

Converting the amount of the prize to its equivalent subjective value only compounds the problem, because now the value of winning (multiplied by the probability of winning) is proportionally far below the value of the cost of the ticket. In other words, the average utility of the gamble is below the average amount. To illustrate, again suppose that $v = \sqrt{A}$. The average utility of the prize is 0.00083 units ($\frac{1}{1,200,000} \times \sqrt{1,000,000}$), or less than a thousandth of the value of the cost of a ticket. If this model were accurate, people would never buy a lottery ticket. Yet we do.

Now consider the case of losses. Buying insurance is equivalent to gambling with the insurance company. If you buy insurance (say, house insurance), you will surely lose a small amount of money — the amount of the premium (say $100). The average amount of your loss would be $100 ($1.0 \times \$100$). If you do not buy insurance, you could lose a lot of money — the replacement cost of your house (say $50,000) — but with a fairly low probability (say $\frac{1}{1000}$). However, the average amount of your loss would be only $50 ($\frac{1}{1000} \times \$50,000$).

We can also calculate average *dis*utilities rather than average amounts lost. The average *dis*utility of buying insurance would be 10 units ($1.0 \times \sqrt{100}$), while the average *dis*utility of refusing to buy insurance would be 0.22 unit ($\frac{1}{1000} \times \sqrt{50,000}$). Even if the numbers used here exaggerate the difference, according to average utility theory it is clearly worse to buy the insurance than to refuse it. Yet we do buy insurance. The lottery and insurance examples illustrate the failure of both average amount and average utility theories to explain how we make decisions among alternatives when high amounts and low probabilities are involved.

A second difficulty with average utility theory is illustrated by the following pair of problems:

III. Which of the following would you prefer?
   1. 80% chance to win $40,   2. $30 for sure
      20% chance to win nothing

IV. Which of the following would you prefer?
   1. 20% chance to win $40,   2. 25% chance to win $30,
      80% chance to win nothing   75% chance to win nothing

Problem III is much like problem I. As with the former problem, people tend to choose the sure thing even though its average amount ($30) is less than that of the gamble ($32). Taken by itself, choice of the sure thing in problem III is easily explained by average utility theory. Still assuming $v = \sqrt{A}$, the average utility of the gamble is about 5.0 units, while that of the (preferred) sure thing is about 5.5 units.

Problem IV was constructed from problem III by retaining the same amounts for both alternatives and dividing each probability of winning (a nonzero amount) by 4. Thus the probability of winning $40 is one-fourth as much in problem IV as in problem III (20 percent versus 80 percent), and the probability of winning $30 is also one-fourth as much in problem IV as in problem III (25 percent versus 100 percent). Given problem IV, however, most people prefer alternative 1 (the former gamble) to alternative 2 (the former sure thing). Average utility theory cannot explain this reversal of preference because the theory proposes that only amounts are transformed by subjective representation (by Equation 4-1)—probabilities are untransformed and act in people's internal cognitive mechanisms just as they do in the real world. Since the amounts are identical in problems III and IV, which involve only the multiplication of relevant probabilities by a constant, average utility theory (the assumption that preference is proportional to average utility) cannot account for the reversal.

The difficulty lies in alternative 2 of problem III. Whereas the other alternatives of both problems all involve various uncertainties (probabilities less than 1), alternative 2 of problem III is a sure win, a certainty ($p = 1$). In general, when certainties are reduced by a given factor, the effect on people's decisions is much greater than when uncertainties are reduced by the same factor. (In problems III and IV, a reduction of certainty actually reverses preference.) Tversky and Kahneman (1981) label this phenomenon the *certainty effect*; it was discovered by Allais (1953) and is found quite reliably in decision experiments—and as shown, it contradicts average utility theory.

PROSPECT THEORY

You will understand prospect theory most easily if you view it not as a separate theory but as an elaboration of average utility theory. Prospect theory essentially places a two-stage representational mechanism in front of the basic calculation of average utility. Once the two stages of the representational mechanism have done their jobs, prospect theory works just like average utility theory.

Figure 4-7 illustrates the processing of a single alternative according to average amount, average utility, and prospect theories. Average amount and average utility theories view perception and evaluation as veridical. According to these theories, once the search process is over, the probability and amount of an alternative pass unaltered through the perceptual mechanism. (The only difference between the two theories is that in average utility theory, amount (A) is converted to its equivalent value (v) before being multiplied by probability (p) to obtain the value (V) of the alternative as a whole, whereas in average amount theory amount is directly multiplied by probability.)

Prospect theory is more elaborate than the other two. First, the perception process works on a given alternative in its content, which may include other alternatives. Kahneman and Tversky (1979) call this perception process the "editing" of the alternative (or prospect). Editing, which we shall soon discuss, results in a probability (p) or amount (A), which may differ from those stated in the problem. After the variables are edited, they are evaluated.

Before discussing these processes, it is necessary to broaden the concept of an alternative slightly. As conceived by decision theories, an alternative offers a stated amount (A) with a stated probability (p). If $p < 1$, then A may not be obtained. In that case, B will be obtained with probability q. We have been assuming throughout that $p + q = 1$, and we have occasionally assumed that $B = 0$. Neither of these assumptions need hold, and prospect theory does not assume that they do. Frequently B is positive (or negative), and less frequently p and q sum to less than 1. (In that case, a third probability, $r = 1 - p - q$, gives the probability that nothing will be obtained).

According to prospect theory, the first part of the decision process after searching is *editing*. The function of the editing mechanism is to transform the language of the problem (whether posed by the experimenter or by everyday life) into a set of *simple prospects* of the form (A, p; B, q). One job of editing is to decide whether each alternative is positive, negative, or zero — a gain, a loss, or a null outcome. If A and B are both positive or both negative, further processing is required to subtract out the common gain or common loss.

Consider the following problem:

V. Which of the following would you prefer?
    1. 50% chance to win $150,   2. $100 for sure
       50% chance to win $50

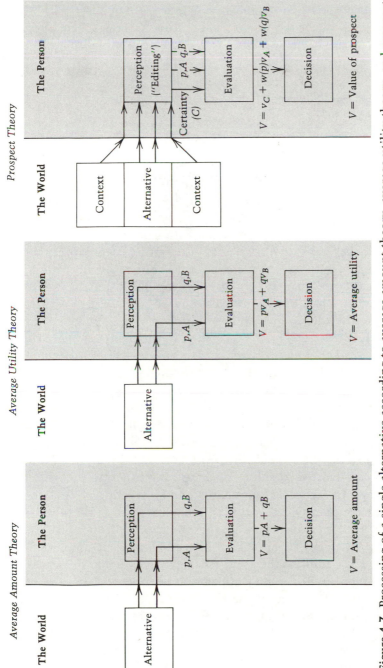

Figure 4-7 Processing of a single alternative according to average amount theory, average utility theory, and prospect theory. Here we assume that $p + q = 1$.

Whichever alternative you choose, you must win at least $50. According to prospect theory, an internal editing process subtracts this certain win from both alternatives before evaluating them. The edited problem is

V'. Which of the following would you prefer? $50 plus:
  1. 50% chance to add $100,   2. Adding $50 for sure
     50% chance to add nothing

Once each alternative has been examined in context to decide whether it involves gains, losses, or both, and once each alternative has been combined and segregated into simple prospects, then the editing mechanism looks across prospects for further simplification. Just as a single prospect may involve a sure gain or sure loss plus a chance of further gain or further loss, so a group of prospects may involve common outcomes that can be edited out of consideration in order to simplify an ultimate decision. In general, a person's preference between any pair of alternatives may be increased or reversed depending on the editing mechanism, which in turn depends on how the alternatives are perceived. This, in turn, depends on their context. At the present time prospect theory provides no hard and fast rules for how the editing mechanism works—just a set of general guidelines that future research may clarify.

The next stage in the decision process, according to prospect theory, is *evaluation*. The input to the evaluation mechanism consists of amounts (A, and B) and probabilities (p and q). The output consists of values (v's) and *decision weights* ($w(p)$ and $w(q)$). Amounts are converted to values by a tapering function like that of the right graph in Figure 4-3. Kahneman and Tversky (1979) do not specify the exact form of this function except to say that when an amount has been encoded as a loss, the function is steeper (in terms of Equation 4-1, s is greater) than when an equivalent amount has been encoded as a gain. As they say, "the aggravation that one experiences in losing a sum of money appears to be greater than the pleasure associated with gaining the same amount" (p. 279). This implies that people would not accept a 50:50 chance of winning $20 and losing $20. Indeed, most people reject such gambles. Furthermore, if forced to choose between the above gamble and a 50:50 chance of winning or losing a lesser amount (say, $10) people usually choose the alternative with the lesser amount. Presumably, the greater the amount is, the greater net aggravation minus net pleasure would be.

The central part of prospect theory is how a probability p is converted to a decision weight $w(p)$. The conversion function has three main characteristics: (1) Certainties are unaltered $(w(1.0) = 1.0)$; (2) most probabilities $(p's)$ are underweighted $(w(p) < p)$; (3) very low probabilities $(lp's)$ are overweighted $(w(lp) > lp)$.

A hypothetical weighting function is shown in Figure 4-8. The discontinuity (the dot at the upper right corner) represents the weighting of certainties $(w(1.0) = 1.0)$; the function (solid line) lying mostly beneath the dotted line represents the underweighting of most probabilities $(w(p) < p)$; the part above the dotted line in the lower left-hand corner represents the overweighting of very low probabilities $(w(lp) > lp)$.

Remember that decision weights $(w(p)'s)$ are not subjective probabilities in two senses. First, they do not represent judgments. That is, you could not report a decision weight or use it as a guide for your own behavior or that of another person; it is not presumed to represent a degree of subjective certainty, nor is it presumed to be accessible to introspection. Decision weights are supposed to mediate between two internal mechanisms, but they are entirely inferred from observations of people's actual decisions. Second, decision weights need not (and generally do not) have the mathematical properties that probabilities must have. In particular, the decision weights of all alternatives of a problem need not sum to 1.0.

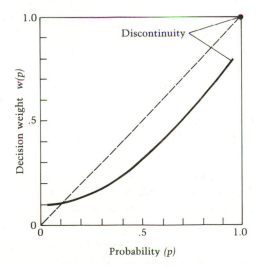

Figure 4-8 A hypothetical weighting function according to prospect theory.

Once the edited amounts of a prospect have been converted to values and the edited probabilities to decision weights, the alternative as a whole is evaluated by multiplying each value by its corresponding decision weight and then adding all the gains and subtracting all the losses. This part of the evaluation process corresponds to the evaluation processes of average amount theory and average utility theory.

Before leaving prospect theory, let us return to the difficulties with average utility theory and see how prospect theory overcomes them. First, average utility theory does not address the influence of context on the perception of the alternatives; prospect theory postulates an active perceptual process (editing) that supplements the initial search process. Coding an alternative as a gain or loss and segregation of certainties from uncertain prospects is assumed to take place at this initial stage. Thus, prospect theory explains the reversals of preference due to the problem's language (its frame).

Second, the intersection of the weighting function and the dotted line in the lower left corner of Figure 4-8 indicates the overweighting of very low probabilities. Thus, gambles with very low probabilities of gain are more attractive than their average amounts would indicate (hence, people buy lottery tickets at prices higher than the average amount of the prize) and highly improbable losses are more aversive than their average amounts would justify (hence, people buy insurance at prices higher than the average amount of their losses).

Third, the discontinuity in Figure 4-8 reflects the fact that our decision mechanisms treat certainties in a special way. Thus, problem III, which contains a certainty, and problem IV, which does not, cannot be simply compared. Because the weighting of the certainty is proportionally higher than the weightings of the lesser probabilities, the certainty in problem III (alternative 2) outweighs the lesser probability (alternative 1). In problem IV, where neither alternative is certain, the difference in the probabilities of the alternatives may be outweighed by the difference in their amounts. Thus, prospect theory accounts for the certainty effect.

This discussion of prospect theory is only an outline. It does not include the quite rigorous mathematical derivation of predictions from assumptions that are characteristic of the theory, and it does not describe several other findings in decision experiments that prospect theory explains. In particular, it does not describe how prospect theory handles chains of decisions as illustrated in Figure 4-6. (Also missing from this discussion are alternatives to prospect theory, such as the cost – benefit analysis of Beach and Mitchell, 1978, the production systems analysis of Pitz, 1977, and the recent, highly promising probability transformations of Machina, 1987.[3] We have intended merely to outline prospect theory and to illustrate how it elaborates upon average utility theory, accounting for decisions that the simpler theory cannot explain (just as average utility theory was designed to account for decisions that average amount theory could not explain). We now go on to discuss the remaining difficulties in explaining human decisions, even with the above elaborations.

THE PREFERENCE REVERSAL EFFECT

Notwithstanding the remarks at the beginning of this chapter about the distinction between judgment and decision, it would be desirable to combine these two areas of research in the study of a single decision process. Perhaps the major obstacle to unifying the studies of judgment and decision is a phenomenon called the *preference reversal effect* (Grether and Plott, 1979; Lichtenstein and Slovic, 1971). We saw in problems III and IV an example of preference reversal. However, the term *preference reversal effect* refers to the following important phenomenon. Consider this problem:

VI. Which of the following would you prefer?
1. $^{34}/_{36}$ chance to win $3,   2. $^{18}/_{36}$ chance to win $6.50,
     $^{2}/_{36}$ chance to lose $2 $^{18}/_{36}$ chance to lose $1

Despite the fact that the expected amount of alternative 2 is slightly higher than that of alternative 1, most people prefer alternative 1, the gamble with the higher probability of winning (and the smaller amount won). Now consider the following two problems (which are essentially judgments):

VII. What is the most money you would pay for a $^{34}/_{36}$ chance to win $3 and a $^{2}/_{36}$ chance to lose $2?

VIII. What is the most money you would pay for a $^{18}/_{36}$ chance to win $6.50 and an $^{18}/_{36}$ chance to lose $1?

Despite preferring alternative 1 to 2 in the decision problem (problem VI), people generally set a higher value in problem VIII than problem VII. How can you prefer what you value less highly to what you value more highly? The fact that most people do is the preference reversal phenomenon. It is a highly reliable and compelling effect that works with many different probabilities and amounts. It works when the gambles are framed in terms of roulette (which is why the probabilities here are expressed in thirty-sixths) or a bingo cage or a dartboard or if they are just presented verbally; it works when people are gambling with real money (in a Las Vegas casino) as well as with hypothetical funds; it works when the same subjects are given both the decision problems and the judgments (disguised by mixing several problems together) as well as when one group of subjects is given the decision problems and another the judgments; it also works when the values being judged are expressed as selling prices ("What is the lowest price at which you would sell . . .") instead of buying prices.

All decision theories postulate an evaluation stage, and although the activity of this stage need not be conscious, it seems that people's evaluations as inferred from their decisions should not be inconsistent with their judgments of value. Nevertheless, they are.

There have been many attempts to explain the preference reversal effect, and we cannot discuss them all here. However, we can say some general things about them. Some explanations focus on differences in people's perception of the two kinds of problems. Note that in the decision problem (problem VI) people prefer the alternative with the higher probability of winning (and lower probability of losing), while in the evaluation problems of judgment (problems VII and VIII) they assign a higher value to the alternative with the higher amount won (and lower amount lost). It is as if something about the context, of the two problems causes people to focus on probability when deciding between them and to focus on amount when evaluating them separately. Perhaps presenting the two alternatives together (as in the decision problem) causes probabilities to contrast with each other (just as bringing a red and green patch of color together makes each more vivid), exaggerates differences in probability relative to amount, and results in decisions based on probability rather than amount.

However, recent experiments in which subjects judged the alternatives by rating them (say, on a scale of 1 to 10) instead of pricing them ("How much would you pay?") cast considerable doubt on the above theory (Tversky, Sattath, and Slovic, 1988). When alternatives are rated rather than priced the preference reversal effect disappears. Rated alternatives are consistent with choice. In pricing the alternatives subjects evidently attended to the monetary values of those alternatives and perhaps used the anchoring and adjustment heuristic discussed in the last chapter. We know that the main problem with anchoring and adjustment is insufficient adjustment. If probabilities were used to make the adjustment probabilities would have been less influential in the ultimate judgment than they should have been. On the other hand, in rating the alternatives, subjects weighted probabilities more strongly, perhaps by anchoring on probabilities and adjusting amounts or perhaps weighting both amounts and probabilities equally. In either case, the pricing-versus-weighting experiments show that the language in which a task is framed can strongly affect performance. We turn to this general issue now.

FRAMING

The *context* (or frame) of the alternatives of a choice plays an important part in making decisions. A vivid example of the effect of frame on a decision is the problem described below, in which an essentially identical pair of alternatives is framed in terms of either gains or losses. Since we know that people tend to avoid risk when alternatives are gains and seek risks when alternatives are losses (the reflection effect), we might expect that such a shift in frame would have a powerful effect on decision.

IX. Imagine that the United States is preparing for an outbreak of an unusual Asian disease that is expected to kill 600 people. Two programs to combat the disease have been proposed. Assume that the exact scientific estimate of the consequences of the programs are as follows:

1. If program 1 is adopted, 200 people will be saved.

2. If program 2 is adopted, there is a one-third probability that 600 people will be saved, and a two-thirds probability that no people will be saved.

1'. If program 1 is adopted, 400 people will die.

2'. If program 2 is adopted, there is a one-third probability that nobody will die, and a two-thirds probability that 600 people will die.

Tversky and Kahneman (1981) posed this problem to a group of subjects using the alternatives on top, framed as gains, and to another group of subjects using the essentially identical alternatives on the bottom, which are framed as losses. As you might expect, the subjects asked about lives saved (gains) avoided risk (72 percent chose program 1), while the subjects asked about people dying (losses) sought risk (78 percent chose program 2'). Figure 4-9 illustrates how the change in the frame of the alternatives shifted the subjects' point of reference on a scale of value. The fact that people's decisions shift with the point of reference is evidence that decisions are made not on the basis of the absolute values of the alternatives but on their values relative to some point of reference provided by the frame. This is a very important finding for research in choice as well as in decision making. Because there is no absolute reference point, alternatives can never be without a frame. When a problem does not specify a frame, subjects may provide a frame of their own, uncontrolled by and unknown to the experimenter.

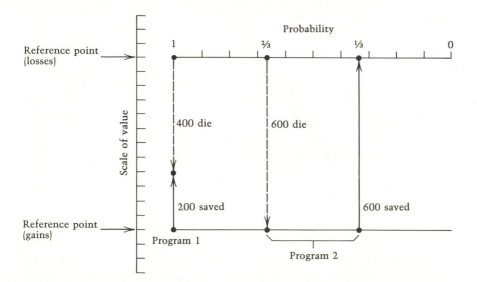

Figure 4-9 How a shift in frame causes a shift in the reference point on a scale of value. The vertical arrows represent amounts (of lives). The position of the arrows on the probability scale indicates their degree of certainty. The solid arrows represent the alternatives framed as gains; the dotted arrows represent the alternatives framed as losses.

The context of a decision need not affect only the valence (positive or negative) of alternatives. It can also affect the amount of an alternative expressed wholly in terms of gains (or wholly in terms of losses). As Figure 4-3 illustrates, a fixed increment in amount ($10 in that figure) is greater in subjective value when it is added to a low amount ($10) than when it is added to a high amount ($90). If alternatives are framed so that a person sets the reference point low on the value scale, a given gain in amount will be valued more than when the reference point is placed high on the value scale. Thus, when a company rewards workers with raises, it usually offers raises of a fixed percent of current salary rather than a fixed amount for each employee. Otherwise, workers with high salaries would be less satisfied than those with low salaries, even though what they buy with the additional money costs the same for both types of worker (and even though Bentham's principle of the greatest good for the greatest number, simply interpreted, dictates the reverse policy).

Symmetrically, if alternatives are framed so that a person sets the reference point at a low value, a given loss will seem less painful than if the reference point were high. You are less likely to worry about a fender dent after a tree has fallen on your car (low reference point) than when that dent is the car's only defect (high reference point).

The effect of the context of a question on a person's decision from a set of presented alternatives corresponds to the effect of the context of a visual scene on a person's perception of that scene. The Gestalt psychologist Karl Duncker showed that when there is a faintly illuminated spot of light within a picture frame in a darkened room, the spot seems to move if the frame is slowly moved even though the spot is standing still. Similarly, subjects' perceptions of the alternatives of a problem change as the frame (and reference point) is changed, even though the alternatives themselves remain the same.

THE DECISION LABORATORY AND THE REAL WORLD

The real-world decisions to which laboratory studies are most relevant are those made at gambling casinos. We have mentioned a few instances where laboratory results correspond to casino behavior. In a way (not to be taken too literally) the casino serves the decision theorist, as the heavens have served the physicist, as a natural laboratory. In the case of physics, the heavens provide examples of the behavior of clearly defined and segregated bodies in a near vacuum. In the case of psychology, gambling casinos provide (relatively) clear motives, clearly defined choices, and clearly calculable outcomes. Just as you would not expect an astronomer to predict the path of a piece of paper dropped in the street on a windy day, you could not expect the decision theorist to predict people's decisions in the very complicated situations of everyday life where motives, choices, and outcomes are all unclear. Although this book uses many examples from everyday life for illustrative purposes, now is a good time to remind ourselves of the dangers of extrapolating from the laboratory to the real world.

Several attempts have been made to study aspects of casino gambling in the psychology laboratory. For ethical reasons, it is not possible to allow the subjects of psychology experiments to lose large sums of money in the laboratory. Yet the possibility of such losses must be a major factor governing casino gambling. Anderson and Brown (1984) measured the heart rate and blood pressure as well as the patterns of betting of experienced gamblers in a casino; they compared those measures to corresponding ones for the same experienced players in a laboratory outfitted with casino equipment and decorated like a casino to create a casinolike atmosphere. They found that physiological measures as well as gambling patterns differed markedly for these experienced players in the two environments as well as between experienced players in the casino and inexperienced undergraduates playing in the laboratory. The only apparent difference between the two situations was the possibility of large losses and gains in the casino and the impossibility of any loss in the laboratory. Chapter 10 will present details of another finding of a difference between behavior in a casino and in the laboratory. These differences between casino and laboratory should not discourage laboratory research, however. As we will see in Chapter 10, the very principles discovered in the laboratory (in this case, the framing effect of gains versus losses) may explain those differences.

Perhaps the most salient example of the difficulty of extrapolation from the laboratory to the real world is a study by Ebbeson and Konečni (1980) called "On the External Validity of Decision-Making: What Do We Know about Decisions in the Real World?" These authors first discuss several differences between the laboratory and the real world that make it difficult to draw conclusions from the former about the latter. Then they present examples of their own failures to duplicate laboratory results in practical situations. The differences cited by Ebbeson and Konečni include the following:

1. In most laboratory decision problems, probabilities of events are presented numerically (in the form of predigested judgments by the person posing the problem), whereas events are usually experienced directly in real life.

2. In laboratory decision problems, monetary gains and losses are, for ethical reasons, hypothetical or of small amount, whereas in life monetary gains and losses are real and sometimes large.

3. In laboratory studies of decision, complex nonmonetary alternatives are often broken down into the components (aspects and probabilities) that the experimenter, on the basis of theory, assumes to be important in real life. If the theory is wrong, those categories are irrelevant to real-life decisions.

4. The theories and models used to explain decision experiments invariably refer to internal variables that cannot be directly observed. Thus, a theory may be correct but still not applicable to everyday life decisions.

5. Time pressures (and other constraints) differ between the laboratory and the real world.

6. In the laboratory, the experimenter observes (or tries to observe) a person's decisions, while outcomes of those decisions are ignored. In real life people are concerned mainly with outcomes (the bottom line, so to speak) rather than the details of the process by which those outcomes may have been obtained.

As one example of the dangers of extrapolating from the laboratory to the real world, Ebbesen and Konečni (1975) described in another article how they tried to create a laboratory simulation of judges' courtroom decisions. Real courtroom judges volunteered to be subjects in the experiment. In the laboratory, the judges were asked to set bail for a hypothetical case after they were given information about the crime of which each prisoner was accused, the recommendation of the district attorney, and the status of the prisoners in their communities. In the laboratory, judges set their (hypothetical) bail based strongly on the prisoner's status in the community — in accord with proper judicial practice. However, leaving the laboratory and returning to their real-life courtrooms, the judges almost always went along with the recommendations of the district attorneys. The actual bail that the judges set in their own courtrooms was unrelated to the prisoner's status in his or her community except as that factor was reflected in the district attorney's recommendation. Thus, in the laboratory, the judges set bail on the basis of one factor, and in the courtroom on another.

What is the reason for this difference? The reader's guess is as good as anyone's. Time pressures were certainly different; in the laboratory the judges had the leisure to go by the book; in the courtroom the heavy caseload demanded quick decisions. Another possibility is that if bail were set too low and the prisoner jumped bail, the judge could avoid blame by claiming merely to have followed the district attorney's advice. Judges may have been reluctant to demonstrate to the experimenters this easily understandable attempt to avoid responsibility. On the basis of this and other examples, Ebbesen and Konečni (1980, p. 37) argue that decision theory must focus more on "what the subjects are *trying to do*" in decision experiments than on inferred internal structures.

We turn now to another psychological approach — behavioral choice theory — to this sort of problem. Behavioral choice theory avoids many of the problems with decision theory that Ebbesen and Konečni pointed out. It is, in fact, primarily focused on what subjects are trying to do in experiments. However, as the reader will see, the behavioral approach has its own problems (largely linguistic). A full understanding of judgment, decision, and choice cannot be attained by either approach alone at present. It is the theme of this book that an enlightened outlook on (if not a full understanding of) these processes can be obtained by combining (and eventually resolving) both approaches.

APPENDIX: MACHINA'S REPRESENTATION OF PROBABILISTIC ALTERNATIVES

Here are problems III and IV again:

III. Which of the following would you prefer?
    1. 80% chance to win $40,   2. $30 for sure
       20% chance to win nothing

IV. Which of the following would you prefer?
  1. 20% chance to win $40,   2. 25% chance to win $30,
     80% chance to win nothing   75% chance to win nothing

Recall that in problem III people preferred $30 for sure (alternative 2) to an uncertain $40 (alternative 1); however, when in problem IV the probabilities of winning $30 or $40 were reduced to one-fourth of their previous values, preference reversed; the $40 alternative was preferred. The independence axiom of probability theory (another form of Luce's assumption of independence from irrelevant alternatives, discussed previously in this chapter) implies that the preference between two alternatives should not change when both are reduced by a common fraction. Thus, the pair of choices in problems III and IV violates the independence axiom.

Mark Machina (1987) has devised a graphical way to represent this violation. Note first that three amounts of money may be won: $40, $30, or $0. There is some probability (which may be zero) of winning each amount. Each alternative may therefore be characterized by a set of three probabilities $(p_0, p_{30}, \text{and } p_{40})$. For each alternative the sum of all probabilities, $p_0 + p_{30} + p_{40}$, must equal 1. Thus we can rephrase these problems as follows:

	p_0	p_{30}	p_{40}
Problem III			
Alternative 1	.2	0	.8
Alternative 2	0	1	0
Problem IV			
Alternative 1	.8	0	.2
Alternative 2	.75	.25	0

The brackets with the arrows indicate the two instances where the probabilities of problem IV are one-fourth of their corresponding values in problem III. Figure 4-10a plots the alternatives of problem III as points on a graph of p_0 versus p_{40}. (Since the three probabilities must add to 1, once you fix two of them, the third is determined by subtracting their sum from 1.) Alternative 1 of problem III (designated III-1 on the figure) is a point on the hypotenuse of the triangle formed by connecting the ends of the axes. All points on this hypotenuse represent alternatives where $p_0 + p_{40} = 1$; hence, on the hypot-

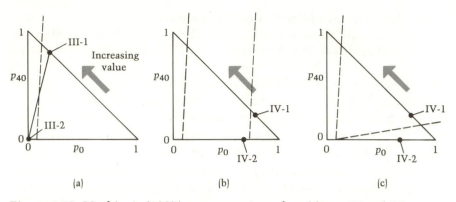

Figure 4-10 Machina's (1987) representation of problems III and IV.

enuse $p_{30} = 0$. Alternative III-2 is plotted at the origin of the axes. At this point both p_0 and p_{40} are equal to 0; hence at the origin $p_{30} = 1$. In the figure the two alternatives are connected by a thin line.

Since we can safely assume that people prefer more money to less, the upper left corner of the triangle (where $p_{40} = 1$) must be the most preferred point, and the lower right corner (where $p_0 = 1$) must be the least preferred. Along the hypotenuse connecting these corners, people would prefer any point to the left and above of any given point because higher points represent higher values of p_{40} and (since $p_{30} = 0$ along this line) lower values of p_0. Machina demonstrates logically and mathematically that the independence axiom implies that there exists in the triangle a set of straight, parallel "indifference lines" leaning to the right. People would be indifferent between two alternatives located on the same indifference line. However, any alternative to the left of a given indifference line would be preferred to any alternative to the right of that line. The upper-left corner, of course, is to the left of all indifference lines in the triangle, and the lower-right corner is to the right of all indifference lines.

Because people generally choose alternative 2 in problem III over alternative 1, an indifference line must exist to the left of which lies point III-2 and to the right of which lies point III-1; one such difference line is drawn as a dotted line in Figure 4-10a. The independence axiom demands that once any indifference line is determined, all others must be parallel to it. Figure 4-10b plots the alternatives of problem IV (p_{30} and p_{40} now decreased). Both points are now on the lower right part of the triangle. The slope of a line between them would remain the same as in Figure 4-10a. Thus, point IV-2 must be to the left of and point IV-1 must be to the right of an indifference line parallel to the one previously drawn. The original indifference line and a parallel one are shown as dotted lines in Figure 4-10b. If indifference lines must be parallel everywhere in the triangle, alternative 2 of problem IV must be preferred to alternative 1. Since the reverse is actually the case, the true indifference lines cannot be parallel.

Machina points out that the preferences in these two problems (as well as several other apparent paradoxes in decision experiments) would be explained by nonparallel indifference lines, such as straight lines fanning outwards from a common point. Figure 4-10c shows a pair of such lines. Relaxing the independence axiom to various degrees would result in indifference lines that fan out on these probability diagrams.

N O T E S

1. For choices among three alternatives, the mathematics of elimination by aspects becomes more complicated, but the principle remains the same. For three alternatives, you should fully count each alternative's unique aspects and discount those aspects it shares with each of the other alternatives by the probability that you will decide to choose that alternative over each of the others. For example, suppose a third alternative, house renovation, is being considered along with the two cars. The aspects of house renovation total 75 units of value and are completely unshared by the two cars. According to elimination by aspects, the preference for the car with the stereo is

$$\frac{2 + 100\,[2/(2 + 1)]}{2 + 1 + 100 + 75}$$

and your preference for the car with air conditioning is

$$\frac{1 + 100\,[1/(2 + 1)]}{2 + 1 + 100 + 75}$$

The terms in brackets are discounts due to shared aspects. Preference for house renovation, because it shares no aspects with the other alternatives, is given in a straightforward way by Equation 4-2:

$$\frac{75}{2 + 1 + 100 + 75}$$

2. Mathematicians call this quantity *expected value.* However, the terms *expected* and *value* both imply subjective (or personal) entities. Value as a subjective quantity may differ from the objective amount, and what a person expects may differ from what the person gets. This book reserves the term *value* (along with *utility*) for subjective or personal quantities and uses the term *amount* for objective quantities. For subjective probabilities we retain the (redundant) adjectival phrase *subjective expected,* but for objective probabilities we substitute the more neutral *average* for *expected.* The following table shows the traditional nomenclature and that used in this book:

Location		Traditional Terms		Terms in This Book	
Probability	*Amount*	*Probability*	*Amount*	*Probability*	*Amount*
World	World	Expected	Value	Average	Amount
World	Person	Expected	Utility	Average	Utility
*Person	World	Subjective expected	Value	Subjective expected	Amount
†Person	Person	Subjective expected	Utility	Subjective expected	Utility

*Usually Bayesian statistics together with actual amounts is considered to exemplify this category. We do not discuss this category in this book.
†Prospect theory falls in this category.

3. The appendix to this chapter shows how Machina's (1987) graphical expression of the independence axiom of probability theory can be used to represent problems III and IV.

REINFORCEMENT
AND
PUNISHMENT

You could draw a line here. The last two chapters presented a cognitive model of judgment and decision; as is typical of cognitive models, nothing was said that distorts our intuitive sense of how these processes work. True, some surprising data were described; people make unexpected yet consistent errors of judgment and decision. Still, the concepts inherent in the very descriptions of those errors are intuitive ones. Human rationality has been shown to be bounded by all sorts of constraints. But then we knew that all along. That is, as they say, why pencils have erasers. Part of the justification for cognitive models is that they conform to intuition—to the phenomenological facts. They may elucidate, they may define, they may even alter a concept here and there for the sake of consistency, but they never fundamentally abandon intuition.

Behavioral models, on the other hand, claim to abandon intuition right from the start. They profess concern, not with conformance to phenomenal facts but with prediction and control of behavior, including one's own. If prediction and control may be obtained only at the expense of phenomenological truth, then, says the behaviorist, phenomenological truth has to go. Of course, as we have seen and will see again, no theory is pure. Cognitivists still want to predict and control behavior and behaviorists cannot yet predict and control behavior well enough to afford abandoning phenomenology altogether.

Nevertheless, the difference is a real one that has real consequences for the reader. Because of the tenuous hold that behavioral models have on intuition, you have to learn a new language (or at least a set of new terms) before you can hope to understand the behavioral model of choice. The purpose of this chapter is to introduce and illustrate that language.

TERMINOLOGY

The behavioral model that we will discuss in the next few chapters is shown in Figure 5-1. The figure repeats the three heavy arrows of Figure 2-2, which represent interaction between a person and the world. Figure 2-2, in accordance with the cognitive model, distinguishes between what people say ("I love you," for instance) as an indication of the state of an internal process and what people do (get married, for instance) as the outcome of a series of internal events. The behavioral model of Figure 5-1, on the other hand, lumps all behavior into one category (arrow 2); it does not distinguish in principle between verbal and other behavior. According to the behavioral model, verbal behavior does not reflect an internal state. Thus, when you say "I love you," you are not simply reporting the state of your heart or mind. Instead, the behavioral model sees verbal behavior as caused by the same sort of process (but not necessarily the same events) that cause any other overt action (like getting married).

Historically, behaviorists have been concerned with two relationships. The first is the relationship between one input and another (arrows 1 and 3 in Figure 5-1). Following Skinner (1938), we call this relationship a *respondent contingency*. In Pavlovian terms (Pavlov, 1927) one of these stimuli is called the *conditioned stimulus* and the other the *unconditioned stimulus*. Which is which is theoretically arbitrary but practically determined by which seems to elicit a strong response more reliably (as, in Pavlov's experiments, food reliably elicits salivation in dogs). This stimulus is the unconditioned stimulus, and the other, the conditioned stimulus. Depending on the tem-

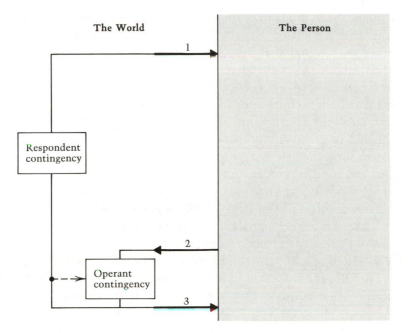

	Judgment	Decision	Operant conditioning	Respondent conditioning
1	Data	Problem alternatives (amount, probability)	Discriminative stimulus	Conditioned stimulus
2	Judgment (value, probability)	Decision	Operant (choice)	Respondent (conditioned response)
3	Verification	Outcome (gain, loss)	Reinforcer, punisher	Unconditioned stimulus

Figure 5-1 Relationships between a person and the world. The four sets of labels for the three arrows show corresponding operations and observations in experiments on judgment, decision, operant conditioning, and respondent conditioning. See the discussion in the text for a description of contingencies.

poral relationship between conditioned and unconditioned stimuli (the respondent contingency), an animal's rate of response (rate of salivation) will change over time. This change in responding is called *respondent conditioning* (also called *classical conditioning* or *Pavlovian conditioning*).

There are three kinds of respondent contingencies: excitation, extinction, and inhibition. In all three, the conditioned stimulus is conceived as a signal that may indicate the arrival of the unconditioned stimulus. A positive relationship (positive contingency or positive correlation) between the conditioned and unconditioned stimuli is called *excitation* or *excitatory conditioning*, a neutral or null (or random) relationship is called *extinction*, and a negative relationship is called *inhibition* or *inhibitory conditioning*. As used by contemporary researchers, these three terms refer to relationships between the conditioned and unconditioned stimuli, not to absolute frequencies of either. For instance, a smoke alarm may go out of order by sounding all the time or by never sounding. Because the smoke alarm no longer signals the presence of smoke in either case, both are technically extinction contingencies.[1]

The study of respondent conditioning arose from Pavlov's experiments on reflexes, conceived in terms of neuronal connections inside people and other animals. Much modern work on respondent conditioning (e.g., Hawkins and Kandell, 1984) retains this conception. However, one of Skinner's earliest contributions to the study of behavior was a conception of a reflex as the relation between a stimulus and a class of responses defined by overt manifestations rather than by neural connections. For instance, a knee jerk, is a reflex, according to Skinner, not because of the neural connections between the sense organ, the nerve, the spinal cord, and the muscles but because the stimulus reliably elicits the response in an intact person. Here we follow Skinner's wholly behavioral conception but note that this conception need not be inconsistent with any particular internal explanation of conditioning (neurological or even cognitive).

There is a conception of choice (Pavlov's own conception, in fact) that sees choice as nothing but the action of respondent conditioning. In this conception each alternative is a conditioned stimulus, the outcome of each alternative is an unconditioned stimulus, and choice is the dominance of a stronger conditioned response over a weaker one. There is something appealing about this conception of choice, because it explains all behavior simply as a set of fundamental reflexes. However, Skinner noted that the kind of behavioral act normally called "voluntary" (which we call choice, such as in selecting between doing X or not doing X or between doing X and doing Y) is more easily explained in terms of the relationship between the act and its consequences than between one stimulus and another. Skinner called such voluntary acts *operants* and defined them in a negative and a positive way. Negatively, operants are acts not apparently elicited by any particular stimulus. Positively, operants are acts that can be controlled by their consequences.

Just as respondent conditioning is the change (over time) in the rate of a respondent brought about through a relationship between the conditioned and unconditioned stimulus, so *operant conditioning* is the change (over time) in the rate of an operant brought about through the relationship between the operant (itself) and its consequences. That relationship is the *operant contingency*. Let us now consider the details of the operant contingency. Unlike respondent conditioning, operant conditioning distinguishes among kinds of outcome (arrow 3). Respondent conditioning treats all outcomes (unconditioned stimuli) in the same way. Operant conditioning classifies outcomes as *reinforcers* and *punishers.* In a later section we will attempt to define these classes, but for the present they can be thought of as relatively pleasant events and relatively unpleasant events, respectively. We will follow typical usage here by using the term *reinforcer* when referring to an event that affects an animal's act and by using *reward* when referring to an event that affects the animal itself. Thus we say "the rat's lever press was reinforced" and "the rat was rewarded." In the case of *punishment*, a single term serves for both usages.[2]

Because operant conditioning distinguishes among different kinds of outcome, each of the three kinds of contingent relationship (positive, neutral, and negative) must be defined for each type of outcome (reinforcer and punisher). Let us consider reinforcers first. A positive contingency or correlation between an operant and a reinforcer is called, logically enough, *positive reinforcement.* When you put a coin in a slot and get a candy bar, your behavior (operant) is thus positively reinforced (and you are rewarded). A neutral contingency or correlation between an operant and a reinforcer is called *extinction* (as in respondent conditioning). When you put a coin in the slot of a broken machine and do not get a candy bar, your behavior is extinguished. Again, as with respondent conditioning, extinction is the absence of a relationship — in this case, between response and outcome. So a broken candy machine that delivers candy bars freely, independently of coins inserted in the slot, would also exemplify an extinction contingency. A negative relationship between an operant and a reinforcer is called *omission* (a poorly named and rarely studied procedure). Here the candy machine analogy breaks down. If you can imagine a candy machine that took a candy bar away from you when you put a coin in the slot, you have an example of an omission contingency.

Now let us consider punishers. A positive relationship between an operant and an unpleasant stimulus is called *punishment.* When a boy is spanked for stealing, the boy's stealing is being punished. A neutral relationship, this time between an operant and an unpleasant stimulus, is again called *extinction.* If the boy were spanked whether he stole or not, the process would be called *extinction.* (*Extinction,* like the other terms here, is defined as a procedure and not as the effect of a procedure on behavior. The labeling of several procedures as extinction does not imply any common behavioral effect.) A negative relationship between an operant and an unpleasant stimulus is called *negative reinforcement* or *escape.* Thus, if you spank a boy when he is not stealing (perhaps spanking him for doing something else) and then stop spanking the boy when he steals, you would be negatively reinforcing the boy's stealing. Negative reinforcement is thus the opposite of punishment. In practice, punishment usually (but not always) reduces the rate of an operant, while negative reinforcement sometimes (but far from always) increases it.

Table 5-1 summarizes the above terminology. The object of behavioral psychology has been and continues to be the study of the effects of these contingencies on the behavior of animals, including human beings. In the behavioral laboratory, first Pavlov (in the respondent case) and then Skinner (in the operant case) attempted to reduce

Table 5–1   Contingencies of Respondent and Operant Conditioning

	Contingency		
	Positive	*Neutral*	*Negative*
Respondent	Excitation	Extinction	Inhibition
Operant			
Reinforcer	Positive reinforcement	Extinction	Omission
Punisher	Punishment	Extinction	Negative reinforcement

these contingencies to their elements. Pavlov's isolated rooms and Skinner's operant chambers (Skinner boxes) are intended to serve for psychology as the vacuum served for physics — a place where the contingencies act simply. For both Pavlov and Skinner, the elements of the conditioning process are individual, discrete stimuli and responses. The relationship that defined the contingency is strict temporal contiguity. Just as Pavlov viewed choice in terms of the competition between individual respondents, Skinner views choice in terms of the competition between individual operants. In a choice situation, Skinner sees each alternative and its outcome as a separate contingency, strengthening or weakening an animal's tendency to make each response. For Skinner, choice among alternatives is not an object of study in itself; it is merely the combination of two individual responses.

As soon as researchers began to study choice systematically in an operant setting (a Skinner box with two possible operants, such as two levers or two keys, and two operant contingencies), it became obvious that choice behavior does not consist merely of the sum of two (or more) individual operants. Rather, as we shall see, choice depends on simultaneous consideration of all the alternatives (Herrnstein, 1970). In other words, individual alternatives of choice have no absolute status; choice by animals can be explained only by viewing each alternative relative to the others. As research on choice has progressed, theory about choice has moved in a direction opposite to Skinner's supposition. Instead of viewing choice as the outcome of individual operants, individual operants may be viewed as the outcome of choices. Thus, even a single operant is viewed as a choice between responding and not responding. All behavior normally said to be voluntary (not elicited by a stimulus) may be conceived of as choice behavior. A rat in a Skinner box with a single lever may be viewed as repeatedly choosing between pressing it and not pressing it. As it turns out, the laws governing this sort of choice are the same as those governing the rat's choice between pressing one of two levers.

There is some dispute about whether this view of individual operant behavior (which will be discussed in detail in the next chapter) is the best view. However, there is no dispute that it is the only one yet proposed that has had any success in explaining individual operant behavior and operant choice behavior with a single set of principles. However, before discussing choice behavior itself (arrow 2 of Figure 5-1) in the next chapter, it is necessary to backtrack and consider the two other elements of the operant conditioning process: discriminative stimuli (arrow 1) and reinforcement and punishment (arrow 3).

DISCRIMINATIVE STIMULI

An important complication of simple operant and respondent contingencies is represented in Figure 5-1 by the small horizontal dotted arrow. In a respondent contingency, the conditioned stimulus (arrow 1) signals the arrival of the unconditioned stimulus (arrow 3), just as the train whistle signals the arrival of a train at a crossing. The relation of the conditioned stimulus to the unconditioned stimulus is independent of any action that a person at the crossing might take. Of course, behavior (arrow 2) depends on the respondent contingency. The important point is that the respondent contingency does not depend on behavior — it simply relates two stimuli.

However, consider a "don't walk" light at a street crossing. What event does that signal? There is no particular unconditioned stimulus (like a locomotive) that invariably follows the onset of the "don't walk" light. A street corner light signals an operant contingency rather than a single event. It says that if you cross the street, you may get a summons or you may get hit by a car. When a stimulus signals the presence of an operant contingency (rather than the arrival of another stimulus), it is called a *discriminative stimulus* (rather than a conditioned stimulus). A discriminative stimulus, according to Skinner, does not cause or elicit a response in the sense that a hammer blow to your patella tendon causes your knee to jerk. Rather, it sets the occasion for an operant (a voluntary act) in the sense that a "don't walk" light at a crossing sets the occasion for you to stop and a "walk" light sets the occasion for you to go.

Discriminative stimuli have been much studied in the operant laboratory. For instance, a pigeon may be trained to peck a disk illuminated with green light (called a green key) by a positive reinforcement contingency and to cease pecking when the illumination is changed to red (red key) by an extinction contingency. If you looked into the Skinner box without knowing what the pigeon's training had been, it would seem to you as though the green light were causing the pigeon to peck (eliciting pecking) and the red light were causing it to stop pecking (inhibiting pecking). However, the process by which this control came about was operant, not respondent, conditioning.

As long as the pigeon's behavior is different in the presence of the green and red keys, the pigeon may be said to be discriminating between the two colors — hence the term *discriminative stimulus*. Now suppose the key is illuminated with blue light (a new color). Most likely the pigeon would peck the blue key, but not as rapidly as it pecked the green key (the color that signaled positive reinforcement). To the extent that it behaves similarly with the green and blue keys, the pigeon is generalizing from one to the other; to the extent that it behaves differently, it is discriminating. Discrimination and generalization are two sides of the same coin. In everyday life we are repeatedly faced with situations that resemble but are not identical to situations that we have experienced in the past. Such situations require fine discriminations and generalizations.

The bridge that this book intends to establish between studies of judgment and decision on the one hand and studies of choice on the other depends strongly on the concept of discriminative stimuli. In the language of operant conditioning, the input to a judgment problem and the presentation of a set of decision alternatives are discriminative stimuli (see the labels at the bottom of Figure 5-1). Human language is, of course, much different from a green or a red key. One difference is the complex grammatical structure of human language and the much simpler structure of the discriminative stimuli to which pigeons are exposed in the laboratory. Nevertheless, the primary function of language in people's everyday lives and the function of the green and red keys in the pigeon laboratory are the same — to signal the presence of a contingency (however complex or simple) between behavior and outcome. (In the case of a decision problem, the question "Which do you prefer, $20 with a probability of .5 or $10 for sure?" functions like two simultaneously available colored keys in a Skinner box.)

THE MECHANISM OF REINFORCEMENT

What is a reinforcer or a punisher? We have so far been getting by with the intuitive notion of reinforcers as pleasant stimuli and punishers as unpleasant stimuli. But a stimulus that is pleasant to one person may be unpleasant to another, and what is pleasant at one time may be unpleasant at another. Furthermore, how do you know what is pleasant or unpleasant to a nonverbal animal? In practice, the definition of pleasant and unpleasant becomes circular: A reinforcer is defined as a pleasant stimulus, and a pleasant stimulus as a reinforcer.

Attempts to break out of this circularity by an independent definition of reinforcement and punishment have been (aside from appeals to intuition) of two kinds: biological and behavioral. The best-known biological definition of reinforcement is the need reduction theory of Hull (1943). According to this theory, anything that reduces a basic need will serve as a reinforcer, and contrariwise, anything that increases a basic need will serve as a punisher. Basic needs, in turn, are defined in terms of goods essential to the animal's survival. In need reduction theory, food reinforces the lever presses of a rat because without food the rat would die.

A problem with need reduction theory is that reducing some animal needs (such as the need for vitamin A) is not generally reinforcing. Another problem is that for many animals, not only humans, many very strong reinforcers do not satisfy needs (that is, you would not die without them). For instance, a monkey can learn to solve a puzzle only for the sake of solving a puzzle. A rat will repeatedly run down an alley at the end of which is only the sight of another rat. Monkeys do not die if they are deprived of puzzles to solve, nor do rats deprived of the sight of other rats. We may infer from their power to reinforce behavior that puzzle solving and rat sighting are pleasant to monkeys and rats, but then we are back to the old circularity.

One attempt to get around problems with defining reinforcement and punishment in terms of biological needs has been to suppose that, in the course of evolution, needs became internalized in animals in the form of instinctive drives. Thus the fact that a rat would die without food is represented inside the rat by a drive or motivation to obtain food. Although originally drives might have corresponded absolutely to needs (and in primitive animals, may do so still), drives are supposed to have gained a certain independence from absolute needs in mammals such as rats, monkeys, and people. An individual monkey would not die without solving puzzles and an individual rat would not die without seeing other rats, but it is probably beneficial for the survival of these species in general for puzzle solving and rat sighting to serve as rewards. In nature, a monkey that likes to solve puzzles might incidentally get the banana down from the tree; a rat that likes to see other rats might incidentally find warmth and sources of food. The concept that drives exist in animals (and that in many animals they do not directly reflect immediate needs) has been useful in ethology in explaining the relation of animal behavior to hormonal and physiological states; the concept has also been valuable as an organizing principle (as in human personality theories such as Freud's).

However, as a theory of reinforcement, the concept of drive suffers from the same problem as the concept of pleasure: It is circular. Just as there is no independent measure of what an animal finds pleasant, there are no independent measures of an animal's drives. So far biological conceptions of reinforcement, like the intuitive conceptions that have gone before them, have raised more questions than they have answered. Now the question of why seeing another rat reinforces a rat's bar presses is accompanied by the additional questions of why a rat gets pleasure from seeing another rat and why a rat has a drive to see another rat. The latter two questions are no less interesting than the first, but they are questions, not answers.[3]

We now turn to a wholly behavioral conception of reinforcement. Its general tactic is to isolate one situation that can serve as a measure by which the power of a reinforcer is assessed. Once this is done, the same reinforcer should serve in other situations. Skinner proposed that a reinforcer of any operant act would work as a reinforcer of any other operant act. Symmetrically, a punisher of any operant act should work as a punisher for any other operant act. The problem with this theory is that reinforcers tend to be situation-specific. The sight of another rat will reinforce a rat's running in an alley or a running wheel, but it might not reinforce that same rat's turning in a maze. In human life, examples abound. You could reinforce my giving you the time of day by a simple "thank you," but that same "thank you" would be a neutral stimulus or even a punisher if I were to receive it instead of my biweekly salary check.

To deal with this problem, Premack (1965, 1971) proposed a relativistic theory of reinforcement. Premack's theory, or some variation of it, is now generally accepted as the best solution we have to the question "What is a reinforcer?" First, all reinforcers are conceived as normally attached to *consummatory responses* — food to eating, water to drinking, air to breathing, and so on. Even the sight of a rat is attached to a consummatory response — the response of looking. For Premack, eating an apple is the reinforcer, not the apple itself. Second, the situation by which the power of a reinforcer is tested is a choice situation. Thus, the power of a reinforcer cannot be evaluated

independently but only in relation to some other potential reinforcer. On the basis of preference in choice situations, all reinforcers
can be placed on a scale of value.

According to Premack, the value of one reinforcer relative to another for an animal is proportional to the time the animal spends
consuming one reinforcer relative to the other in a test situation
(where both reinforcers are freely available). To discover how a person (at a given state of deprivation) values apples relative to oranges,
you could deprive the person of fruit for a week, then put him or her
in a room with a barrel of apples and a barrel of oranges and then
measure the time the person spends eating each kind of fruit. The
more time a person spends eating one type of fruit, the higher its
value.

Just as all potential reinforcers may be conceived of as (consummatory) acts, all acts may be conceived of as potential reinforcers.
Playing with puzzles, looking at conspecifics, pressing a lever, even
jumping in the air may be first withheld and then made freely available in Premack's choice test. Relative values can then be
determined.

Finally, the values of any pair of acts may be used to predict the
effectiveness of an operant contingency where one of the pair serves
as the operant (arrow 2 of Figure 5-1) and the other serves as a
potential reinforcer (arrow 3). According to Premack, any act higher
on the value scale will positively reinforce (increase the rate of) any
act lower on the value scale upon which it is contingent. Symmetrically, any act lower on the value scale will punish (decrease the rate of)
any act higher on the value scale upon which it is contingent.

According to Premack, the reason a rat's lever pressing is reinforced by food is that, given a free choice between pressing a lever
and eating food, the rat spends more time eating food. This is a
noncircular but wholly behavioral answer to the question "What is a
reinforcer?" Usually consumption of food is high on an animal's
value scale and mechanical manipulation of a lever is low, but if the
rat has just eaten its fill in a place where physical movement of its
paws is limited, this preference may be reversed. In such a case, given
a free choice the rat will spend more time pressing a lever than
eating, and if lever pressing is made contingent on eating (if the lever
is withdrawn until the rat has eaten some food and then made available for a brief period), eating should be reinforced by lever pressing
(eating should increase in rate). Premack and his students have demonstrated this principle many times.

In one demonstration with human children rather than rats as subjects, Premack (1971) found in a choice test that the children spent more time pulling the plunger of a pinball machine than eating candy (both machine and candy were freely available). Later (as Premack predicted), when playing pinball was made contingent on eating candy, the children's rate of eating candy increased (positive reinforcement). Here is a case of a manipulative response (pinball playing) reinforcing a consummatory response (eating candy) — just the opposite of the typical relationship between manipulative and consummatory responses.

In practice there are some problems in using Premack's choice test to predict contingent behavior. First, some consummatory acts (sex, for example) so quickly lead to satiation that one or two reinforcers serve to drastically lower the value of these acts. Other consummatory acts (listening to a concert, for example) take a while to occur. The value of the former type of acts can only be measured veridically in a very brief choice test, while the value of the latter can only be measured at all with a relatively long choice test. How can you predict the result when one of these consummatory acts is made contingent upon the other? One solution is to discover a third consummatory act that maintains its value over brief and long durations and to compare the other two to that third act. In the case of rats, such an act is running in a wheel. In the case of humans, the act of paying money might do.

However, that last example brings us to a second practical problem with Premack's theory. The value of low-valued consummatory acts cannot be measured in a free-choice test. For Premack, aversive stimuli (like electric shock) are aversive not because of what they make you feel but because of what they make you do. A low-valued act is, by definition, not freely done. If an animal does not do an act in a free-choice test, we know it is low in value but we do not know how low. For instance, if put in a room with the opportunity to jump high in the air and to bang your head against the wall, you would probably do neither. But one of these acts is probably valued higher than the other. In testing between high-valued acts (like eating apples and oranges) the test situation may harmlessly allow a third alternative — doing neither. In testing between low-valued acts, the test situation must be structured to preclude that third alternative; in practice, this is often difficult to arrange.

Finally, some reinforcers and punishers are not clearly attached in practice to consummatory acts. For instance, very mild electrical stimulation in certain areas of the brain can reinforce lever pressing of rats. What is the consummatory act for the brain stimulation? If lever pressing is said to be the consummatory act, then lever pressing and brain stimulation together must be considered as the reinforcer. But then how can the within-reinforcer relation between lever pressing and brain stimulation be studied? Similarly, it is possible to reinforce a series of turns by a rat in a maze by injecting milk directly into the rat's stomach. Here the natural consummatory act of the rat (drinking) is bypassed, yet the reinforcer is still effective. Why? Premack's theory does not say.

When we discuss economic theories of behavior in Chapter 8 we will consider another theory of operant conditioning that avoids the concept of reinforcement (and some of its problems) entirely.[4] Meanwhile, Premack's theory of reinforcement is the most complete one now available.

TWO KINDS OF VALUE SCALE

The concept of value is as important in the study of choice as it is in judgment and decision. According to Premack (1971), the greater the difference in value between an operant act and a reinforcer or punisher, the more effective the reinforcer or punisher is. Figure 5-2 shows two ways to conceptualize value. We will call one "objective" and the other "subjective." The objective scale places the lowest-valued events at zero. On this scale being tortured would presumably be down near the bottom and winning a million dollars far above it. There is no essential difference on this scale between positive reinforcement and negative reinforcement. The former (shown in Figure 5-2 by a transition from a to b) is the contingent relation between an operant and a positive reinforcer, as when a rat presses a lever to obtain food. The latter (shown in Figure 5-2 by a transition from c to a) is the contingent relation between an operant and the removal of a punisher, as when a rat presses a lever to remove electric shock. In both cases, the transition is from a state of lower value to a state of higher value. Correspondingly, on the objective scale there is no essential difference between omission (the removal of a positive reinforcer) and punishment (the presentation of a punisher). The former is represented in Figure 5-2 by a transition from b to a, and the latter by a transition from a to c.

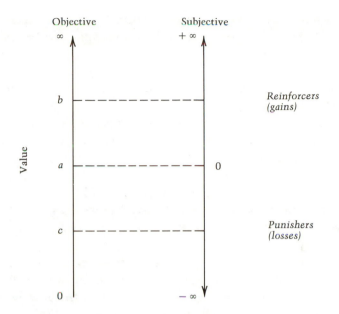

Figure 5-2 Objective and subjective value scales.

In Premack's theory, operant responses are not neutral stimuli; they each have a position on the objective value scale. Premack has shown that, for a rat, a single kind of response — running in a wheel — may serve as an operant (as when wheel running is reinforced by eating or punished by electric shock), a reinforcer (as when the wheel, normally locked, is unlocked by pressing the lever), or a punisher (as when the wheel, normally free, is motorized to go at a high speed by pressing the lever). What counts, in this theory, is the value of an act relative to another act, not its absolute (or objective) value. In general, the greater the difference between the value of a reinforcer or punisher and the value of the instrumental act, the greater its effectiveness as a reinforcer (to raise the rate) or as a punisher (to lower the rate) of the instrumental act.

Yet, subjectively, there is a great deal of difference between positive reinforcement and negative reinforcement and between punishment and omission. It makes a difference to us whether we work as free people for wages or whether we do the same work as slaves to avoid being whipped. The carrot and the stick may both make the donkey move, but there is certainly a difference between them as far as the donkey is concerned. This difference is shown in Figure 5-2 on the subjective scale of value. Premack's theory of reinforcement sets the instrumental act (upon which a reinforcer or punisher is contingent) at the zero point of the subjective scale. All acts above it are reinforcers with respect to it, and all acts below it are punishers with respect to it. Thus, each instrumental act effectively sets up a separate subjective scale.

As we have seen in the last chapter, simply rephrasing a decision problem from a context of gains to a context of losses can reverse a decision. In terms of Figure 5-2, the effect of a problem's frame is to shift the zero point of the subjective scale. If the zero point is at the level of a, as shown, then a shift from a to b is positive reinforcement. If the subjective scale were moved upwards so that the zero point were at b, the same shift from a to b would be negative reinforcement.

The position of the zero point of the subjective value scale is important even if we confine our attention to one side of it. A shift from a to b might have one effect on behavior if the zero point were at a but quite another if the zero point were at c. As Tversky and Kahneman (1981) indicate, a decision whether to buy a rug alone (a shift from a to b with the zero point at a) may be quite different from a decision whether to buy a rug when already buying a house (a shift from a to b with the zero point far below a). As we have seen in the study of decision and as we will see in the study of choice, the subjective scale is the scale that counts.

Conditions of satiation and deprivation shift the value of reinforcers and punishers relative to the zero point. Just as a $1000 prize has a different value for a millionaire than for a pauper, a pellet of food has a different value for a satiated than for a hungry rat. The value of reinforcers and punishers relative to the zero point depends not only on an animal's recent consumption but also on the animal's current situation, including the other available alternatives. For instance, a choice between $1 and $2 sets your zero point lower than it would be if you were offered a choice between $2 and $2000. With the latter choice, your zero point might well be above $2; if for some reason you received the $2 instead of the $2000, you would be disappointed, to say the least.

A classic experiment by Tinklepaugh (1928) nicely demonstrates the effect of context on the position of a monkey's zero point. Tinklepaugh was teaching monkeys simple discriminations between geometric shapes (e.g., squares and circles) drawn on the covers of boxes. He rewarded the monkeys with lettuce leaves and pieces of banana for picking up the correct box. As long as one monkey was rewarded with lettuce leaves and another with banana, both learned the discriminations quickly and accurately. However, when one monkey normally rewarded with banana picked up a box and found instead a lettuce leaf underneath, not only was the discrimination destroyed but the monkey got very angry (and threw the lettuce at the experimenter). In terms of Premack's theory, the monkey's zero point (along with the value of the operant, picking up the box) shifted relative to the value of the lettuce leaf — from below it, in the context of the lettuce leaf alone (which then reinforced the operant), to far above it, in the context of the banana (so that the lettuce leaf now punished the operant).[5]

The subjective scale of value, with its slippery, shifting zero point, is the true one. Unless we assume a shifting zero point of value, we cannot explain the dramatic swings in preference with either past or present contexts of reinforcement. Cycles of consumption and deprivation, in everyday life and the laboratory, constitute the clearest examples of such swings.

In practice, in experiments with nonhuman animals, the animals are deprived of rewards before the experiment begins and are kept far from satiation during the experiment. The intent of this procedure is to bring the instrumental response, hence the zero point of the subjective scale, into line with zero amount of reinforcement and keep it there for the experiment's duration (just as in human decision experiments, where the frame of the problem establishes the zero point to which gains are added and losses taken).

Shifting from the objective to the subjective scale of value requires a change in the application of Equation 4-1 (p. 81), which relates the amount of a reward to its value. The subjective value of a reinforcer would be the value as calculated by Equation 4-1 minus the value of the operant response. In many of Premack's demonstrations, the value of the operant is manipulated, and consequent changes in the subjective value of the reinforcer are observed. In most laboratory experiments, reinforcers are chosen so that the operant is worth close to zero amount of the reinforcer. (That is, the reinforcer is valuable, but emitting the operant at low rates is neither very valuable nor very costly.) Thus, in most practical cases, objective and subjective values of the reinforcer are equal. Henceforth, unless specifically indicated, we will assume this to be the case. With typically used punishers such as electric shock, we may again assume that the value of the operant is about equal to zero amount of shock. However, the amount A in Equation 4-1 is negatively related to the intensity of the punisher. In cases of punishment, where the outcome is worth less than the operant, subtracting the value of the operant results in negative subjective values.

NONCONTINGENT EFFECTS OF REWARD

Imagine the following experiment: You are an eccentric multimillionaire. You decide to be an anonymous benefactor to two unemployed single men. The men, let us call them Arthur and Bob, do not know each other. You will give them each $60,000 per year (in twelve payments each year of $5000) for the rest of their lives. When the time comes for a payment, your representatives will track down each man, wherever he is, and give him the cash without a word. Neither man will know who you are, why the payments are coming, or if and when they will stop. The difference is that Arthur will be paid regularly at noon on the first of every month, but Bob will be paid irregularly (randomly, from his point of view). Sometimes he will get two, three, and even four or five payments a month; sometimes many months will go by without a payment. For both men, let us assume, your beneficence is their only income. Furthermore, neither man will be allowed to save. If anything is left over from the previous payment, it will be subtracted from the present one.

Such an experiment has never been done with humans, so we have to imagine the results. It is likely that the regular deliveries of money would allow Arthur to organize his life much better than Bob could. On the strength of his regular income, Arthur might rent an apartment or buy a house (with a low down payment) or get married. He might try to be in the same place each month so your representative would have no trouble finding him. (If I were Arthur, I would be sure to be home at noon on the first day of each month, and I would make sure that the doorbell was working.) Arthur would be a man of regular, predictable habits. At least he would have the opportunity to live such a life.

Bob, on the other hand (unless he had remarkable powers of self-control), would have to live the life of a gambler. Periods of feast and famine would prevent him from making commitments. He might be restless and travel widely in a futile attempt to track down the source of his income, or he might never leave his house, fearful of missing a payment.

Although no such experiment has been done with humans, it has been done with animals (on a much-reduced time scale). Staddon and Simmelhag (1971) observed the behavior of two groups of pigeon subjects under the following conditions. All of the pigeons were hungry (kept at 80 percent of their free-feeding weight). Each member of one group (the fixed-time group) was fed a very small amount of food (2 seconds of access to a hopper of grain) every 14 seconds for an hour each day. Each member of the other group (the variable-time group) was fed at the same overall rate but erratically; sometimes 2-second hopper accesses would follow each other rapidly, sometimes minutes would go by without a delivery.

In terms of Table 5-1, both groups of pigeons were undergoing operant extinction. Reward was independent of their behavior. However, the fixed-time pigeons were undergoing respondent excitation. Reward was contingent on a stimulus—a fixed temporal interval (Pavlov showed that fixed temporal intervals act as conditioned stimuli). The variable-time pigeons, on the other hand, were undergoing respondent as well as operant extinction.

The question that interested Staddon and Simmelhag was what the pigeons did between food deliveries. All in all, in the Skinner box with nothing in it but a magazine (the hole in one wall through which food was made available), there were sixteen different acts that the pigeons did, ranging from "an orientation response in which the bird's head and body are directed toward the wall containing the magazine" through "flapping wings" through "preening" to "walking about in no particular direction."

The pigeons that got the fixed-time food deliveries (the "Arthurs") tended to divide the interfood period into two distinct parts. During the first part they engaged in what Staddon and Simmelhag call "interim activities" — such things as preening, flapping their wings, and walking about. However, as the time of food delivery approached, the birds generally oriented themselves to the magazine wall and often began to make pecking movements in the air. Staddon and Simmelhag call these acts "terminal activities."

To Staddon and Simmelhag, interim activities seemed to be somewhat higher valued, in and of themselves, than terminal activities. Terminal activities (technically, the pigeon's conditioned responses) seemed not valuable in themselves but rather a means of preparing for the oncoming food. (Putting it another way, the food was more valuable if it had been obtained right after a terminal response than if it had been obtained right after an interim response.) Indeed, when a response that does have high intrinsic value, like drinking water, is made available, pigeons perform it during the interim period and abandon it as food delivery becomes imminent (during the terminal period). In short, the fixed-time pigeons' lives in the Skinner box were well organized. There was a time for preening, wing flapping, and other apparently mildly enjoyable activities and a time for serious business — getting ready for the oncoming food.

For the other pigeons, the variable-time pigeons, life in the Skinner box was much less organized. They spent almost all of the time between food deliveries making terminal responses. Their rate of (intrinsically valuable) interim activities was much lower, and their rate of terminal activities (less intrinsically valuable because they are rarely chosen when no food is available) much higher than that of the fixed-time pigeons. Not knowing when food was coming, the variable-time pigeons had to be continuously ready for it. If you believe that happiness is a concept that can apply to pigeons, and if you agree with the ancient Greek philosophers that a harmonious (well-ordered) life is by definition a happy one, then you would have to say that the fixed-time pigeons were happier than the variable-time pigeons.

Staddon and Simmelhag's results show that rewards can have strong effects on the behavior of an animal even when, as with respondent conditioning, they are delivered independently of the animal's actions. When rewards are dependent on the animal's actions, as with an operant contingency other than extinction, the effect of the contingency must be measured as a difference in behavioral organization between the respondent and operant contingencies.

Let's go back to the example of Arthur and Bob. Imagine that you have become still richer and want to add a third unemployed man, Charlie, to the roll of your dependents. You pay Charlie regularly, like Arthur, but Charlie's payments are contingent on his coming to a certain spot — say, the top of the Empire State Building. The main difference between Charlie's and Arthur's behavior is likely to be that instead of being at home at noon on the first day of every month like Arthur, Charlie at that time would be at the top of the Empire

State Building. The basic organization of Charlie's behavior (assuming that it is the same as that of Arthur) would have to be attributed to the respondent contingency (regular payment) rather than to the operant contingency (dependency of payment on behavior). Charlie's behavior has to be understood as composed of the effects of the contingency of payment on it (unique to Charlie), the effects of the regularity and predictability of payment (common to Charlie and Arthur), and the effects of the payments themselves (common to Charlie, Arthur, and Bob). To try to separate these effects with pigeons, Staddon and Simmelhag studied the behavior of a third group. The experimenters delivered food at fixed times to this third group just as they did to the first group, but these pigeons (analogously to Charlie) had to peck a key to receive their food deliveries when the deliveries were due. The pigeons in this third group, called the fixed-interval group, behaved exactly like those in the first, fixed-time group. Just after a food delivery, the fixed-interval pigeons engaged in the same sorts of interim activities as the fixed-time pigeons did. As a food delivery became due, the fixed-interval pigeons, like the fixed-time pigeons, ceased their interim activities and began terminal activities. The only difference was that for the fixed-interval pigeons the terminal activity was always the same thing — pecking the key.

In our everyday lives, some regularly occurring significant events (like sunrise) are independent of our actions and some (like our salaries) are dependent. Regularly occurring action-dependent events may strongly affect the actions they depend on. Such effects are composed of three parts: the effects of the dependency (operant conditioning), the effects of regularity (respondent conditioning), and the effects of the events themselves (respondent and operant extinction). It is not always obvious which particular contingency causes or maintains a given act. For instance, most of us attribute our work habits (such as they are) to the contingency of our income on our work. However, many people discover after they retire that the organization of their lives (of which work habits are an important part) was maintained not by the work-dependent nature of their income but by its work-independent regularity (along with other work-independent but regularly occurring events). Since retirement is marked by a release of the work dependency but not of the various regularities, retirees frequently find old patterns of work much harder to break than they had supposed.

A MOLECULAR CONCEPTION OF
REINFORCEMENT AND PUNISHMENT

Laboratory experiments are often divided into segments — brief questions and answers, trials, stimulus presentations, and so on. However, real life flows along continuously. A bite of cake is an act in itself but may also be part of eating a slice of cake. Eating the slice of cake may be part of eating a meal, which in turn is part of a person's general pattern of eating. A person's general pattern of eating takes its place in a general pattern of life, consisting of sleeping, social relationships, and work as well as eating.

Suppose you are trying to control your weight. Relationships at every level of behavior from the molecular bite to the molar pattern of life can maintain overeating. On the molecular level, each forkful lifted to your mouth is positively reinforced by the eating of the cake. On a more molar level, the dessert as a whole may reinforce the eating of the rest of the meal. (Perhaps in your childhood the contingency between eating a meal and eating dessert was strictly enforced by your parents.) Although it is true that on a more molar level a pattern of overeating is punished by bad health and the social consequences of being overweight, it is also conceivable that, on a still more molar level, being overweight serves a function in the overall pattern of your life. Being fat could be a way of avoiding or escaping sexual competition and sexual temptation, hence the jealousy of a spouse. All this from a bite of cake. (And we have mentioned only operant contingencies. Respondent contingencies, such as temporal patterns of food availability and stimuli signaling the presence of food, and abnormalities in the zero point of your particular value scale — perhaps you have a lot of fat cells — undoubtedly also play a part.) No wonder so many of us are overweight.

On the molecular level, the fundamental relationship between an operant and a reinforcer or punisher is temporal contiguity. A discrete individual act (like lifting a forkful of cake to your mouth) may be followed by a discrete reinforcer or punisher either immediately or after a delay. The effect of delayed reinforcement and punishment on an operant is well-known. As the delay increases, the value of the reinforcer or punisher approaches zero on the subjective scale. In other words, the value of the reinforcer or punisher approaches the value of the operant and thus loses its reinforcing or punishing power. The mathematical function by which delay diminishes the effect of reinforcers and punishers is a matter of interest and debate (see Commons et al., 1987).

In one experiment by Mazur (1986), pigeons chose between rewards of different amounts that were delayed by various time intervals from the choice response (the operant). For one alternative, amount and delay were both fixed. For the other, amount was fixed but delay varied. If the pigeon chose the first alternative, the delay of the second was decreased on subsequent trials (presumably making it more attractive). If the pigeon chose the second alternative, its own delay was increased on subsequent trials (presumably making it less attractive). By this method Mazur could determine a pair of delays that would exactly counterbalance a pair of amounts in the sense that the pigeon would be indifferent between one alternative (of a given amount and delay) and the other. This procedure is called a *titration procedure.* (Its details involving balancing and exposure of alternatives do not concern us here.) Mazur found, as expected, that the effect of delay on choice — the value of a delayed reinforcer — was an inverse function of the time interval between the choice (the operant) and the reinforcer; in other words, the more the reinforcer was delayed, the less it was worth. This result generally confirmed the findings of many experiments with people and other animals. It also reflects our everyday economic experience. A $10,000 bond maturing in ten years can be bought now for, say, $7000. The $10,000 delayed by ten years is, essentially, worth only $7000 now. You could say that the $10,000 is discounted by its delay.

Because reinforcers are discounted by delay, the value relationship expressed by Equation 4-1 and already modified in this chapter (by subtracting the value of the operant) must be further modified to account for delay. The following equation fits Mazur's results and those of other investigators:

$$v = \frac{\text{value of amount}}{\text{value of delay}}$$

The value of the delay may be determined by an equation similar to Equation 4-1 where delay (D) is substituted for amount (A) and different constants for the coefficient and exponent.[6] We distinguish between the amount exponent and the delay exponent by subscripts $(s_A$ and $s_D)$. Combining the amount and delay versions of Equation 4-1 we get

$$v = k\frac{A^{s_A}}{(1 + D)^{s_D}} \tag{5-1}$$

where k is now the quotient of the individual amount and delay coefficients. A constant of 1 is added to the delay so that when delay is zero, the denominator of the equation is 1.0 and Equation 5-1 reduces to Equation 4-1. (The units of D must be determined empirically. For Mazur, $D = k'd$ where d might be minutes, seconds, etc.)

This equation says that the subjective value of a reinforcer (its power to reinforce an operant) varies directly with the amount of reinforcement (the amount of reinforcer A of Equation 4-1 minus the value of the operant converted into equivalent units). However, now the amount value is discounted; it is divided by a delay term. The exponents s_A and s_D reflect the animal's sensitivity to amount and delay. When an exponent equals 1.0 sensitivity is linear—value is directly proportional to amount or inversely proportional to delay. (For the pigeons in Mazur's experiment, $s_D = 1.0$.) As the exponent decreases from unity to zero, sensitivity decreases until, at zero, the animal is insensitive to the variable (amount or delay).

Because punishers are lower in value than the operant on which they are contingent, the numerator of Equation 5-1 is negative in the case of punishment; hence, the subjective value of a punisher is negative. Regardless of whether the consequence of an operant is a reinforcer or a punisher, the denominator of Equation 5-1 remains the same. Just as the power of a reinforcer to reinforce an operant is diminished by delay, so is the power of a punisher to punish an operant. Figure 5-3 shows the symmetry of reinforcement and punishment as they are affected by delay.

According to Equation 5-1 we may ignore the delay between an operant and a reinforcer or punisher on two occasions. The first is when response and outcome are temporally contiguous; in this case $D = 0$ and the denominator of Equation 5-1 becomes unity. The second is when the animal is completely insensitive to delay; then $s_D = 0$ and the denominator of Equation 5-1 again becomes unity. On those occasions, Equation 5-1 reduces to Equation 4-1. In real life, delays between an act (like putting a quarter into a slot) and a reinforcer (like a cup of coffee) are often negligible, but when they are not, we are rarely indifferent to them. That is, D sometimes equals zero (or close enough not to matter) but s_D rarely equals zero.

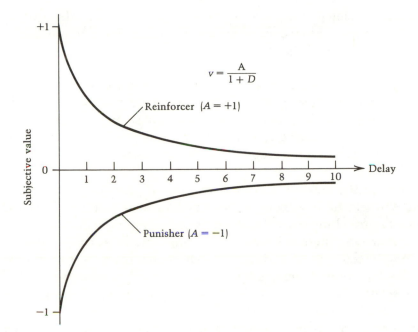

$$v = \frac{A}{1 + D}$$

Reinforcer (A = +1)

Punisher (A = −1)

Subjective value

Delay

Figure 5-3 Values of a reinforcer and a punisher as functions of delay according to Equation 5-1 (all constants and exponents assumed to equal unity).

PROBLEMS WITH THE MOLECULAR CONCEPTION

The main problem with an entirely molecular conception of respondent and operant contingencies is that it is difficult to apply to even mildly complex situations. A more molar conception of this relationship allows better prediction and control (hence a better explanation) of complex behavior. *Adopting a molar point of view does not necessitate rejecting the molecular point of view.* The meteorologist knows that air and clouds consist of molecules. Eventually the science of meteorology may be based entirely on molecular (or atomic or subatomic) physics.[7] Meanwhile, meteorology proceeds on a much more molar level—jet streams, cloud formations, and so on. The general advantage of molar points of view, in psychology as well as in meteorology, is that they embrace context more easily than molecular viewpoints because the relationships they describe are wide in scope. The essence of the molar conception of reinforcement and punishment is that the behavior of animals is sensitive to contingencies as a whole rather than to their elements. Just as you recognize your father on a molar level, all at once, when you meet him without comparing his nose to your recollection of his nose, his mouth to your recollection of his mouth, and so on, so your behavior is sensitive to positive reinforcement, punishment, and extinction without taking into account particular individual operants or reinforcers.

Perhaps the greatest difficulty we have in predicting and controlling the behavior of others and of ourselves is the fact that a given act (like taking a bite of cake) may, at the very same time, be an element of events at different levels (like eating dessert, eating a meal, or eating in general). In Chapter 3 we discussed the problem of a witness who reported seeing a Blue cab in an accident in a city in which the relative base rates of the cabs are 85 percent Green and 15 percent Blue. One reason that you might not take base rates into account in evaluating the witness's report is that the witness may already have done so when making the report. The accident as it occurred before the witness's eyes was relatively molecular in the sense that it was a brief, singular event. However, it was also part of several other, more molar events: Blue and Green cabs in accidents or Blue and Green cabs passing the corner or Blue and Green cabs in the neighborhood or Blue and Green cabs in the city or Blue and Green cabs in the world. Because the witness may have some information about the relative frequency of Blue and Green cabs at any of these levels, the information available at one level may contradict that at another. None of the information is certain. In order to base an action on the information (in the terms of this chapter, in order for the information to function as a discriminative stimulus), each level has to be balanced against the others.

Base rates can affect not only our reports to each other but also the actions that those reports can serve to guide. Rachlin and Baum (1972) demonstrated the action of base rates of reinforcement by simultaneously presenting two kinds of reinforcement schedule to hungry pigeons. First, variable-interval schedules were used, in which brief reinforcers were presented at variable intervals averaging a certain number of seconds between presentations. Each reinforcer was dependent upon the pigeon's peck on a key. With variable-interval schedules, operants (pigeons' key pecks in this experiment) during the interval have no programmed effect; the first operant after the (variable) interval is over produces a reinforcer immediately; then a new interval begins. Superimposed upon the variable-interval schedules were variable-time schedules, in which brief reinforcers were presented independent of the pigeon's behavior at variable times averaging a certain number of seconds between presentations.

Before discussing the simultaneous effects on behavior of variable-time schedules (of extinction) and variable-interval schedules (of positive reinforcement), let us consider the effects of variable-interval schedules alone. In an experiment, Catania and Reynolds (1968) presented hungry pigeons with variable-interval schedules of positive reinforcement alone, varying the average minimum interval between reinforcers. Figure 5-4 shows the operant response rate of the pigeons in this experiment as a function of the time between reinforcers. As the figure shows, the faster the maximum rate of reinforcement (the smaller the minimum interval between reinforcers), the faster the pigeons pecked the key.

This behavior by Catania and Reynolds's pigeons is easily explained by a molecular theory based on Equation 5-1. The average delay between a random peck and the very next variable-interval

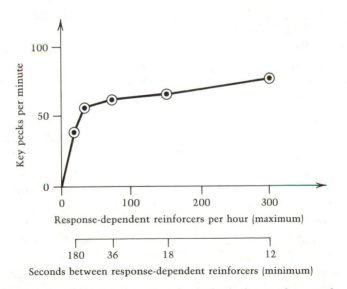

Figure 5-4 Rate at which hungry pigeons pecked a key with several variable-interval schedules, each presented individually (from Catania and Reynolds, 1968).

reinforcer would be about equal to the average interval between the reinforcers. The shorter the interval between reinforcers, the less the delay between any particular peck and reinforcement and the higher the subjective value of the food reinforcer relative to the peck (according to Equation 5-1). The higher the subjective value of a reinforcer relative to an operant, the higher the rate of the operant (according to Premack's theory). Thus, a molecular theory explains the increase in rate of pecking with a decrease in the length of the interval between reinforcers.[8]

The advantage of molecular theory is that it explains the effect of a reinforcement (or punishment) operant contingency without supposing that animals are at all sensitive to something so complex as a contingency. The animal need be sensitive only to its own individual operant responses and the delays between each of them and subsequent reinforcement. Assuming that the amount of the reinforcer and the value of the operant remain constant, Equation 5-1 predicts that the rate of operant responding varies inversely with average delay, as it did in Catania and Reynolds's experiment.

Now suppose that the variable-interval schedule parameter (call it X) is held constant. Rather than decreasing X, we will add other reinforcers independent of responding according to a variable-time schedule (with an average interval, Y between reinforcers). Equation 5-1 predicts that the extra reinforcers, even though independent of pecking, should cause the rate of pecking to increase and, furthermore, the more rapid the rate of peck-independent reinforcers (the smaller the interval Y), the more the rate of pecking should increase.

Baum and I (Rachlin and Baum, 1972) tested this prediction. We added response-independent, randomly programmed (variable-time schedule) reinforcers to a basic variable-interval schedule of positive reinforcement of key pecking of hungry pigeons. Then we systematically decreased the interval (Y) between the response-independent reinforcers (thus decreasing the average delay between pecking and food). However, instead of increasing their rate of pecking, the pigeons in our experiment decreased their rate of pecking. The more response-independent reinforcers we added (the lower we made Y), the slower the pigeons pecked. Figure 5-5 shows the data.

It would be difficult for a wholly molecular theory to account for both the Catania–Reynolds (1968) and the Rachlin–Baum (1972) results. Why should the two experiments change the rate of pecking in opposite ways when the molecular variable, the average delay

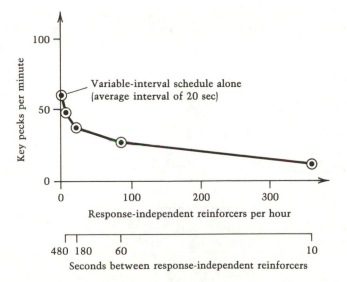

Figure 5-5 Rate at which hungry pigeons pecked a key with several variable-time schedules, each superimposed on a single variable-interval schedule (from Rachlin and Baum, 1972).

between pecking and food, varied in the same direction in both experiments?

A molar theory, on the other hand, easily explains these results. The molar theory takes it as given that animals are differentially sensitive to different contingencies. The pigeons in the Rachlin–Baum experiment were to some degree able to discriminate between those reinforcers dependent on their own actions and those that were independent. The former type of reinforcers increased the pigeons' rate of pecking while the latter decreased it.

A MOLAR–MOLECULAR CONCEPTION

Imagine that you have just graduated from college and are offered a job in your chosen field paying $25,000 per year. You are weighing whether to take the job. If a theory of behavior is to have any meaning in the real world, it ought to be applicable to an operant response defined as "taking a job." However, a job is not a single event, it is a situation in which you will behave in certain ways and experience certain consequences. With such long-term situations two contingencies must be explained: first, on a molar level, the contingency of the situation on behavior (of the job itself on your seeking and acceptance of the job) and second, on a more molecular level, behavior and its consequences within the situation (your actions on the job and the rewards and punishments contingent on them).

To account for outcomes that are temporally extended, like a job, in addition to those that are brief, like a food delivery, the value equation (Equation 5-1) has to be modified once again (and for the last time)

$$v = \frac{\text{amount term}}{\text{delay term}} \times \text{rate term}$$

$$= k \frac{A^{s_A}}{(1 + D)^{s_D}} \times R^{s_R} \tag{5-2}$$

where R is the rate of reinforcement or punishment over some time interval unspecified by the equation and the exponent s_R is sensitivity to this new variable. In everyday life, rate (R) and delay (D) of reinforcement or punishment are often the inverse of each other. For instance, if you move to Arizona, where the rainstorm rate is low, the delay will probably be long between your move and the first rainstorm. If you move to Oregon, where the rainstorm rate is high, the delay between your move and the first rainstorm will probably be short. Sometimes, however, the strict inverse relationship between delay and rate is broken. For instance, in the army you may be paid at a low rate relative to many jobs, but you get an enlistment (or reenlistment) bonus so that the delay between signing up and your first paycheck is very short. In taking a job, you would probably be much more sensitive to the rate of reinforcement over a relatively long period (given by A and R) than to the delay to the first paycheck (given by D). So, in calculating the subjective value of the job, s_A and s_R would be relatively high while s_D would be relatively low.

Like Bayes' rule of Chapter 2, Equation 5-2 is a hybrid of immediate (molecular) and overall (molar) variables. The pecking of keys by pigeons in a Skinner box, like the judgments of people in a psychology laboratory, sometimes takes the molar variable into account and sometimes does not. Like people who fail to take molar variables into account, pigeons, who likewise fail, may be said to be making a mistake. Just as you would be making a mistake if you took a bad job because the first paycheck (perhaps an enlistment bonus) came early, so a pigeon is making a mistake when its behavior is sensitive to delay to the next reinforcer rather than to the overall rate of reinforcement or punishment. We have seen that human judgments may reflect base rates when immediate conditions are unknown (as in the lawyer–engineer problem in Chapter 3 when people are not given a description on which to base their judgment) or when people have a lot of experience with that type of problem. Similarly, when immediate consequences of a peck are variable or when pigeons have a lot of experience in a certain situation, pigeons' pecking can be sensitive to the overall rate of reinforcement or punishment.

In some situations, immediate contingencies and base rates demand a single course of action, as when satisfaction of immediate pleasure coincides with ultimate self-interest. However, in many cases they do not coincide. In such cases, if people or other animals are more sensitive to molecular than to molar contingencies, we tend to say that those people or animals are impulsive and lack self-control. When people or animals are more sensitive to molar contingencies, we tend to say that they are restrained and have self-control. We will discuss the concept of self-control in humans and other animals in a later chapter. For our purposes here, note that in the behavioral conception of self-control, the difference between restraint and impulsiveness is not a distinction between control from within an animal and control from without, but rather a distinction between control by wider contingencies, operating over an extended temporal interval (the overall molar situation), and control by narrower, molecular contingencies, operating over a limited temporal interval (the immediate molecular situation).

Although pigeons and people may both be sensitive to overall and immediate situations, perhaps the most striking difference between pigeons and people is the strong sensitivity of pigeons (and other nonhuman animals) to molecular contingencies and their relative insensitivity to molar contingencies (their impulsiveness). In contrast, people exhibit strong sensitivity to molar contingencies (despite their frequent insensitivity to base rates in laboratory judgment problems) and relative insensitivity to molecular contingencies (their restraint). The other distinguishing characteristic of humans — our complicated language — may be seen as the possession of a highly useful, highly complex tool by which we bring ourselves into contact with wider, more molar contingencies than could otherwise affect our behavior.

The concept of language as a tool is the essence of Plato's and Wittgenstein's (1958) approaches to language, as well as Skinner's (1975). In Skinner's terms, language is a discriminative stimulus for behavior, sometimes for other linguistic behavior (A: "How are you?" B: "Fine."), sometimes for nonlinguistic behavior (A: "Please pass the salt." B: then passes the salt.). Complex units of language (paragraphs, stories, and books) are discriminative stimuli for complex molar patterns of behavior that could extend over a lifetime. Simple units of language (words and sentences) are discriminative stimuli for less complex, less molar units of behavior. Of course, this is just putting a label on a very ill-understood process. Nevertheless, this particular label will enable us to relate the simpler (but complex enough) behavior patterns of pigeons to the very elaborate and (almost) incomprehensible behavior patterns of people.

N O T E S

1. Usually the term extinction refers to a special case of a null contingency between conditioned and unconditioned stimuli — the case where the rate of the conditioned stimulus is above zero but the rate of the unconditioned stimulus is zero. In other words, extinction usually refers to the presentation of the conditioned stimulus without the unconditioned stimulus. However, modern research in classical conditioning (since Rescorla's paper of 1967) conceives of a random relationship between conditioned and unconditioned stimuli as a baseline from which excitation and inhibition are measured. It will be convenient here to call this relationship extinction and to use the term *zero-rate extinction* for the special case where the rate of the unconditioned stimulus is zero.

2. Thorndike (1911) used the term *reinforcement* to refer to a literal strengthening of an internal connection between stimulus and response. For Skinner and for modern researchers, nothing particular is strengthened by reinforcement except the abstract tendency of the animal to make the response. (You could say, "There is a strong tendency for earthquakes to occur in California," without implying any particular connection or process.) This difference distinguishes Skinner from other behaviorists such as Hull (1943), who, like

Thorndike (and like modern cognitive psychologists), was chiefly concerned with describing internal processes, the nature of which was inferred from overt behavior. Because these processes, the objects of their theories, are said to mediate internally between stimulus (S) and response (R), Thorndike and Hull may be classified as S – R theorists. In this sense of the term, Skinner is not an S – R theorist.

3.   A biologist's answer to both these questions is that seeking pleasure and reducing drives enhances the survival of the species. Such an answer is noncircular only if it is accompanied by an adequate theory of environmental selection. The psychologist, correspondingly, needs a specific theory of reinforcement.

4.   To anticipate, economic theory sees all situations as choice situations with various kinds of constraints on behavior. Thus, Premack's (1965) choice test would constitute one kind of constraint, while the operant contingency would constitute another. Either situation could thus be used to establish the values of the alternatives, and these in turn could be used to predict behavior in the other situation (with the other set of constraints).

5.   The effect of context on value has long been recognized. Gestalt psychology has continually focused on context. The adaptation level theory of Helson (1958), an attempt at quantifying these effects in both perception and choice, eventually became overly complex. More recent attempts to quantify context, such as matching or economic choice theory, (to be discussed later) may be seen as outgrowths of Helson's efforts.

6.   It may seem strange to speak of delay as having value in itself. However, the value of a delay means no more than the subjective effect of the delay. Although it is convenient to imagine this effect as distinct from the effect of amount, it is of course impossible for the delay of a reward to affect choice independently of the reward itself. The same remarks apply to consideration of probability as being independent of amount of outcome in decision experiments.

7.   However, recent work on meteorological predictions shows the weather to be "chaotic." Vast variations in future conditions in one place depend on minute changes in present conditions in another. As James Gleick (1987, p. 8) puts it, "a butterfly stirring the air today in Peking can transform storm systems next month in New York."

Complex physical events may never be predictable in molecular terms, and human behavior may be no less chaotic.

8. According to molecular theory, the decrease in delay between a peck and food, hence the gain in value, as the interval decreases between food deliveries does not come only by means of the pecks contiguous with reinforcement. For contiguous pecks, delay always equals zero. As the interval length decreases, more and more of these zero delays are averaged in. According to molecular theory, the increase in value of pecking comes also by means of pecks not contiguous with food. For those pecks, delay decreases with the increased rate of food deliveries.

CHOICE

The previous chapter introduced behavioral concepts and illustrated their use. The present chapter taxes the reader's patience a bit further by introducing still more new terms specifically relevant to choice. Near the middle of the chapter, a theory of behavior called *matching* is at last described. Although the theory itself is quite simple, it has several important consequences when applied to specific cases.

THE BEHAVIOR OF CHOOSING

One common measure of choice is the *behavior ratio* (BR) introduced by Tolman (1938). The numerator of the behavior ratio is the number of times an animal chooses one alternative and the denominator sums the total choices of all alternatives. In the case of two alternatives (1 and 2) we have

$$BR = \frac{B_1}{B_1 + B_2} \qquad (6\text{-}1)$$

where B_1 and B_2 are the number of choices of alternative 1 and of alternative 2, respectively. The behavior ratio is like a probability in that it varies from unity (when alternative 1 is chosen exclusively) to zero (when alternative 1 is never chosen). Another common measure of choice is the fraction B_1/B_2, the *relative choice* (*RC*):

$$RC = \frac{B_1}{B_2} \qquad (6\text{-}2)$$

It is important to note that mathematically the behavior ratio and the relative choice are just two forms of the same relationship. Sometimes it is convenient to use one form and sometimes the other.

In the laboratory, choice is commonly studied with a Skinner box containing two operant alternatives. Figure 6-1a shows two lines, one for each alternative, during a hypothetical interval of time T. Each pip on a line represents a single operant, say a pigeon's peck on one of the two available keys. Counting the pips, the behavior ratio for alternative 1 is $10/15$; that for alternative 2 is $5/15$. The relative choice for alternative 1 is $10/5$ and for alternative 2, $5/10$.

In calculating these measures, behavior ratio and relative choice, it is assumed that each peck constitutes a choice between the available alternatives (between pecking one or another key). Both measures rely on the counting of pecks and are thus measures of the relative number of pecks during an interval of time T. Dividing the number of pecks at each alternative by the time T gives us the *overall operant rate*. Thus the overall operant rate for alternative 1 is $10/T$. If T were 60 seconds, the overall operant rate for alternative 1 would be $10/60 = 0.167$ peck per second; the corresponding overall operant rate for alternative 2 would then be $5/60 = 0.83$ peck per second.

TIME ALLOCATION

Figure 6-1b shows the same pattern of operants as Figure 6-1a. Here the interval T is divided into alternating periods, t_1 and t_2, marked by the first in a string of successive emissions of each operant.[1] In the pigeon example with two keys, when the pigeon switches from pecking key 1 to pecking key 2 or vice versa, the shading in the figure changes. Time is thus divided (somewhat arbitrarily) into time

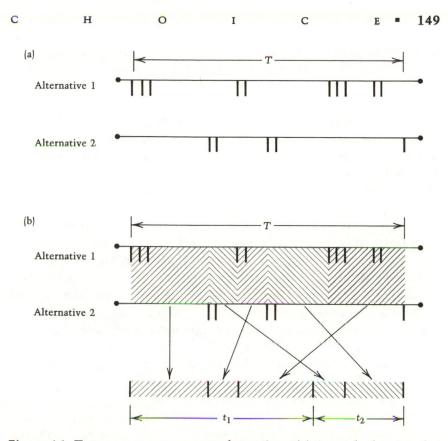

Figure 6-1 Two concurrent operant alternatives. (a) A graph showing the number of emissions of an operant. (b) The same pattern of behavior divided into time spent emitting each operant.

spent emitting one operant (pecking key 1) and time spent emitting the other (pecking key 2). For alternative 1, behavior ratio and relative choice become

$$BR = \frac{t_1}{t_1 + t_2} = \frac{t_1}{T} \qquad (6\text{-}3)$$

$$RC = \frac{t_1}{t_2} \qquad (6\text{-}4)$$

The division of T into time spent emitting one operant (t_1) and time spent emitting the other (t_2) provides another measure of behavior — *local operant rate.* The local rate of operant 1 is $10/t_1$, and that of operant 2 is $5/t_2$. In Figure 6-1, $t_2 = \frac{1}{2}t_1$. Assuming $T = 1$

minute, we get $t_1 = 40$ seconds and $t_2 = 20$ seconds. In this hypothetical case, the local rate of operant 1 ($^{10}/_{40}$ response per second) equals that of operant 2 ($^5/_{20}$ response per second).

In laboratory studies of operants such as licking at a drinking tube or pressing a lever by rats, pecking a key by pigeons, or pressing a button by humans, local operant rates are often found to be equal across alternatives regardless of their relative attractiveness. Figure 6-1 illustrates this common result; there are twice as many emissions of operant 1 as of operant 2, and twice as much time is spent emitting operant 1 as operant 2.

The great advantage of the time allocation measure is that it applies to situations where discrete operant responses are nonexistent or incommensurate. Consider three kinds of situation. First, one set of contingencies of reinforcement or punishment might apply when an animal is in one of two sections of the experimental area, and another set of contingencies when the animal is in the other. It is easy to measure how much time an animal spends in one or another place, but in this situation there is no specific operant response emitted by the animal that can be counted. Similarly, we can measure how much time a person spends on vacation or at work, but there is no corresponding countable pair of operants.

Second, time allocation can be used when measuring preference among behaviors of different topography. We call such choices asymmetrical. A rat's choice between pressing one lever versus pressing another is symmetrical, as is its choice between licking at a tube of water with one concentration of sugar versus licking at a tube with another concentration. However, its choice between licking a tube of water and chewing a pellet of food is asymmetrical. With symmetrical choices, local operant rates usually remain equal (which is an advantage of using a common operant like bar pressing when measuring choice). In contrast, when you try to compare chewing of food with licking of a drinking tube, local operant rates usually differ. Even if they were equal, the equality would have no meaning (equality of what?). Time allocation provides a meaningful measure between asymmetrical operants that are otherwise impossible to compare. You could say that the rat spent so much of the session eating (t_1/T) and so much drinking (t_2/T).

Third, time allocation can be used to compare the symmetrical choice between operants (as between a pigeon's pecking one key or another) with the asymmetrical choice between emitting an operant and not emitting it (as between a pigeon's pecking a key and not pecking it). This is a very important comparison, because it is the basis for saying that all behavior is choice behavior. Whether the principles that explain an animal's choice between two operant contingencies can be extended to explain an animal's choice to respond or not within a single operant contingency is an empirical question that we will try to answer later. Figure 6-2 shows how the emission of a single operant during a period of time T may be broken up (again somewhat arbitrarily) into the time spent emitting the operant (t) and time spent not emitting the operant ($T-t$).

This sort of temporal division makes sense only if the rate of operant emission *when the animal is emitting operants* is constant (when the local operant rate during t is constant). Many studies of individual operants have found local operant rates surprisingly constant. Cotton (1953) studied rats running in straight alleys with food at the end. The more food in the goal box at the end, the less time the rats took to get there. However, they did not run faster with more food. Rather, with more food in the goal box, they ran more consistently, pausing less frequently to sniff around in the alley. When they did run, they always ran at the same speed, regardless of how much food was in the goal box. Gilbert (1958), studying rats licking at drinking tubes containing various concentrations of saccharin, found that they always licked at the same rate (about 7 licks per second) but for a higher fraction of the time when the saccharin concentration was ideal compared with higher or lower concentrations. In human life as well, many activities (say, chopping wood) are

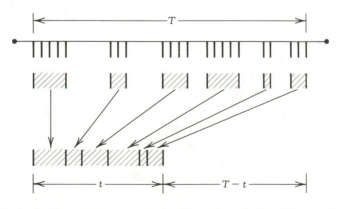

Figure 6-2 A single operant seen as the allocation of time (T) to emitting the operant (t) and not emitting the operant ($T-t$).

performed at a constant rate when they are performed. When we do them less, we tend to do them for less time rather than at a lower local rate. To take another example, I am spending about four hours every day trying to write this book. Some days I write more pages than others, but not because I write faster. Rather, on those days I spend less of the four hours daydreaming, sharpening pencils, and so on.

Finally, note that just as all behavior ratios, whether of relative number or of relative overall operant rate add to unity for a given set of alternatives, so the behavior ratios of relative time for a given set of alternatives add to unity. Just as any individual operant must be a choice of one alternative or another, so an animal must always be engaged in some behavior, even if that behavior is defined as "doing nothing," "not responding," "resting," or "leisure."

FEEDBACK FUNCTIONS

Consider a simple single-operant schedule not discussed in the last chapter — a variable-ratio schedule. With a variable-ratio schedule, a reinforcer is delivered following the first operant that is emitted after a variable number of responses have been made. For instance, a variable-ratio schedule of 10 delivers a reinforcer after a number of operants, determined randomly but averaging 10, have been emitted. Figure 6-3 shows feedback functions for three different variable-ratio schedules of reinforcement. With a variable ratio of 2, half of the operants emitted are reinforced. When a flip of a coin is the operant and an outcome of heads signals a reinforcer, then coin flipping is a schedule with a variable ratio of 2. The probability of winning at coin flipping or any other gamble is given by the slope of the variable-ratio feedback function (in this case, 0.5). Just as probabilities are limited in range between unity and zero, so variable-ratio schedules of reinforcement are limited by the case where every emitted operant is reinforced and the case where none is.

Let us assume that $T = 1$ minute and the local rate of emission of the operant is constant at 100 per minute. In other words, we assume that if the animal spent all of its time emitting the particular operant being studied, the rate of emission would be 100 per minute. (A rat emits lever presses at about that rate when it is continuously pressing the lever.) Another scale can then be constructed showing the overall rate of reinforcement (R) as a function of the fraction of time

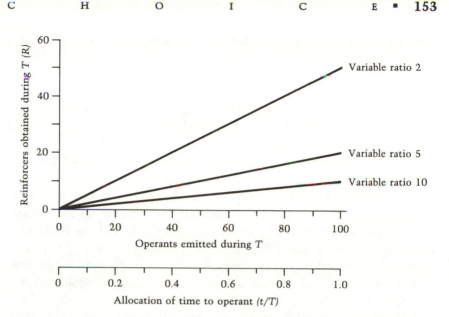

Figure 6-3 Feedback functions of three variable-ratio schedules. Each function indicates the overall rate of reinforcement that would be obtained under each schedule were an animal to emit operants at the rate shown on the abscissa. The lower horizontal scale assumes that an animal spending all its time emitting operants emits operants at a rate of 100 per minute.

the animal spends emitting the operant. As we indicated in the last section, many discrete operants (of humans as well as rats) can be converted into time allocations. Furthermore, other activities, which can easily be measured in terms of time allocation (like standing on one side or the other of the chamber), have no corresponding discrete operant. Thus, in constructing feedback functions, the lower x-axis scale of Figure 6-3, based on time allocation, is generally more useful than the upper one based on the overall number or rate of emitted operants.[2]

The feedback functions of ratio schedules are straight lines because ratio schedules enforce a proportionality between behavior and reinforcement (or punishment). Another schedule whose feedback function is a straight line is the variable-time schedule used by Staddon and Simmelhag (1971). The variable-time schedule is an extinction schedule that delivers reinforcers at a given rate regardless of the animal's behavior. Thus its feedback function is a straight horizontal line at a level on the ordinate corresponding to the rate of delivery of the reinforcer.

The feedback function for the variable-interval schedule is not a straight line but a curve that starts at the origin, rises very rapidly at first, and then tapers off to become nearly horizontal. In nature, an animal foraging in an area with depletable but renewable resources (like a cow grazing in a field) obtains reinforcers by a variable-interval schedule. The animal's foraging depletes the resources, but, over time, they are renewed.

Figure 6-4 shows a family of feedback functions.[3] There has been considerable debate about the exact shape (and mathematical expression) of the feedback functions for various schedules of reinforcement commonly used in the operant laboratory (Nevin and Baum, 1980). The variable-interval curve of Figure 6-4 may not be exactly the function determined by commonly used laboratory programming. Nevertheless, the curve resembles the contingencies of real life as closely as the laboratory schedule does. After all, a feedback function does not reflect anything about people or other animals — it is a fact about the environment (the operant contingency of Figure 5-1). As such, the shape of the function and its mathematical expression might be anything that nature or an ingenious experimenter can construct.

Note that at each time allocation (at each point on the abscissa) in Figure 6-4, the variable-time feedback function is highest, followed by the variable-interval feedback function and then the variable-ratio feedback function. This means that, for a given allocation of time to

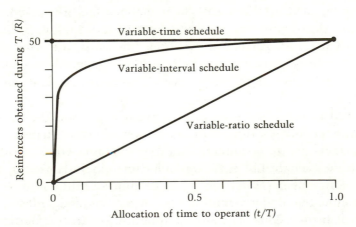

Figure 6-4 Feedback functions for three different single schedules of reinforcement.

the operant (t/T), the variable-time schedule provides the highest rate of reinforcement. With that schedule, all the animal has to do is sit around and wait for free reinforcers (independent of t); no operants need be emitted. The variable-interval schedule is like the variable-time schedule in that reinforcers are earned by waiting, but the animal must eventually emit an operant (some of T must be allocated to t). The variable-interval schedule is like foraging. In the case of an animal foraging for food, the food grows (or prey reproduces) while the animal waits, but the animal will obtain no food at all unless it hunts sometimes. A variable-ratio schedule, on the other hand, is more like manufacturing than foraging. Reinforcement is proportional to the operants emitted (proportional to t). The less time the animal devotes to the operant, the less reinforcement a variable-ratio schedule provides.

Figure 6-4 shows feedback functions for the case illustrated in Figure 6-2, where an animal is exposed to only a single available operant (for instance, a pigeon in a Skinner box with a single key and a single schedule of reinforcement). There the alternatives are to emit the operant (t) or not $(T-t)$. Now we go back to Figure 6-1, which illustrates the case where two alternatives are available (for instance, a pigeon in a Skinner box with two keys and two schedules of reinforcement). There the alternatives are to emit one operant (t_1) or the other (t_2). What is the feedback function for the two-alternative case?

To determine the overall rate of reinforcement from two concurrent schedules, we add the feedback functions of the two schedules.[4] Figure 6-5 plots feedback functions for concurrent variable-time/variable-time, variable-interval/variable-interval, and variable-ratio/variable-ratio schedules. In correspondence with the single-alternative functions of Figure 6-4 (assuming a given set of parameter values), concurrent variable-time schedules provide the highest rate of reinforcement, concurrent variable-interval schedules the next highest, and again, concurrent variable-ratio schedules the least. If you were exposed to a pair of concurrent variable-time schedules, each would provide reinforcers dependent on time but independent of your behavior. It would be as if you had two rich aunts who both periodically sent you presents regardless of what you did.

With concurrent variable-ratio schedules, reinforcers from each alternative come only when you allocate time to that alternative. It would be as if each of your rich aunts thought about giving you presents only when you visited her. (Out of sight, out of mind.) Since

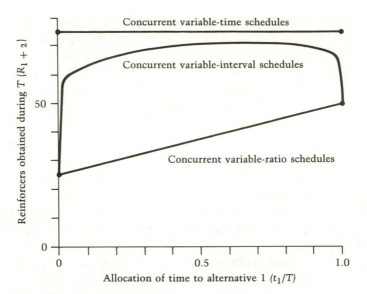

Figure 6-5 Feedback functions for three different pairs of concurrent schedules of reinforcement. The time not spent choosing alternative 1 is assumed to be spent choosing alternative 2.

a person can only visit one aunt at a time (assuming that the aunts do not live together), your highest rate of receiving presents would be achieved by staying 100 percent of the time with whichever aunt was more generous.

Finally, concurrent variable-interval schedules are somewhere between the other two cases. Variable-interval aunts both buy presents for you whether you visit them or not (like variable-time aunts), but instead of sending them to you, they hold them until you come for a visit (like variable-ratio aunts). You would have to shuttle between aunts to pick up the presents. If you were quick on your feet, you could do pretty well for yourself, but since the interval between presents is unpredictable, both for the variable-interval aunt you are with and for the one you are not with, you could never know exactly when to make your move. There would inevitably be some time when a present was sitting at an aunt's house, unpicked up. Thus, with variable-interval aunts, your rate of reinforcement might approach but could never equal that from a pair of variable-time aunts who sent you presents wherever you were.

Feedback functions for choice between concurrent schedules (two alternatives, t_1 and t_2), like those for choice between emitting and not emitting an operant with a single schedule (one alternative, t, and its refusal, $T-t$), are molar properties of the environment and may be of any shape that nature provides or people can invent. The ones illustrated in Figures 6-4 and 6-5 have formed the basis for extensive laboratory studies of choice and have parallels in the everyday life of humans and other animals. Subsequent chapters will show a further parallel — to studies of decision in the laboratory with human subjects.

MATCHING

Behavioral choice theory views the interaction between a person and the world as a reciprocal relationship. Half of that relationship is how the world takes the actions of animals and reflects their consequences back upon them. That half consists of operant contingencies. We have just made some particular contingencies explicit in terms of feedback functions. Now we turn our attention to the other half — the choice process itself, or how animals take aspects of the world and reflect them back upon the world by their behavior. Feedback functions were properties of the environment; we now turn to properties of the organism. For behavioral theory, the key subjective variable is value.

In cognitive theory the value of an alternative is the state of an internal process, an intermediary state, coming after a representation and before a decision. In judgment tasks, people are often asked to report values — how much such-and-such is worth. In laboratory decision tasks, sometimes the observer infers value from a subject's decisions (Tversky and Kahneman, 1981), and sometimes a subject reports value as part of a series of introspections about an ongoing decision process (Ericsson and Simon, 1984). In behavioral theory, value is used to predict an animal's choices in one situation from its behavior in another. In Premack's (1965, 1971) behavioral reinforcement theory, the value of one act relative to another is inferred from the animal's choices when the act is freely available; value is then used to predict behavior when choice is restricted, that is, when the act (as a reinforcer or punisher) is contingent on another act or when the other act is contingent on it (as an operant).

In the present chapter, Premack's concept of value is broadened. The value of a reinforcer or punisher may be inferred from behavior in any situation and used to predict behavior in any other situation.

The outcome of a series of observations is an expression relating the parameters of reinforcers or punishers (amounts, delays, or rates) to their values. From experiment to experiment, this expression has been refined to better summarize previous results and better predict future ones. Thus, in behavioral theory, value is a stage of a process that the observer goes through rather than the subject. It is a sort of accounting method used to summarize the results of previous observations in a form that can be easily used to predict future observations.[5]

According to Herrnstein's (1970) behavioral choice theory, animals (such as we) take aspects of the world and reflect them back upon the world by the process of *matching*. With two alternatives (1 and 2), matching says that the following relationships hold:

$$BR_1 = \frac{B_1}{B_1 + B_2} = \frac{v_1}{v_1 + v_2} \tag{6-5}$$

$$RC_1 = \frac{B_1}{B_2} = \frac{v_1}{v_2} \tag{6-6}$$

where v_1 and v_2 stand for the values of the alternatives. Herrnstein's matching law says that an animal's relative choices match the relative values of the alternatives. If one alternative has twice the value of another, the animal will choose that alternative twice as frequently as the other; if it has half the value, half as frequently.

Equations 6-5 and 6-6 are nothing but behavioral versions of Luce's (1959) decision model as given by Equation 4-2 (p. 84). Just as Luce's model had to be modified when we considered alternatives of various degrees of qualitative similarity (see Figure 4-5 and the accompanying discussion), so we will have to modify Equations 6-5 and 6-6 when we consider reinforcers and punishers that differ in degree of similarity. Meanwhile, let us assume that all reinforcers or punishers are identical in quality (are completely similar) and differ only in the quantitative parameters of amount, delay, and rate; further, we will assume that the two concurrent responses by which the alternatives are chosen are equal in value. Then, combining Equation 6-6 with Equation 5-2 (p. 142) we get

$$\frac{B_1}{B_2} = \frac{v_1}{v_2} = b\left(\frac{A_1}{A_2}\right)^{s_A} \times \left(\frac{1 + D_2}{1 + D_1}\right)^{s_D} \times \left(\frac{R_1}{R_2}\right)^{s_R} \tag{6-7}$$

The constant b in this equation (where $b = k_1/k_2$) stands for *bias*. In a perfect experiment, only the intended variables would be varied; that is, all alternatives should be equal in every way except with respect to the variables at issue. However, no experiment can be perfect. An animal may be biased towards one alternative or another by factors that are unaccounted for, whether innate preferences or past experiences. The constant b accounts for the action of such factors taken together. Note that bias acts like any other term comprising relative value — it is multiplied by the other terms. That is, factors that are unaccounted for are presumed to act on choice in the same way as factors that are accounted for.

Equation 6-7 looks complicated because it assumes that all three variables accounted for (amount, delay, and rate) are varied at once; in this sense it is a generalized matching law. In practice, however, all three variables are rarely varied together. Herrnstein's (1961) initial studies kept the molecular variables (amounts and delays) constant across alternatives and varied only the molar variable, the rate of reinforcement (the base rate in cognitive terms). When amounts and delays are constant we get

$$\frac{B_1}{B_2} = b\left(\frac{R_1}{R_2}\right)^{s_R} \tag{6-8}$$

Figure 6-6 shows average results that Herrnstein obtained with three pigeon subjects, each exposed to five pairs of concurrent variable-interval schedules of food reinforcement. The results are plotted on log–log coordinates, where the slope of a straight line represents the exponent s_R.

Figure 6-7 shows average results that Baum and I (Baum and Rachlin, 1969) obtained with six pigeons, each exposed to nine pairs of concurrent variable-interval schedules of reinforcement. Here Herrnstein's (1961) procedure was employed except that instead of pecking keys to obtain food reinforcement, the pigeons had to walk from one side of the experimental chamber to the other. In both experiments, relative choice was found to be proportional to relative reinforcement rate ($s_R = 1$), but in the Baum–Rachlin experiment there was a bias towards one side of the chamber ($b = 0.6$ as measured by the distance from the solid line to the dashed line fitted to the points), whereas in Herrnstein's experiment there was no bias towards either key ($b = 1$).

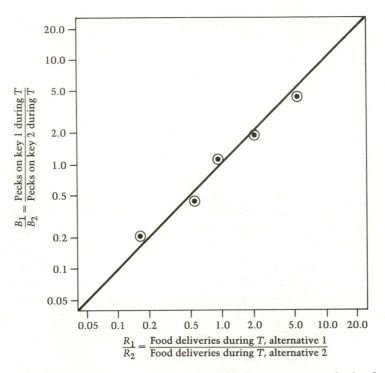

Figure 6-6 Data from an experiment in which pigeons matched relative choice to rate of reinforcement. The time T is the duration of the experimental session (about 1 hour) minus time spent eating.

Both studies used an experimental procedure called a *changeover delay*. A changeover delay holds reinforcers for a short period after the animal changes over from one alternative to the other. (It is as if your aunt did not give you a present she had been saving for you until you had visited her for at least three days. You can understand why.) Changeover delays have molecular and molar effects. On a molecular level, they delay reinforcement from a changeover, defined as a discrete operant in itself, thereby discouraging rapid changeovers. On a molar level, with concurrent variable-interval schedules, changeover delays create a more sharply peaked feedback function instead of the rather flat-topped function of Figure 6-5. We will see later (Figure 8-7) why the shape of the feedback function may be important.

The results shown in Figures 6-6 and 6-7 and many others like them (reviewed by de Villiers, 1977) testify to the empirical strength

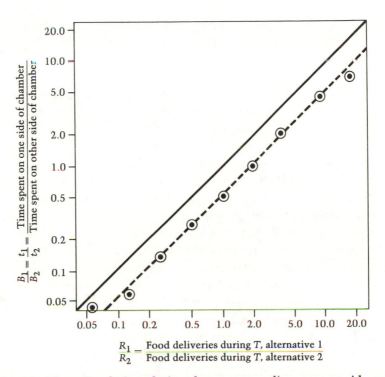

Figure 6-7 Pigeons' relative choices between standing on one side or the other of the experimental chamber versus relative rate of reinforcement on each side.

of the matching relationship.[6] Equation 6-7 contains several constants, but that equation is a generalized one designed to apply to complex cases. The results of most laboratory experiments can be explained in much simpler terms. Herrnstein's (1961) data are described by

$$\frac{B_1}{B_2} = \frac{R_1}{R_2} \tag{6-9}$$

where B_1 and B_2 are rates of pecking on two keys. The Baum–Rachlin (1969) data are described by

$$\frac{B_1}{B_2} = \frac{t_1}{t_2} = b\frac{R_1}{R_2} \tag{6-10}$$

Equations 6-9 and 6-10 are both versions of Equation 6-7, the more general matching relation. In both sets of data, the exponent s_R was found to be about equal to unity and could therefore be ignored. However, the exponents of the matching equation have been found to deviate from unity in two kinds of choice circumstances. First, when the alternatives are not so clearly defined as in the above experiments, the rate exponent s_R does not equal unity. We will show one such example later in this chapter. Second, when the alternatives are qualitatively dissimilar, the amount exponent s_A deviates from unity. We will discuss this case in Chapter 8.

The variables on the right-hand side of Equation 6-7 are not truly independent variables because it is not generally possible to manipulate them directly. Rather, as we have been conceiving behavior here, the environment consists of (abstract) *contingencies*, not (particular) values of variables. With the concurrent variable-interval schedules used in both of the experiments whose data are shown in Figures 6-6 and 6-7, the distinction between a variable and a contingency is not important. As Figures 6-4 and 6-5 show, over most of the range of possible behavioral allocations, the reinforcers obtained during T with variable-interval schedules are almost constant (and are only slightly less so with changeover delays). In other words, the slope of the feedback function for concurrent variable-interval schedules is close to zero (the function is close to a horizontal line) over most of its range. For variable-ratio schedules, however, the reinforcers obtained are directly proportional to behavioral allocations. There, feedback functions make a big difference.

Equation 6-7 says that behavior depends on reinforcement, but the feedback function says that reinforcement depends on behavior, which in turn depends on reinforcement, and so on. The relationship is circular. Equation 6-7 and feedback functions such as the equation in note 4 form a *system*. In the case of concurrent variable-interval schedules, as we see from Figures 6-6 and 6-7, with each pair of schedules tested, the system becomes stable at some point of behavioral allocation (B_1/B_2) between zero and infinity. However, with concurrent ratio schedules, the system does not become stable anywhere between the extreme values of complete allocation to one alternative or the other.

Remember, concurrent ratio schedules are like having two aunts, each of whom buys you presents only when you are visiting her. If aunt 1 bought you a present every day while you were visiting her and aunt 2 bought you a present every week while you were visiting her, you might try to match their generosity by your visits, spending seven weeks with aunt 1 and one with aunt 2. But over those eight weeks ($T = 8$ weeks) you would get an overall number of 49 (7×7) presents from aunt 1 and only 1 from aunt 2. You could then try again to match, spending 49 weeks with aunt 1 and one week with aunt 2. But over those 50 weeks (a new T) you would get 343 (49×7) presents from aunt 1 to 1 from aunt 2. Given no other considerations except the presents, you would soon be spending all of your time with aunt 1 and none with aunt 2. Although you may very well have considerations other than the presents and would visit both aunts no matter what, animals exposed to concurrent variable-ratio schedules of food reinforcement eventually allocate their time and effort exclusively to the better-paying one (Herrnstein and Loveland, 1975). When the two variable-ratio schedules are equal, animals sometimes allocate their time exclusively to one schedule and sometimes divide it equally between them — either pattern of choice is consistent with matching and the ratio feedback function.

As another way to see the difference between concurrent interval and concurrent ratio schedules, remember that an interval elapses no matter what you do, while a ratio accumulates only when you allocate your choices to it. An animal exposed to a pair of concurrent interval schedules is like an animal in the wild, foraging in two adjacent patches. The animal may spend more time in the richer patch but eventually depletes that patch and moves over to the poorer one, going back only when the richer patch has replenished itself. Concurrent ratio schedules are like patches that do not become depleted. If a patch does not become depleted, there is no reason to abandon the richer patch for the poorer one. Analogously, a gambler with a better-paying and a worse-paying slot machine has no reason ever to play the worse one.

Both the Herrnstein (1961) and the Baum–Rachlin (1969) choice experiments of Figures 6-6 and 6-7 kept amount and delay of reinforcement constant and varied the schedule of reinforcement. This procedure caused the rate of reinforcement to vary between the two alternatives. In the next chapter on self-control, we will discuss the case where amount and delay are varied and the rate of reinforcement is held constant.

Consider now the correspondence of a symmetrical choice among more than one alternative operant and an asymmetrical choice between emitting an operant and not emitting it. The Herrnstein and Baum–Rachlin experiments of Figure 6-6 are cases of symmetrical choice, whereas the Rachlin–Baum (1972) experiment of Figure 5-5, where a pigeon pecked a single key, is a case of asymmetrical choice.

In the Rachlin–Baum experiment, there were two sources of extrinsic reinforcement, the food deliveries contingent on pecking the key (variable-interval schedule) and the food delivered freely (variable-time schedule). These two sources of reinforcement may be thought of as concurrent schedules — a variable-interval schedule providing reinforcers at an overall rate R_1 and a variable-time schedule providing reinforcers at an overall rate ER (for "extra reinforcers"). Applying Equation 6-8 to the asymmetrical case we get a direct relation between B_1 (pecking the key) and R_1 (peck-contingent reinforcers) and an inverse relation between B_1 and ER (extra reinforcers) corresponding to the upward and downward curves of Figures 5-4 and 5-5, respectively.

In the symmetrical case, B_1 was the number of operants or time allocated during T to one alternative, and B_2 was the number of operants or time allocated to the other. In the asymmetrical case, there is no number of operants allocated to the other alternative (there is no specific other alternative); therefore, B_1 and B_2 must both be expressed in units of time (as in Figure 6-2), where T is time spent emitting the operant and $T - t$ is the remainder.

Before applying Equation 6-11 to the Baum–Rachlin (1969) data in more than a qualitative way, you would first have to decide how to convert the number of pecks on the key during T that we measured into the fraction t of time T that the pigeon spent pecking. As a rough guess at this parameter, we can use an estimate by de Villiers (1977), who exposed each of six pigeons to a series of variable-interval schedules without variable-time schedules superimposed (see Figure 5-4). From Catania and Reynolds's (1968) data, de Villiers estimated that a (median) pigeon pecking a key 100 percent of the time would peck 80 times per minute.[7] Using this value, Figure 6-8 plots relative choice as a function of relative rate of reinforcement for a pigeon choosing between the alternatives of pecking the key and not pecking it.

In the Herrnstein (1961) symmetrical-choice experiment of Figure 6-6, both bias (b) and sensitivity (s_R) were about 1.0, and in the Baum–Rachlin (1969) symmetrical-choice experiment of Figure 6-7, s_R was about equal to 1.0. In contrast, in the Rachlin–Baum (1972) asymmetrical-choice experiment, both constants deviated from unity. There is considerable bias towards pecking the key (perhaps because of terminal responding) and a lack of proportional sensitivity to reinforcement (s_R is about 0.75). Remember, in the symmetri-

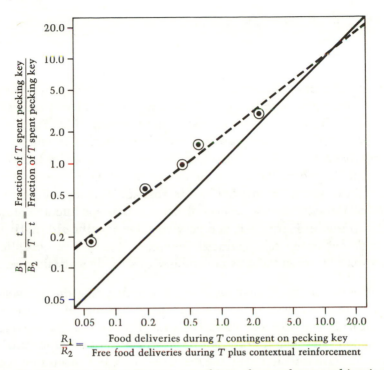

$$\frac{R_1}{R_2} = \frac{\text{Food deliveries during } T \text{ contingent on pecking key}}{\text{Free food deliveries during } T \text{ plus contextual reinforcement}}$$

Figure 6-8 Pigeons' choices between pecking a key and not pecking it as a function of the relative rate of reinforcement for pecking the key and not pecking it. The time T is the duration of the session minus time spent eating.

cal cases, the source of each reinforcer was clear. In the Herrnstein experiment, reinforcers followed immediately upon pecks of one of two different keys of different colors; in the Baum–Rachlin experiment, the food reinforcers, contingent on the pigeon's presence on either side of the chamber, were delivered from separate hoppers on the two sides. In the asymmetrical case, the pigeons had to tease apart reinforcers dependent on their pecking from those delivered freely. Considering the difficulty we humans have in making corresponding discriminations (say, a student teasing apart what fraction of a grade comes from his or her own efforts and what from the teacher's generosity), it may be surprising that the pigeons were sensitive at all to these contingencies.

N O T E S

1. Although, T has been divided between time allocated to t_1 and t_2 in Figure 6-1b, you could argue that it should be divided in three parts: t_1, the time allocated to one alternative; t_2, the time allocated to the other alternative; and t_3, the time allocated to neither. The animal might make two choices in a hierarchy (like Figure 4-6): whether to emit an operant or not and then whether to allocate it to alternative 1 or 2. In some cases, such a model is required to explain an animal's choice behavior. However, three-alternative cases are beyond the scope of this book. We restrict ourselves here to two cases of two-alternative choices: between two specific alternatives, as illustrated in Figure 6-1, and between one specific alternative and "other" behavior, as illustrated in Figure 6-2. More complicated cases may be considered as concatenations of these basic ones.

2. The molar–molecular view from which Equation 5-2 was derived sees rate R as a more molar form of amount A. If a series of identical-unit reinforcers (pellets to a rat, for instance) is delivered at a specified rate, then the amount of reinforcement obtained during T is just the rate multiplied by the duration of T. If T is a unit duration (as we assume) then rate (pellets per unit time) during T and amount (number of pellets) during T are identical. Unless otherwise indicated, the feedback functions that follow are assumed to be variable (interval and ratio) rather than fixed (interval and ratio) because with variable schedules, rate of reinforcement is constant regardless of the actual duration of T. (Fixed schedules involve temporal discriminations, the explanation of which is currently under debate and beyond the scope of this book.) The reader need only remember that we follow the convention introduced in Chapter 5 of using A to refer to the amount of an individual reinforcer and R to the number of individual reinforcers per unit time (T).

3. The functions of Figure 6-4 are power functions. Power functions were used in previous chapters to characterize another relationship, that between the amount, delay, and overall rate of a reinforcer and the value of the reinforcer. An advantage of using power functions to characterize feedback functions is that different schedules can be represented by different exponents, and different values of the same schedule can be represented by different coefficients. In the feedback function

$$R = m\left(\frac{t}{T}\right)^n$$

R is the rate of reinforcement (reinforcers obtained during an interval T); t/T is the allocation of time to the operant, m is the coefficient, and n is the exponent. When n is 0, this equation characterizes feedback functions of variable-time schedules; when n is 1, the equation characterizes feedback functions of variable-ratio schedules; when n has a low value, about 0.1, the equation characterizes feedback functions of variable-interval schedules.

4. When both schedules are of the same kind, they have the same value of n:

$$R_1 + R_2 = m_1\left(\frac{t_1}{T}\right)^n + m_2\left(\frac{t_2}{T}\right)^n$$

When both are variable-time schedules, $n = 0$; when both are variable-interval schedules, $n = 0.1$; when both are variable-ratio schedules, $n = 1.0$.

5. Philosophical readers will detect that this sort of behaviorism is operationism, a theory of science propounded by Bridgman (1927). One argument against operationism is the fact that there is a difference between the temperature of an object and the observation of that temperature (by reading a thermometer, for instance). However, operationism distinguishes between defining operations and incidental operations. A more serious objection to Bridgman's operationism is that it apparently ignores values. However, this objection cannot apply to an operationistic account of value itself.

6. If Equation 6-7 and those equations derived from it are to be useful in predicting behavior, the exponents s_A, s_D, and s_R must remain constant as the variables A_i, D_i, and R_i change. Research on this question (summarized recently by Davison, 1988) indicates that the individual exponents do not remain constant under all conditions. For instance, with a pair of alternatives of unequal amounts of reinforcement but equal delays, Equation 6-7 says that preference for the higher amount should be constant regardless of the delays (which cancel out). Yet a study by Duncan and Fantino (1970) and several subsequent studies with pigeons and rats have found that preference for the greater amount is somewhat stronger when both delays are

long than when both are short. In other words, sensitivity to amount (s_A) is not constant but depends to some extent on delay. It may be that once complications of standard choice procedures (such as changeover delays, local satiation effects, and response requirements) are accounted for, Equation 6-7 will be confirmed. Meanwhile, despite some serious disconfirmations, this equation remains the best generalization we have of the extant data on choice.

7. The Catania–Reynolds (1968) experiment with "simple" variable-interval schedules actually involves a kind of asymmetrical choice that we have not yet discussed in detail—between explicitly programmed food reinforcers and other reinforcers obtained in the operant chamber. In the case of a pigeon, these other reinforcers may consist of preening, scratching on the floor of the cage, and other interim activities (Staddon and Simmelhag, 1971). De Villiers (1977) assumed that such reinforcers (RO) could be converted to units equivalent to food and compared with food reinforcers. Figure 6-8 was constructed using deVilliers's estimate of RO as equivalent to 9 reinforcers per hour; that is, I added 9 to each programmed rate (ER). However, as we will see in a later chapter, qualitatively different reinforcers such as food and preening cannot simply be added. For our purposes, the various estimates used to construct Figure 6-8 are rough guesses and not to be taken too seriously. However, the general form of the figure would be about the same with all reasonable estimates.

C H A P T E R ▪ S E V E N ▪

SELF-CONTROL

Behaviorists distinguish between actions and passions, discussed in Chapter 1, in terms of their consequences, not in terms of the human soul or underlying mechanisms. According to the behaviorist, actions and passions are both overt behaviors, the former controlled by their distant consequences and the latter by their immediate ones.

Equation 6-7 (p. 158) provides two ways to conceive of the temporal aspect of consequences, one molecular and the other molar. The molecular conception focuses on conflict between amount and immediacy of reinforcement—choice between an alternative with a larger amount and one with a briefer delay. A person who chooses a larger, more delayed reinforcer (two candy bars tomorrow) over a smaller, less delayed reinforcer (one candy bar today) is exhibiting self-control in the molecular sense. With punishers, a person who chooses a smaller, more immediate punisher (a dental checkup today) over a larger, more delayed punisher (a toothache tomorrow) is exhibiting self-control in the same molecular sense.

A molar conception of self-control consistent with Equation 6-7 would focus on the overall rates (R's) of reinforcers or punishers in general as opposed to the amounts and delays of a single reinforcer. The conflict, in the molar conception, is between choice based on the first few of a series of reinforcers or punishers (perhaps a single reinforcer or punisher) and choice based on an extended series of reinforcers and punishers (corresponding to the conflict in cognitive decision problems, such as the Blue and Green taxicab problem, between immediate probabilities and base rates). You can think of a person choosing between eating an ice cream sundae and not eating it as facing the alternative of a single, discrete, highly pleasurable reward (the taste) followed by undesirable but vaguely connected aftereffects (being overweight) or the alternative of a more desirable but also vaguely connected series of events extended in time (being thin). Most studies of self-control have concentrated on the molecular view of self-control as a paradigm case, assuming that more molar cases may be constructed from molecular elements. Let us take up that view first; then we will discuss the more molar view.

A MOLECULAR CONCEPTION OF SELF-CONTROL

For most of the previous chapter, we have been ignoring punishment. Now let us consider it along with reward. Imagine two choices. The first is between rewards: Alternative 1 is a large, delayed reward, and alternative 2 is a small, immediate reward. The second choice is between punishers: Alternative 3 is a small, immediate punisher, and alternative 4 is a large, delayed punisher.

In accordance with the molecular view of self-control, the outcome of each alternative is only a single event, a single reinforcer or punisher. Therefore, in determining the subjective value of each outcome, we ignore the rate of outcome (R) and consider only the amount (A) and delay (D) of the single reinforcer or punisher.

Figure 7-1 shows how delay interacts with amount in determining the value of each reinforcer and punisher. Figure 7-1 corresponds to Figure 5-3 (constructed from Equation 5-1); the difference is that in the earlier figure the point of choice was held fixed at zero on the x-axis, and distances along that axis represented various delays of reinforcers or punishers. Here the x-axis represents time rather than delay; the time of delivery of the reinforcer or punisher is assumed to be fixed (just as the maturity date of a bond is fixed), and the point of

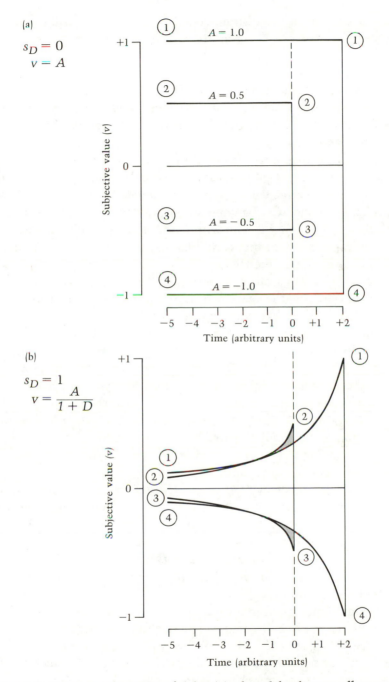

Figure 7-1 Value as a function of delay (a) when delay has no effect and (b) when reinforcers and punishers are discounted by delay. Bias is assumed equal to unity.

choice is conceived to be somewhere along the axis (when you buy the bond). When choice is at the point marked zero (time = 0), alternatives 2 and 3 are immediate while alternatives 1 and 4 are delayed by 2 (arbitrary) units of time. If the point of choice were moved 5 units back (time = −5), alternatives 2 and 3 would be delayed by 5 units of time and alternatives 1 and 4 by 7 units of time. (There are always 2 units of time between alternatives 1 and 2 or between 3 and 4.)

Figure 7-1a shows how alternatives would be valued if delay had no effect on value ($s_D = 0$). Regardless of delay, the decreasing rank order of the subjective values of the alternatives would be 1,2,3, and 4. It is hard to conceive of any person or any animal at all so indifferent to delay. With $s_D = 0$, you would choose two candy bars delayed by a million years over one candy bar right now. Only a computer could make a choice like that.

Figure 7-1b shows a more realistic situation. There, the attractiveness of a reward and the aversiveness of a punisher decay proportionately to delay. Note that as the figure was drawn (with the constants as assumed), the values of the larger, more delayed reward and punisher are lower at time 0 than the values of the smaller, more immediate reward and punisher. The order of values at time 0 is 2, 1, 4, and 3. Since matching (Equations 6-5 and 6-6) says that actual choice is proportional to relative obtained value, with the constants as assumed in Figure 7-1b, animals choosing between rewards at time 0 should choose the smaller, more immediate one (alternative 2) and animals choosing between punishers at time 0 should choose the larger, more delayed one (alternative 4).

As sensitivity to delay (s_D) varies, choice varies. Animals sometimes behave impulsively and choose the smaller immediate reinforcer (the single candy bar today) or the larger delayed punisher (the toothache tomorrow); sometimes behavior is not impulsive (it is "under control," or "restrained") and the larger delayed reinforcer (the two candy bars tomorrow) or the smaller immediate punisher (the dental checkup today) is chosen. The behaviorist thus conceives of self-control not as an inner quality that a person or animal has or does not have but as a direct consequence of the sensitivity of behavior to delay (Logue et al., 1984). When we are impulsive, our behavior is highly sensitive to delay, and our choices may be described (by value equations and matching equations) using a relatively high delay exponent (s_D). When we are under control, our behavior is relatively less sensitive to delay, and our choices may be described using a relatively low delay exponent.

Pigeons and rats, as you might suspect, are generally impulsive. In many experiments with these animals (see Commons et al., 1987) in which delays and amounts of reinforcement were varied, the delay exponent was found to be unity or close to unity (more like Figure 7-1b than 7-1a). Adult people in the confines of the laboratory, choosing among the trivial rewards we offer and facing delays measured in seconds, tend to be much more restrained than are pigeons. The delay exponents of children most likely lie somewhere between those of pigeons and those of adult people.

Mazur and Logue (1978), using a fading procedure, were able to train pigeons over months of daily experiments to abstain from pecking a key (which produced a small, immediate food delivery) and to wait 10 seconds for a larger reward. You could say that Mazur and Logue trained pigeons to become less sensitive to delay.

Experiments using punishment have not corresponded, either in extensiveness or in precision, with experiments using reward. Nevertheless, in a qualitative way the results are similar. For instance, a rat will choose to take a series of three electric shocks later (10 seconds after the choice) rather than a single electric shock of the same intensity right now (Lambert et al., 1973).

In a sense, this behavioral analysis does no more than pin a label on pigeons' and people's self-control or lack of it. Its advantage is that it provides a quantitative measure of self-control and places it on a continuum with all choices. It replaces an intuitive dichotomy with an objectively measurable scale. Second, it has many implications and makes several predictions that have been confirmed. One implication has to do with *commitment*, both in the animal laboratory and in human clinical psychology. We will briefly discuss this implication now.

COMMITMENT

In Figure 7-1b, when the point of choice is at time 0, the smaller rewards and punishers are immediate, the larger ones are delayed by 2 units of time, and the descending order of their current values is 2, 1, 4, and 3. The last section argued that this ordering resulted in impulsive choices both between rewards and between punishers.

Now suppose the point of choice is moved back 5 units of time to time −5. In this case the smaller rewards and punishers are delayed by 5 units of time, the larger ones by 7 units, and the descending order of their values is 1, 2, 3, and 4. The change in ordering with the backward movement of the point of choice is due to the crossing of the curves at time −1. With the point of choice between 0 and −1 (the shaded areas), the smaller alternatives have higher (positive and negative) values than the larger ones, resulting in impulsive choices. With the point of choice back further than −1, relative values revert again to an order proportional to the amounts of the alternatives. This is the same order as when sensitivity to delay is low, resulting in nonimpulsive (i.e., restrained) choices.

In other words, when the point of choice is close to the more immediate alternative (between −1 and 0) choice is impulsive; as the point of choice moves back, choice is less and less impulsive until, beyond where the curves cross (beyond time −1), choice is the same as it would be with no sensitivity to delay — it is perfectly under control. Analogously, a child's choice of one chocolate bar today over two chocolate bars tomorrow would tend to reverse when the choice is between one chocolate bar a week from now versus two chocolate bars in a week and one day from now. The moral judgment that it is better to have self-control (in this molecular sense) than not to have it is equivalent to the moral judgment that what should count in making a choice are the amounts of the alternatives, not their delays. Delays are often seen, morally, as only causing confusion rather than legitimately discounting the value of the reward.[1]

Ainslie (1975) noted that the crossing of the discount functions of Figure 7-1b implies the possibility of commitment to the less impulsive choice. In everyday life, you frequently have not just one choice but a series of choices at different stages (sometimes discrete, sometimes continuous) that are between a single pair of alternatives fixed in time. By making your choice at an earlier stage, you commit yourself in the sense that it may be difficult or impossible to reverse the choice later as the consequences come nearer. It is as if you were traveling along the time axis of Figure 7-1b from time −5 (or beyond) to time 0. If you make an irrevocable choice before the curves cross, you will be unable to reverse it later. So, for reasons of duty, you promise to visit a (non-present-giving) aunt a month from now. When the time comes around and you really do not feel like going, you are already committed and have to go. The classic example of commitment is Odysseus' tactic of stopping up the ears of his crew and tying himself to the mast of his ship; later, when the ship sailed past the Sirens, he heard their song but, although irresistibly tempted to sail his ship into the rocks, could not alter his earlier choice.

Ainslie reasoned that if the curves of Figure 7-1b apply to animals in general, any animal should be capable of commitment. Once the alternatives are made available at an earlier time, commitment involves nothing but the choice, at that time, of the high-valued alternative.

In Ainslie's experiment with pigeons, periodic brief illuminations of a single key with red light constituted temptations. If the pigeon pecked the key when it was red, the pigeon would receive an immediate but small delivery of food. If it did not peck the red key, it would receive a larger delivery of food after the red light went out. Several seconds prior to the illumination with red light, however, the key was illuminated with white light. If the pigeon pecked the key when it was white, the red illumination would be cancelled and the pigeon would be committed to obtaining the larger but more delayed food reward. Ainslie's pigeons (like Greek sailors) could not resist temptation. Whenever the red key was presented, it was pecked; the pigeons got the small, immediate food delivery and lost the larger, delayed food delivery. However, most of the time the pigeons did peck the white-illuminated key, thus cancelling the red key and receiving the larger reward.

Another experiment with pigeon subjects by Green and myself (Rachlin and Green, 1972) was similar to Ainslie's except that choice was symmetrical (pecking key A versus pecking key B) rather than asymmetrical (pecking versus not pecking). Our experiment is diagrammed in Figure 7-2. The pigeons had two choices. Choice Y at time 0 was between a small (2 seconds of access), immediate food delivery obtained by pecking a red key and a large (4 seconds of access) food delivery delayed by 4 seconds, obtained by pecking a green key. As in Ainslie's experiment, the pigeons nearly always succumbed to temptation and pecked the red key. Choice X at time −10 was between access to choice Y 10 seconds later and commitment to the larger reward. At point Z, only the green key was available.

In effect, choice X was between a 2-second food delivery delayed by 10 seconds (obtained after pecking the left [white] key and then almost invariably pecking the red key at choice Y) and a 4-second food delivery delayed by 14 seconds (obtained after pecking the right [white] key and then pecking the green key at point Z). The delay

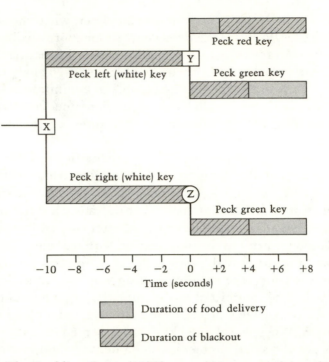

Figure 7-2 The Rachlin–Green (1972) commitment experiment in which pigeons could choose at decision point X between choice Y, where they could subsequently choose between a small, immediate versus a large, delayed reward, and Z where they were committed to the large, delayed reward.

gradients of Figure 7-1b correspond fairly well to those found with pigeons. Thus, a time of −10 seconds should be well before the point at which the curves cross. In fact, the pigeons in our experiment did predominantly choose the larger, more delayed reward at X—they did choose commitment. When we later varied the interval between choice X and points Y and Z, we found that the shorter the interval, the less the pigeons chose commitment, as Figure 7-1b predicts.

Although people generally have more self-control (less sensitivity to delay) than pigeons, the difference between Odysseus and the pigeons of our experiments is not in self-control but rather in inventiveness. Our pigeons, in the course of choosing the reward currently of highest value, made use of a commitment device provided by us. Odysseus invented his.

A MOLAR CONCEPTION OF SELF-CONTROL

As powerful as the above molecular conception of self-control is, it does not capture the full meaning of the term. We control ourselves not only when we choose the delayed over the immediate, but also when we choose the general over the concrete. When you turn down a tempting ice cream sundae in order to be thin, you have no particular reward in mind. Being thin is not in itself a reinforcer, and even if it were, there is no measurable delay between a particular act (such as turning down the sundae) and the general state of being thin. In fact, it is not possible to attain the general state of being thin through any particular act (as some of us know through bitter experience). Rather, if we generally turn down tempting desserts, we will generally be thin. The relation of eating to weight is not complicated — the less you eat, the less you weigh. The same goes for the relation between drinking and alcoholism — the less alcohol you drink, the less likely you are to be an alcoholic. What makes these relationships into self-control problems is the pitting of a single, discrete, molecular, immediately reinforced alternative against another alternative that is delayed in some sense but, more accurately, is molar rather than discrete.

Most adult humans are pretty good at choosing between two molecular alternatives when the consequences of one are larger and more delayed than those of the other. For instance, we can easily balance a worse movie at a local theater against a better movie at a theater a half-hour drive away. The issue is hardly one of self-control at all. The person who argues for the closer movie might be called lazy but would not be deemed impulsive or immature by his more energetic friends. Similarly, we are not bad at choosing between a pair of alternatives both with molar consequences, like a better but easier school versus a worse but harder school. (In the judgment problem of the Green versus Blue cabs, people would easily judge between two immediate witnesses or between two base rates.) The difficulty arises when you are choosing between one alternative with a discrete molecular reward (like going to the movies) and one with a vague molar reward (like doing your homework). In judgment tasks, an example would be choosing between a witness going in one direction and a base rate going in the other.

The philosopher Ryle (1949), in his book *The Concept of Mind*, discusses a mistake we often make, which is called a "category mistake." As an example, he tells the following story:

> A foreigner visiting Oxford or Cambridge for the first time is shown a number of colleges, libraries, playing fields, museums, scientific departments and administrative offices. He then asks "But where is the University? I have seen where the members of the Colleges live, where the Registrar works, where the scientists experiment and the rest. But I have not seen the University in which reside and work the members of your University." It has then to be explained to him that the University is not another collateral institution, some ulterior counterpart to the colleges, laboratories and offices which he has seen. The University is just the way in which all that he has already seen is organized. When they are seen and when their co-ordination is understood, the University has been seen. His mistake lay in his innocent assumption that it was correct to speak of Christ Church, the Bodleian Library, the Ashmolean Museum *and* the University, to speak, that is, as if 'the University' stood for an extra member of the class of which these other units are members. He was mistakenly allocating the University to the same category as that to which the other institutions belong. (p. 16).

When we come to explain human behavior, Ryle argued, our attempt to place molar, abstract categories (like believing X is true) alongside molecular, concrete ones (like saying "X is true") leads us to invent interior mental constructs. Since the statement "X is true" is a discrete act, it seems reasonable that the belief that X is true should be a discrete act, too. Finding no overt discrete act corresponding to a belief, we infer the existence of a covert one. However, according to Ryle, we should conceive of a belief as a molar act, that is, as an organization of more discrete but completely overt acts, just as the university is an organization of more molecular entities. By such a conception we would not have to invent covert activities within our heads to explain our beliefs.

As you see, Ryle's argument is behavioristic. A corresponding behavioristic argument extends Ryle's concept to behavior conceived as choice. We are always having to choose between one alternative (like eating an ice cream sundae) that leads to a discrete reward and another that leads to a much more vague reward (like being thin). We can point to the ice cream sundae as the object controlling our eating of it; if a person does eat the sundae, we are content to say that the person's behavior was controlled by the external reward. However, when the person turns down the sundae, we have no corresponding discrete external reward to point to as the source of control. Hence, we invent a mentalistic entity, an internal source of control, an nonmaterial self (or a purely physiological self) that we say controls the person's choice of the molar alternative. But just as the concept of a belief as an organization of overt actions obviates the need for a mental action, so the concept of a molar reward (an organization of discrete rewards) obviates the need for a nonmaterial self. According to the behaviorist, the opposition we are discussing here is not between control from without and control from within but between control by a molecular relation between behavior and its consequences (a molecular contingency, or a molecular feedback function) and control by a molar relation between behavior and its consequences (a molar contingency, or a molar feedback function).

Several experiments with pigeons have directly pitted choice of an immediate, small food reinforcer against an overall higher rate of food reinforcement (see, for instance, Logue, Smith, and Rachlin, 1985). The results are uniform — pigeons succumb to temptation and reduce their overall rate of reinforcement. A more interesting series of experiments uses a schedule called a *concurrent chain*, which varies both the overall rate of reinforcement and the local consequences of choice. We do not have the space here to discuss these schedules in any detail. In general, they offer a choice not between individual reinforcers, as simple concurrent schedules do, but between temporally extended exposures to one or another single schedule. Concurrent-chain schedules stand to simple concurrent schedules as choosing a cook stands to choosing a meal or as choosing a husband or wife stands to choosing a date for the evening. Choosing one meal or another occurs almost at the same time as eating one meal or another. The act of choice is followed by a brief act of consumption. But after you choose a cook (or a spouse), you have to live (for at least a while) with the object of your choice. Thus, with concurrent-chain schedules, there are two distinct conditions: the condition during which choices are made and consequences are unavailable (called the "initial link") and the condition after the basic choice has been made, during which consequences are experienced (called the "terminal link").

With simple two-alternative concurrent schedules, choice is always symmetrical. With concurrent-chain schedules, choice is symmetrical only during the initial link, when choosing between either of two terminal links (as when choosing between two cooks). During either terminal link, choices may be made, but they are asymmetrical (as when dealing with the chosen cook). The terminal links are never available together.

Fantino and Abarca (1985) have argued that concurrent-chain schedules correspond to the patterns of animals foraging in the wild as they hunt in one of two patches or spend time traveling between them. Fantino and Davison (1983) have shown that pigeons' choices in this situation depend not only on the rate of reward provided by each of the (more molecular) conditions between which the animal chooses but also on the (more molar) rates of reward in the experimental situation as a whole. This result has been quantified in various ways, none entirely satisfactory. Fantino has proposed a kind of matching to the relative difference between the overall and immediate rates rather than to the relative rate of reinforcement. Equation 6-7 accounts for the relative influence of overall and immediate consequences in terms of a difference between rate and delay exponents (between s_R and s_D), where R stands for the rate of reinforcement during the experimental session as a whole (initial and terminal links combined) and D stands for the delay between entering into a terminal link and reinforcement.[2]

It should be pointed out that the generalized matching law deliberately leaves the definition of rate of reinforcement (R) vague. Rate of reinforcement is the number of reinforcers divided by time in a given situation. But what is a situation? In animal laboratories, it is common to feed each animal after an experimental session in inverse proportion to what it ate during the session so that it will be about equally hungry tomorrow regardless of what happened in today's experiment. A "smart" pigeon might not peck the key at all; even if that meant no food during the session, the lack would be made up right afterward. If a pigeon exposed during the experiment to a single variable-interval schedule of reinforcement could view the situation as including the few minutes after removal from the experimental chamber and was sensitive to the overall rate of reinforcement during that entire situation, it would not peck the key. However, no matter how sensitive to overall rate of reinforcement a pigeon may be (and that is not too much), no pigeon to my knowledge has ever been smart enough to add those extra few minutes onto the denominator by which it calculates rate of reinforcement.[3]

In human affairs, the boundaries of a situation are obviously much more flexible than those in the affairs of a pigeon in a Skinner box. A man is hammering a nail. Is he just hammering the nail, or is he building a wall, constructing a house, or earning a living? He could be doing all at once — but he is still just hammering a nail. In a review of S. Naipaul's novel *North of South*, Anatole Broyard says:

> Perhaps the best comment on Africa is the one given to Mr. Naipaul by a Culture Ministry official in Tanzania. The author has asked for permission to visit a Ujama village, and the official warns him not to expect too much. "It's people planting," he says. "That is all. Why do you want to see people planting?" "But what about the spirit of socialism and self-reliance?" Mr. Naipaul asks. The official sighs. "The spirit of socialism and self-reliance is there," he says. "But you cannot see it. All you will see is people planting" (*New York Times*, April 21, 1979, p. 21)

This passage can be interpreted in two ways. One reason you might not be able to see the spirit of socialism and self-reliance is because it is hidden in the hearts and minds of the people planting. Another is because it is in the context or the background of their planting and gives meaning to it, as the illumination of a room, which is not usually seen as such, affects the brightness of the objects in it.

As we said previously, language is a discriminative stimulus that signals the presence of a contingency. If an experimenter is telling a subject to do something, the experimenter's language determines the contingency that forms the context for the subject's act. An experimenter could say to one subject, "Hammer that nail," to another, "Build a wall," and to a third, "Begin to construct a house." All subjects could do the same immediate thing — take up the hammer and hammer the nail in. Suppose you stop the experiment at that point. Did they all do the same thing? In a molecular sense, they did. But the cognitivist and the behaviorist agree that, in a larger sense, the three subjects did different things. The cognitivist says that the difference among the subjects lies in their thoughts. The behaviorist agrees up to a point: The difference among the three subjects is indeed their thoughts, but the subjects' thoughts (like their spirits of self-reliance and socialism, if any) are not in their heads (or not only in their heads) but in the overt contexts of their actions. Each subject's past experience forms the context of his or her present act. The question the behaviorist asks is "Where does the act belong in the subject's long-term pattern of behavior?"[4] The experimenter's verbal instructions, according to the behaviorist, put the subject's act into its context.

To illustrate how powerful the effect of context can be, consider Mischel's classic experiments on self-control with four-year-old children as subjects (summarized in Mischel, 1984). Each child chose between a preferred reward (for instance, two marshmallows), which could be obtained by waiting for the experimenter to come into the room, and a less preferred reward (for instance, one marshmallow), which could be obtained by just reaching out. The data are the number of minutes that the children waited before taking the less preferred reward. (After 15 minutes the experimenter would come in, but most children did not wait that long.) Mischel and his colleagues varied both the stimulus conditions during the waiting period and what the experimenter said to the child before she left the room

The two main stimulus conditions of waiting were with the rewards exposed where the child could see them and with the rewards covered up and out of sight. If nothing more was said to the child than merely the rules of the experiment, the children with the exposed rewards waited about 30 seconds on the average, while the children with the hidden rewards waited about 13 minutes.[5] The order of difference (about 25:1) is great, but it could be completely reversed by what the experimenter said to the children before leaving the room. When children with exposed rewards were told to "think fun" (say, to think about mommy swinging them on a swing), their average waiting time jumped to around 13 minutes; when children with covered rewards were told to think about consuming the rewards (eating the marshmallows), their average waiting time shrunk to around 1 minute. Other verbal manipulations had the same reversing effect. Mischel (1984) summarizes the results (using pretzels rather than marshmallow rewards) as follows:

> If the preschoolers ideate about the rewards for which they are waiting in consummatory or "hot" ways (focusing on their taste, for instance, by thinking how crunchy and salty the pretzels are), they cannot delay long (Mischel and Baker, 1975). But if they focus on the unconsummatory or "cool" qualities of the rewards (on their abstract features, thinking of the pretzels as if they were sticks or tiny logs, for example) they can wait for them easily. (p. 354)

As a cognitive psychologist, Mischel opposes the environmental stimulus — the exposed rewards — to the internal stimulation from the children's own ideas. He says.

> An enduring general concern underlying the research is to try to understand how persons can overcome "stimulus control" — the power of situations — and achieve increasing volitional control over their own behavior even when faced with compelling situational pressures. (p. 353)

For the behaviorist, the opposition is not between the situation and the person's volition but between the situation in a narrow context and the situation in a wider context. The words that the experimenter says to the child establish a context; that is, they are discriminative stimuli for actions appropriate to various situations.[6] Thinking about consuming a pretzel and thinking about playing with a pretzel may be characterized metaphorically as hot and cool ideas in behavioristic as well as cognitive terms. Imagine yourself in a situation where your potential actions under control of their narrow context are in conflict with your potential actions under control of their wider context (say you are driving a car and someone cuts in front of you from another lane). If you get "hot under the collar," your actions in that situation are, by definition, set in a narrow context — your relations with that particular person at that particular time. If you are "cool under pressure" or "cool under fire," your actions, also by definition, are set in their wider context — your relations with other drivers and with other people in general.

In summary, the molecular conception of self-control, as presented in the previous section, rejects the dichotomy between control from within the self and control from outside the self. It sees behavior ordinarily thought to be controlled by the self as controlled instead by distant rewards. The molar conception of self-control goes a step further and virtually abandons the concept of control in its ordinary usage. Rather, it looks at each act in its context as part of a pattern of behavior. When the act fits with certain behavioral patterns (say, patterns of consumption), it is seen as impulsive. When the act fits with certain other, more abstract behavioral patterns (say, patterns of play) it is seen as less impulsive; ultimately, when the act fits in with behavior extending over a person's lifetime, it is seen as goodness, fulfillment, maturity, true happiness, and so on.[7]

The matching equations of the previous chapter are descriptive rather than normative. They say how animals do act, not how they should act. They describe molecular self-control in terms of an opposition between amounts and delays of individual reinforcers and punishers. The equations describe molar self-control in terms of an opposition between an individual reinforcer or punisher and a more abstract overall rate of reinforcement or punishment. At a still more molar level, the equations allow rate of reinforcement to be calculated with various time bases. As the time base expands, wider and wider environmental patterns can be accounted for.

Abstractly interpreted, the matching law is nothing but the statement that patterns of choice match patterns of events in the environment; all acts of choice are acts of matching. So much is dogma. The empirical part of the matching law is its use in discovering what the reinforcers and punishers are — what people and other animals want, or what you yourself want. Many, but not all, of the choices made by "lower" animals like rats and pigeons in very simple environments match aspects of the environment — aspects that are quite narrowly confined — within a few seconds of the choice. Some, but not many, human choices in the real world are similarly confined in scope. In the last chapter we will consider some human choices (gambling choices) with delays measured within a few minutes. Other human choices match wider aspects of the environment.

You may look down on pigeons (metaphorically speaking) for their almost invariable impulsiveness, but it is not their impulsiveness per se that makes them inferior to you. The contingencies of our experiments with pigeons often create choices analogous to that between spending and saving. In those situations, pigeons are invariable spenders. But it would make still less sense to be an invariable saver. What makes you and me superior to pigeons is our ability to balance spending and saving — impulsiveness and restraint. It is to that general issue, the question of balance itself, that we now turn.

NOTES

1. The medieval prohibition against charging interest on a loan directly reflects this morality. That attitude may in turn reflect the strain of Neoplatonism in medieval thinking. In the early dialogue *Protagoras*, Plato says, "The same magnitudes seem greater to the eye from near at hand than they do from a distance" (356C). At that

point, as in the shaded area of Figure 7-1b, "appearances lead us astray" (356D). For this reason, Plato says, we should not allow our choices to be guided by our perceptions. We should guide them instead by calculations: "Like an expert in weighing, put the pleasures and pains together, set both the near and distant in the balance, and say which is the greater quantity" (356B). In his later dialogues, however, Plato explicitly abandons this purely molecular conception of self-control, which he calls "intelligence," and advocates a more molar conception, a harmonious mixture of intelligence and pleasure. (See Rachlin, 1985, for a discussion of the relation of Plato's concept of the Good to modern behaviorism.)

2. For instance, with concurrent variable-interval, 1 minute schedules in the initial links, the initial links would last an average of 30 seconds. (With two chickens each laying eggs at about 1 per minute, the time between eggs would average 30 seconds.) Suppose one terminal link was a single variable-interval, 50-second schedule, and the other a single variable-interval, 100-second schedule. The ratio of the overall rates of reinforcement (R_1/R_2) of alternatives 1 and 2 would be $(30 + 100)/30 + 50)$ and the inverse of the ratio of the delays (D_2/D_1) would be 100/50. Most of the evidence against the generality of Equation 6-7, mentioned in note 6 of the previous chapter, comes from experiments with concurrent-chain schedules.

3. However, when no issue of self-control is involved (when there are no temptations), events during one session may influence a rat's or a pigeon's behavior the next day or even months or years later (Skinner, 1938). Even when reinforcement is immediate, its effects persevere over long periods. An animal's vision of the future may be said to be narrow, but that narrowness does not usually become evident until the animal is faced with a choice involving self-control. From a behavioral point of view, the difference between what a rat knows and what it does is really a difference between what the rat does in one versus another set of circumstances. A behaviorist would say that a rat knows how large the distant reward is (because it chooses that reward over a smaller distant reward), but when the same reward is pitted against a much smaller but immediate reward, the rat chooses the latter. In that sense the rat knows one thing but does another.

4. This point is one where Ryle (1949) differs from behaviorists. Ryle says that the difference lies in what the subjects would have

done had the experiment continued (dispositions). The behaviorist does not deny that the three subjects would have done different things but prefers to define mental terms as actual events (what the subjects have done) rather than potential ones (what they will do). The writer Italo Calvino (1988, p. 77) quotes Hoffmannsthal as follows: "Depth is hidden. Where? On the surface." Hoffmannsthal must have been a radical behaviorist.

5. Grosch and Neuringer (1981) repeated this experiment with pigeons under comparable conditions — exposed versus nonexposed rewards during a waiting period — and obtained comparable results.

6. Of course, the words are represented in and processed by the child's nervous system. The nature of this processing is highly significant. Nevertheless, the interest of the behaviorist is focused, as usual, not on how the words are internally represented but on what they externally represent.

7. In Plato's central dialogues, he abandons the molecular concept of self-control, which had characterized the early dialogues, and adopts a molar view:

> There are two patterns, my friend, in the unchangeable nature of things, one of divine happiness, the other of godless misery — a truth to which their [unjust people's] folly makes them utterly blind, unaware that in doing injustice they are growing less like one of these patterns and more like the other. The penalty they pay is the life they lead, answering to the pattern they resemble. (*Theaetetus*, 176e–177a)

An ideal state, according to Plato, would arrange contingencies so that conflicts never arise. Acts of consumption, for instance, would fit into the pattern of all acts, much as the notes of a symphony fit into its overall structure. In the real world, however, contingencies are such that conflicts inevitably arise. About this Plato says, "It makes no difference whether [an ideal state] exists now or will ever come into being. The politics of this city only will be his [the wise man's] and of none other." (*Republic* 9.592b).

ECONOMICS
AND CHOICE

IN ONE OF HIS LATER DIALOGUES, *Philebus*, Plato says:

> Why, it's just as if we were supplying drinks, with two fountains at our disposal: one would be of honey, standing for pleasure, the other standing for intelligence, a sobering unintoxicating fountain of plain salubrious water. We must get to work and make a really good mixture. (61c)

Of course, Plato was speaking about the way a person should live, and the honey-water mixture is only an analogy. However, let us take it literally for a while. The choice Plato asks us to make is among an infinity of degrees of mixture of honey and water, not all or none, not between honey and water as such. That sort of choice is quite different from those we have been considering. First, the alternatives, each a particular proportion of honey and water, are infinite in number. Second, the two extremes are qualitatively different from each other. We have been concentrating thus far on schedules of reinforcement — on the contingencies of the choice situation itself — assuming that the rewards (or punishers) differ only in amount, delay, or rate; we have been dealing with qualitatively identical consequences of choice. But water and honey are qualitatively different. Where alternatives differ qualitatively in addition to the other parameters, a theory of choice needs to take that qualitative difference — and its converse, the degree of similarity — into account. Chapter 4 briefly discussed a cognitive theory of qualitative difference and similarity based on identical elements. This chapter presents a more elaborate theory based on *substitutability* in trade.

SUBSTITUTABILITY

Imagine yourself setting out to take Plato's advice literally. You begin with 10 cups of honey and no water. Figure 8-1a represents your state at point *A*. A man comes along with a supply of water that he is willing to trade for honey. He asks you, "How much honey would you be willing to give me for 1 cup of water?" Because you have no water and a lot of honey, 1 cup of water is worth a lot to you, so you offer him 3 cups of honey for it. He agrees and you trade. You are now at point *B* of Figure 8-1. Then the same man asks you, "How much honey would you give me for another cup of water?" This time you are less eager to part with honey, since you have less of it than you had before and you already have a little water. So now you offer him only 2 cups of honey for a cup of water. Suppose he agrees and you trade again. Here, at point *C*, you have 5 (10 − 3 − 2) cups of honey and 2 cups of water, summing to only 7 cups of the two drinks together.

Although you had 10 cups when you started, you are no less happy than you were at the beginning (assuming that each trade was an exactly even trade for you). The loss of 3 cups of drinkable liquid is compensated (let us suppose, exactly compensated) by the advantage of having a mixture rather than only one liquid to drink. Suppose the man keeps offering to trade. For the third cup of water you give only 1½ cups of honey. At this point (point *D*) you have a honey – water mixture that seems almost perfect to you. You have 3 cups of water and 3½ cups of honey. Now you have become much stingier with your honey. You are just barely willing to trade cup for cup, progressing to point *E* (4 cups of water to 2½ cups of honey), but now,

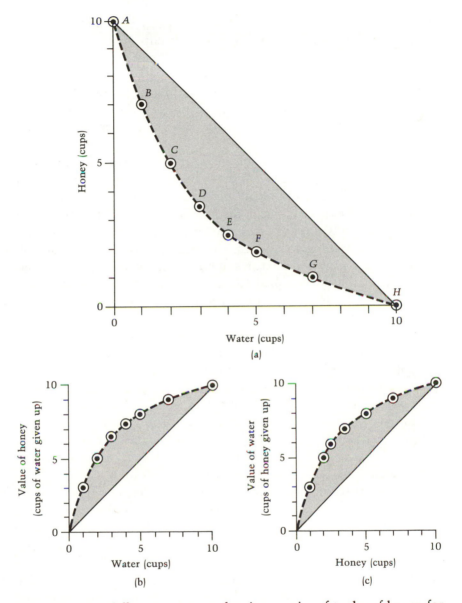

Figure 8-1 (a) Indifference contour showing a series of trades of honey for water. (b) Value function of water (in terms of honey). (c) Value function of honey (in terms of water). Value functions derived directly from the indifference contour.

moving away from your perfect proportions, you demand to be compensated by more water. For the next cup of water, you offer only half a cup of honey, moving to point F. Then you want 2 cups of water for a cup of honey, moving to point G; finally, for your last cup of honey, you demand 3 cups of water, ending up at point H, with 10 cups of water and no honey. At each point, let us say, you are just as happy as you were at any other. What you got in each trade exactly compensated for what you gave.

The string of points traced out by your several trades is called, in economics, an *indifference contour*. By our assumption, you are absolutely indifferent among all mixtures of honey and water along the contour. The space between the straight solid line (representing a constant sum of 10 cups of drinkable liquid) and the curve represents what you are willing to give up in terms of volume of drinkable liquid in order to obtain mixtures of honey and water. When you had all honey or all water you had 10 cups, but as you approached closer and closer to an ideal proportion, you were willing (just willing, we assume) to sacrifice total volume for variety of the mixture.

The curvature of your indifference contour is a direct measure of your preference for variety. If the two fluids had been very similar, say Coke and Pepsi, you might not have cared about variety so much as total volume. Thus, with Coke and Pepsi, you might well have been willing to trade cup for cup, and your indifference contour would have been right on the straight line from point A to point H. Even if you did perceive some qualitative difference between the two cola drinks, your indifference contour would likely be much closer to a straight line than your honey – water contour was.

The curvature of a person's indifference contour between two rewards (economists call them *goods*), like honey and water or Coke and Pepsi, is an indication of the degree to which the two goods are *substitutable* for each other in trade. If two goods were perfectly substitutable, you would not care whether you had all of one, a mixture of the two, or all of the other. You would just be concerned about volume. The concurrent-schedule choices of animals discussed in the previous chapters — for instance, those of pigeons between a hopper full of food after pecking one key and a hopper full of the same food after pecking another key — were between perfectly substitutable goods. In such cases, the parameters of amount, rate, and delay (comprising the equivalent of total volume) were our only concern. However, choices with single schedules of reinforcement — for instance, choices by pigeons between a hopper full of food after pecking a key and the opportunity to engage in interim behavior such as preening or scratching around the floor of the cage—are between goods that are not perfectly substitutable. In such cases choice is affected by substitutability.

The indifference contour of Figure 8-1 is nothing but a symmetrical version of the bent-over value function of Figure 4-3 (the law of diminishing marginal utility). There we assumed that the value of a good was a specific function of the amount of that good. Here value is a relative concept. A single good, like honey, has no value by itself. Rather, it has (economic) value only relative to some other good, like water, that can be exchanged for it.[1]

If you consider water as a measure of the value of honey, then the more honey you have, the less valuable a cup of honey is relative to a cup of water. If you consider honey as a measure of the value of water, then the more water you have, the less valuable a cup of water is relative to a cup of honey. In Figure 8-1a you could think of a turned-around honey axis (the inverse of the honey given up) as value and the water axis as amount, or you could think of a turned-around water axis as value and the honey axis as amount. Either way, you would get a bent-over curve like those of Figures 4-3 or 4-4. The curve in Figure 8-1b places water on the horizontal axis and turns the vertical axis around relative to the curve in Figure 8-1a; it shows the value of water as measured by honey given up (as if honey were money—no rhyme intended). The curve in Figure 8-1c places honey on the horizontal axis and shows the value of honey as measured by water given up (as if water were money) on the vertical axis.

Had you started the trading process with 20 cups of honey instead of 10, you would have traced out another indifference contour roughly parallel to the one shown but higher. Had you started with 5 cups of honey, you would have traced out a lower indifference contour. By definition, the mixture represented by each point on a given indifference contour is worth exactly as much as the mixtures represented by every other point on that same contour. Therefore, each mixture on a 20-cup indifference contour would be worth more than each of those on the 10-cup contour, which in turn would be worth more than each of those on a 5-cup contour. In general, the higher the indifference contour (relative to both axes) the higher its value. Figure 8-2a shows three hypothetical indifference contours (much like that of Figure 8-1a) of different values. You could think of them as you would of altitude contours on a map of a hill rising upwards and to the right from the origin.

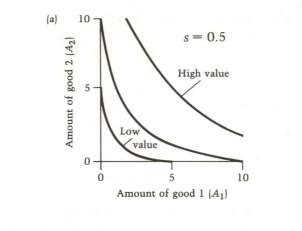

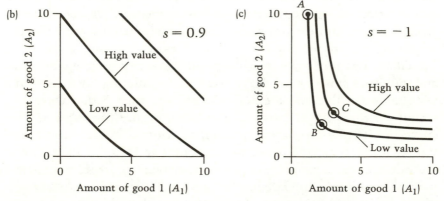

Figure 8-2 Indifference contours of different values with (a) moderate substitutability, (b) high substitutability, and (c) complementarity. Amounts are in arbitrary units of the good.

The curvature of the contours is a measure of how desirable variety is. With honey and water, you would prefer some variety (we assume), so your indifference contours would be curved as in Figure 8-1a and 8-2a. With Coke and Pepsi, you would care much less about variety, so your indifference contours would be much closer to a straight line, as in Figure 8-2b. Honey and water are somewhat substitutable, but Coke and Pepsi are almost completely substitutable. The more substitutable two goods are, the more their indifference contours approach a straight line.

Figure 8-2c shows a set of indifference contours near the opposite extreme from complete substitutability — *complementarity.* Two goods are complements when a mixture is not just desirable, but almost necessary. Examples include left shoes and right shoes or bicycle frames and pairs of bicycle wheels. The sharp bends of the indifference contours of complements reflect the greater need for variety with such goods. For instance, if you had 10 bicycle frames and 1 pair of bicycle wheels, you might well be willing to trade 8 of those frames for a single pair of wheels (assuming there was no other way you could get the wheels). In Figure 8-2c the circled point nearest to 10 frames and 1 pair of wheels (point A) would then be on the same contour as the point corresponding to 2 frames and 2 pairs of wheels (point B). Point C, representing 3 frames and 3 pairs of wheels (three bicycles) must be on a higher contour than point B, representing only two bicycles. Being high and to the left on a given contour means having too many (almost worthless) frames, while being low and to the right means having too many (almost worthless) wheels.

The curvature of indifference contours means the same thing as the bending over of the value functions in Chapter 4. As you have more and more of any good, additional units of that good are worth less and less to you. In Chapter 4 we considered absolute worth. The only difference here is that now we are considering *relative* worth — worth in terms of combination with another good.

In Chapter 4 we used a power function with an exponent less than 1 to characterize the bending over of the value function mathematically. In this chapter we use a power function with an exponent less than 1 to characterize the substitutability between two goods. Here the outcome of various allocations of choice between two alternatives consists of a *package*, so to speak, of two goods (1 and 2) in various proportions rather than of different amounts of a single good. Assuming that we can simply add values of two goods, a mathematical expression (consistent with Equation 4-1) that can express the sum of the values of two different goods is

$$v_A = k_1 \, (A_1)^s + k_2 \, (A_2)^s \qquad (8\text{-}1a)$$

where v_A is the value of the package consisting of an amount A_1 of one good plus an amount A_2 of another good, k_1 and k_2 are constants representing the relative contributions of units of the goods to the value, and the exponent s represents the substitutability between good 1 and good 2.[2]

All the functions of Figure 8-2 are plots of amount of good 1 versus amount of good 2. Just as Equation 8-1a will give you the value of any combination of A_1 and A_2, so every point within the three sets of axes of Figure 8-2 must fall on some indifference contour (equal-value contour). The indifference contours drawn are only a sample of an infinite number of contours. (Similarly, the equal-altitude contours and equal-temperature contours on maps are samples. Every point on the map is conceived as having a single altitude or a single temperature.) The commodity space (as defined by the axes in Figure 8-1 and 8-2) is assumed to be full of indifference contours of ever-increasing value as they are higher in the space.

In the operant laboratory the overall amount of a good is usually varied by altering the rate R of reinforcers, each of identical individual amount, over a given time period T. When overall amount is varied in this way, we can express Equation 8-1a as

$$v = k_1 \ (R_1)^s + k_2 \ (R_2)^s \tag{8-1b}$$

Both Equations 8-1a and 8-1b mean the same thing. If you double either A (the amount of an individual reinforcer) or R (the rate of reinforcement), you double the overall reinforcement obtained during T. If you halve either A or R, you halve overall reinforcement during T.

Either form of Equation 8-1 is only one of a number of conceivable utility functions that express the value of a pair of goods that can vary in substitutability. We discuss this particular function here for several reasons: (1) As we shall soon see, it helps explain much of the data obtained in studies of animal choice; (2), it is consistent with Equation 4-1, which, Chapter 4 claimed, expresses the value of a good as a function of the amount of that good; and (3) economists are fond of it because of its simple mathematical properties (it is easy to differentiate) and its ability to explain many molar and molecular economic and social phenomena.

The constants k_1 and k_2 used to draw the indifference contours of Figure 8-2 are each assumed to be unity. The values of s are indicated on each figure part. If goods 1 and 2 were completely substitutable for each other, the exponent s would equal 1.0, and Equation 8-1 would express a simple proportionality between value and amount. In other words, the value of a pair of completely substitutable goods (when considered as alternatives of a single choice) is simply proportional to the sum of the two (weighted) amounts.[3] Therefore, if you were choosing between two completely substitutable goods, and if you were trying to maximize the value of your choice, and if all other variables (probability, delay, and rate) were equal, and if your choice were not constrained by extraneous factors, you would simply choose the alternative of highest amount. If you were choosing among an infinity of alternatives, each consisting of a package of two completely substitutable goods (and if those other ifs applied), you would simply choose the package with the highest total amount of the two goods. However, if all of these assumptions did not apply, your choices could not be described so simply. When goods are not completely substitutable ($s < 1$), your choices would depend on both amount and substitutability, as given by Equation 8-1. Furthermore, they would depend critically on any extrinsic constraints that might apply. Let us now consider how extrinsic constraints affect choice. First, we show a way of representing constraints on the same axes used in Figures 8-1 and 8-2.

CONSTRAINTS

Imagine that instead of starting out with 10 cups of honey and trading with some stranger, as you did above, you were given a certain fixed amount of money, say $5, and could spend it on water and honey. Suppose honey costs $1 a cup and bottled water costs 20¢ per cup. If you spent the entire $5 on honey, you could buy 5 cups; if you spent the entire $5 on water, you could buy 25 cups. Or, you could buy a mixture (as Plato advises). Line XY (the middle line) of Figure 8-3 connects the extremes (5 cups of honey and 25 cups of water) and traces out the locus of combinations of honey and water you could buy. Given that you have to spend the whole $5 on honey and water (and that cups can be infinitely divided), line XY delimits your choices. You are constrained to choose among the points along that line, each point representing a specific mixture (or package) of the two goods. You cannot choose any of the mixtures below the line because you have to spend all of your money, and you cannot choose any of the mixtures above the line because they are too expensive. Thus, the line represents the *constraint* on your choice. The more money you have to spend (your budget), the higher the constraint line; the less, the lower. Line X'Y' (the lower line) of Figure 8-3 shows the constraint with a budget of $2.50 and the same prices for honey and water as before. When your budget changes and prices remain constant, your constraint line moves up or down correspondingly to the budget. Note that line X'Y' is parallel to line XY with a different budget but equal prices.

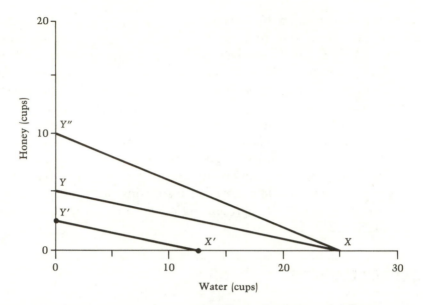

Figure 8-3 Three constraint lines with different budgets and different prices of honey and water. Lines XY and X'Y' have the same prices but different budgets. Lines XY and XY" have the same price of water but different prices of honey.

Changes in price, however, may cause changes in the slope of the constraint line. Line XY" (the upper line) shows the constraint with a budget of $5 and a reduction in the price of honey to 50¢ per cup. Although budget changes move the constraint upward or downward in a parallel fashion, changes in relative price alter the slope of the constraint.[4]

Constraints need not be only straight lines. For instance, if honey and water came in bottles of various sizes, larger bottles being proportionately cheaper (the large "economy" size), the constraint would sag in the middle — you could buy a little more if you bought the large size of either good and sacrificed variety. In the laboratory, a constraint may be any shape that an experimenter arranges. A constraint, after all, is only a set of alternatives. If there are alternatives to choose among, there must also be limits to choice. Later we will consider some nonlinear constraints.

The constraints of Figure 8-3 represent objective sets of facts. We drew Figure 8-3 without making any assumptions about what a person would do. To draw the constraints, we needed no person at all. Constraints are exactly analogous to schedules of reinforcement or punishment; graphical representations of constraints, such as those of Figure 8-3, are exactly analogous to feedback functions such as those of Figures 6-3, 6-4, and 6-5. Both constraints and feedback functions represent the alternatives available for choice, and both say nothing about what an animal or a person will do when faced with those alternatives.

Just as we needed a subjective assumption — an assumption about the choice process — to predict choice given a set of feedback functions (we used matching), so we need a corresponding subjective assumption about the choice process to predict choice given a constraint. The assumption of maximization of utility serves this purpose. We will discuss later whether matching and maximizing (the two subjective molar processes that have been assumed by theories of choice so far) make the same predictions or different predictions about actual choices in corresponding situations. Now let us focus our attention on maximization.

MAXIMIZATION

Maximization theory says that an animal, given a set of alternatives (as represented by a constraint line), will choose among them so as to maximize subjective utility. In terms of Figures 8-2 and 8-3, the animal will choose a package of goods on the highest utility contour possible with those alternatives (under those constraints).

The reason for drawing constraint lines differently from feedback functions (even though they are the same thing, that is, a representation of alternatives) is to put the objective constraint lines on the same axis as the subjective utility contours so that they can be compared. Figure 8-4 puts an arbitrary set of constraint lines (one straight, one curved, and one right-angled) on the same set of axes as a set of indifference contours. Obtainable packages of goods are represented by points on the constraint line. Each point has a value as given by the indifference contour that intersects it. Maximization says that, given a set of obtainable packages (points on the constraint line), an animal will choose the one of highest value. As we have drawn them, the highest-valued point on each constraint line is the one where the line touches the highest possible indifference contour. Because the space is full of indifference contours (every point has a value), every point on the constraint line is also on an indifference

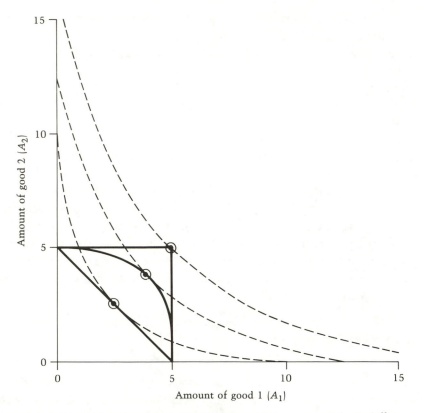

Figure 8-4 Maximization (circled points) at highest possible indifference contours (dotted lines) that can be reached with a given set of constraints (solid lines). Amounts are in arbitrary units of the good.

contour (even though the latter may not be drawn). In Figure 8-4 the highest indifference contour that each constraint line intersects is drawn as a dotted line, and the point of intersection is circled. You can see that on a given constraint line (solid line), all points other than that circled will fall on a lower indifference contour. Thus, given the alternatives represented by the points (packages) on each constraint line, maximization theory predicts choice of the circled point.

If an animal did indeed choose the highest-valued alternatives among those attainable and if that animal's (subjective) indifference contours were known, it would be a simple matter to predict its choices. Therefore, the first step in predicting a person's choice among a set of alternatives is to discover that person's indifference contours. However, economists studying people's behavior in real-world marketplaces and psychologists studying animal behavior in the laboratory have found it difficult to determine indifference contours directly. Instead, the following steps are taken in the example of a marketplace:

1. A consumer with a fixed budget to be spent on various goods at various prices allocates his or her purchases among the goods. The economist may observe (relatively easily) the consumer's budget and the prices of available goods. These observations comprise a constraint, which limits the packages of goods that the consumer can buy. Then the economist observes the actual package that the consumer does buy. This last observation represents the consumer's choice — the allocation of the budget among available goods at specific prices.

2. Then the economist assumes the existence of a utility function (such as Equation 8-1). The consumer's observed allocation "reveals" the parameters of his or her utility function to the economist (Samuelson, 1973).

3. Having assumed a set of parameters of the consumer's utility function (hence, the indifference contours), the economist can predict the consumer's allocation with any new constraint (new set of budget and prices) that might be imposed. The economist further assumes that, within the confines of the constraint, the consumer will choose the package of goods (the allocation) with the highest attainable value — the one on the highest attainable indifference contour. This will usually be the one tangent to the constraint line.

4. Now the economist observes the consumer's allocation of purchases with the new constraint (the new prices and budget). If the allocation is the one predicted (or close to it), the economist's assumption about the form and the parameters of the utility equation (i.e., the shape of the indifference contours) was correct. However, if the observed new allocation differs from the one predicted, the economist revises the utility function (assumed in step 2) until a set of indifference contours is discovered that accounts for both the old and the new allocations. Then the economist goes on to use this new utility func-

tion to predict allocations with still newer constraints, and the process continues.

This process is just a version of the procedure that any theory of choice must use. Underlying the procedure in this case are two basic assumptions. First, given a set of alternatives, people choose the one of highest value. Second, a person's utility function (hence, his or her indifference contours) remain constant from one situation (set of constraints) to another. The economist's job is to discover that utility function. The first assumption, the assumption of maximization, is not only a firmly held assumption of economists; it is virtually built into the English language. To say that people always choose the alternative of highest value—the alternative that seems best to them—is tautological. It is impossible for most of us to conceive of a person choosing an alternative that seems worse over one that seems better.[5] (People who say that alternative 1 is better than alternative 2 and who nevertheless choose alternative 2 are thought to be lying to us, lying to themselves, or making a mistake about their own values.) The second assumption, that people's values remain stable across situations, is less axiomatic but underlies the practice of economics as much as the first; this assumption allows a utility function (a set of indifference contours) that is revealed under one set of constraints to be used to predict people's choices under another.

Perhaps the furthest extension of this economic program is that of Becker (1976), who explains much human social behavior, including marriage, divorce, and prejudice, in terms of an economic model. In Becker's extension of economics to human social life, people are seen as spending not money but time and energy (sometimes convertible to money, sometimes not) on activities that reward them in various monetary and nonmonetary ways. We have no time (or energy) here to explore in depth such social extensions of the economic model, but it is worth emphasizing that they rely on the stability of people's values from situation to situation.

As an example, consider Stigler and Becker's (1977) explanation of addiction. If any example of a drastic change in a person's values could be found, it would seem to be in the case of the addict. People who become addicts seem almost by definition to value the thing they become addicted to much more than they did before. According to Stigler and Becker, however, the real change that occurs in addiction is a change in price (in constraints), not in value. According to these economists, addictions (to such substances as alcohol, heroin, and cocaine) result when two factors coincide. First, the substance must satisfy a basic need in the sense that the person's demand for it is inelastic. A demand for a good is inelastic, according to economists, when equivalently priced substitutes for that good are unavailable. Thus, the demand for milk is often inelastic, while the demand for fur coats is often elastic. A given person's demand, according to Stigler and Becker, is not so much for the good itself as for the kind of satisfaction that the good provides. Substances such as alcohol, heroin, and cocaine may satisfy basic needs for security or acceptance normally available through contact with friends and relations. The living conditions of some people, however, may be so bad that these social rewards are unavailable to them. Such people, according to Stigler and Becker, are likely to become addicts.

The second part of an addiction is a process of rapid habituation; the more the good is consumed, the less satisfaction it offers. (The veteran alcoholic needs a quart of hard liquor to get as drunk as the neophyte drinker does from a glass of wine.) Even if the monetary cost per unit remains constant, the real price, in terms of the cost of achieving a given level of satisfaction, goes up and up as the person consumes more and more of the substance. According to Stigler and Becker, it is the combination of inelastic demand and increasing real price that causes an addict to consume more of a substance—not a change in his or her values.[6] The addict's satisfaction from the substance is necessary and requires more and more of the substance as more and more is consumed. An addict differs from a nonaddict, according to Stigler and Becker, not because the addict's values are different from those of the nonaddict nor because the addict has less self-control, but because the addict has come to satisfy some basic need (shared by all of us) in a way that becomes ever more costly with time.[7] The critical component of addiction, according to Stigler and Becker, is therefore a change in price, not a change in value.

ECONOMICS AND THE CHOICES OF ANIMALS IN THE LABORATORY

Research in the animal laboratory using an economic model may follow the same steps taken by the economist in observing consumers in the marketplace. The following two experiments (Rachlin et al., 1976) were undertaken to demonstrate this procedure. We used thirsty rats as subjects of the first experiment. The rats chose among goods by pressing levers. Two levers were available in the Skinner box for each rat to press. After a certain number x of presses on the left lever, a small dipper (0.05 milliliter) of Tom Collins mix (nonalcoholic and fizzed out) was delivered to the rat. After a certain number y of presses on the right lever, a small dipper of root beer (also nonalcoholic and fizzed out) was delivered. After a certain number z of total presses the day's session ended—the levers were withdrawn and the rat was taken out of the box.

You can think of the rat's situation in either of two ways: as an economic situation or as an operant-choice situation. In economic terms, lever presses were like money. The price of Tom Collins mix was x lever presses per dipperful; the price of root beer was y lever presses per dipperful; the rats' budget was z lever presses to be spent on Tom Collins mix and root beer. In operant terms, the rat chose between two ratio schedules of reinforcement, ratio x for Tom Collins mix and ratio y for root beer.

Following the steps outlined above, we first imposed on the rat a set of schedules (prices and a budget). That is, we fixed x, y, and z and observed the rat's allocation of lever presses to the two alternatives (the rats' purchases of "packages" of Tom Collins mix and root beer). Then we changed the schedules and criterion for ending the session (the prices and budget) and observed a second allocation. From the two allocations we could estimate the parameters of a utility function (Equation 8-1b, in this case). Then we again changed the schedules and the criterion for ending the session (prices and budget) and again observed the rat's allocation—the third allocation. Then we revised, usually only slightly, our estimate of the utility function parameters to fit the third point.

Figure 8-5a shows two of the three constraint lines (feedback functions in operant-choice terms) as solid lines. The point on each line represents the rat's consumption of Tom Collins mix and root beer. We selected the prices and budget for the second constraint so that its line would run through the point marking the rat's allocation under the first constraint. Thus, we changed the prices but left the budget about the same.

The dotted lines of Figure 8-5a show indifference contours tangent to each line at each point. The utility function (Equation 8-1) maximized by the rat appears in the box along with the curves. For the sake of clarity, two constraint lines and two indifference contours are shown instead of the three actually imposed. The first constraint line imposed is the steeper one shown. The shallower line represents

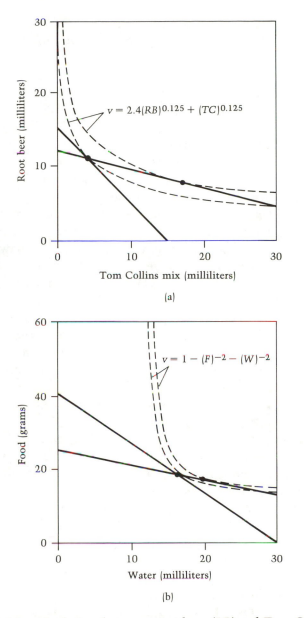

$v = 2.4(RB)^{0.125} + (TC)^{0.125}$

$v = 1 - (F)^{-2} - (W)^{-2}$

(a)

(b)

Figure 8-5 (a) A rat's choices between root beer *(RB)* and Tom Collins mix *(TC)*. (b) Another rat's choices between food *(F)* and water *(W)*.

an increase in the price of root beer relative to Tom Collins mix. The movement of the point down and to the right shows that with the change in prices, the rat purchased less of the more expensive root beer and more of the cheaper Tom Collins mix.

The other constraint imposed (not shown) was a decrease in the price of root beer relative to Tom Collins mix. Under that constraint, the rat purchased more root beer and less Tom Collins mix than with the first constraint. The utility function shown on the figure predicts all three allocations quite precisely. Thus, we were able to derive a set of Tom Collins – root beer indifference contours for this rat indirectly by imposing constraints and measuring choices. A more direct method would have been to give the rat some amount of one good and to ask the rat (by means of imposed constraints) to trade the other good for it — as we imagined with honey and water at the beginning of the chapter. However, such direct methods are difficult even in the laboratory; they would be virtually impossible in the real world.

The second experiment we did was very much like the first except that the new rat subjects were hungry as well as thirsty, and the two goods (rewards) were food (in the form of pellets) and water (delivered by dipper) rather than Tom Collins mix and root beer. We assumed that food and water would be complements rather than the substitutes that the Tom Collins mix and the root beer were. The results confirmed this assumption.

Figure 8-5b shows the results of the food – water experiment. Note that the food – water indifference contours approach right angles much more than do those for Tom Collins mix and root beer. The parameter of the utility function (Equation 8-1) that represents substitutability (s) was closer to 1.0 (perfect substitutability) for the Tom Collins – root beer choice ($s = 0.125$) than for the food – water choice ($s = -2$). The negative substitutability in the food – water case indicates that, as economic goods, food and water are complements rather than substitutes.[8] With Pepsi and Coke, which we assume to be substitutes, the more Pepsi you have, the less Coke you need. However, with bicycle frames and bicycle wheels, which we assume to be complements, the more frames you have, the more wheels you need. Correspondingly, the more Tom Collins the rats bought, the less root beer was worth, whereas the more food they bought, the more water was worth.

Green and I did several other experiments with rats choosing among other commodities and found corresponding results in the sense that maximization with a single set of indifference contours (as given by a single set of parameters of Equation 8-1) described the results. By using a somewhat different equation, children's allocation of time playing with toys could be explained by the same principles (Rachlin and Burkhard, 1978).

MAXIMIZATION AND SCHEDULES OF REINFORCEMENT

Looking at the above experiment in operant-choice terms, the rats were exposed to a pair of concurrent ratio schedules. The constraint lines of Figure 8-5 are the same as the feedback function line labeled "concurrent variable-ratio schedules" in Figure 6-5 except that in Chapter 6 the rewards (goods) obtained from each alternative could be lumped together because they were qualitatively identical ($s = 1.0$). In Figure 6-5 the vertical axis represents the sum of rewards from the two alternatives. An animal that maximized the sum of the two rewards would choose the allocation corresponding to the highest point on the feedback function of Figure 6-5. In that figure, for the feedback function for the concurrent variable-ratio schedules the highest point is the rightmost point. In other words, as we said in Chapter 6, with concurrent ratio schedules of completely substitutable reinforcers, an animal both matches its behavior to obtained value and maximizes total reward when it chooses one alternative exclusively—the one delivering the higher rate of reinforcement (the lower ratio).

In Figure 8-5 it is not possible to lump the now not-completely-substitutable reinforcers together. Instead, the two rewards are separated on the two axes. Maximization here does not correspond to the highest point on the constraint line (which would be the point where the line touches the vertical axis) but to the point where the constraint line touches the highest possible indifference contour. Thus, with concurrent ratio schedules and nonidentical rewards, maximization predicts that animals will not allocate their effort or their time 100 percent to one alternative.

This finding accords with common sense. To see how, let us go back again to your two generous aunts. Remember the analogy: Just as the rat allocates its presses between two levers, you allocate your time between your two aunts. With concurrent ratio schedules, it is as if each aunt thinks about you and buys you presents only when you are with that aunt. (These were the out-of-sight, out-of-mind aunts.) Suppose both aunts bought you only shirts of identical color and style. In other words, suppose the gifts of your two aunts were completely substitutable for each other. Then (again assuming all you cared about were the gifts) you would spend all of your aunt-visiting time with the one who bought you gifts at a higher rate, as we said in Chapter 6. But now suppose one aunt bought you shirts while the other bought you slacks (complementary rather than substitutable presents). Now you would distribute your time between the aunts, going from one to the other according to your needs for shirts and slacks, even though the amount or rate or delay of one aunt's gifts was higher than that of the other.

With concurrent interval schedules of reinforcement, represented in Figure 6-5 by the curved line (your aunts buy you gifts wherever you are but save them for your visits) together with completely substitutable rewards, we said that you would distribute your time between the alternatives proportionally to the rates of the rewards (matching). When the rewards are not completely substitutable (like those considered in this chapter), your distribution would be affected by the substitutability of the rewards. We now address the question of how the substitutability (or lack of it) of the rewards interacts with the schedule of reinforcement (the feedback function) to determine choice.

Let us consider choice to be the allocation of time as we did in Chapter 6 (the rats in the above experiment would be seen as allocating time rather than lever presses to the two levers). With two concurrent operants, we assumed that t_1 and t_2 were the time allocated to each and that T was the sum of t_1 and t_2. Figure 8-6 is just another version of Figure 6-5 but with R_1 and R_2 separated on the two axes. Figure 6-5 shows the sum of R_1 and R_2 as a function of time allocation (t_1 and t_2). Figure 8-6 takes each allocation, determines R_1 and R_2 separately for each allocation (according to Equation 6-5), and plots one amount against the other.

Concurrent variable-time schedules deliver reinforcers from two sources independent of the animal's behavior; no choice is required. With these schedules, the constraint may be represented as a point at the intersection of the two rates of reinforcement. With concurrent ratio schedules, as used in the root beer–Tom Collins and food–water studies just described, the constraint line is straight — the rate of reinforcement from each alternative is directly proportional to the choice of (the allocation of time to) that alternative. The constraints

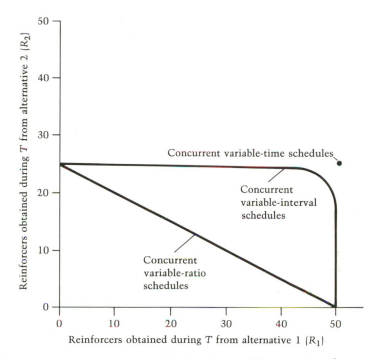

Figure 8-6 Constraints on R_1 and R_2 for three different pairs of concurrent schedules of reinforcement characterized by a power function with different values for its exponents. Points along each line represent various allocations (values of t_1/T).

imposed by concurrent interval schedules lie between those of concurrent ratio and concurrent time schedules corresponding exactly to the feedback functions of Chapter 6. Once the constraint line is determined for a pair of concurrent schedules, the animal's choice is predicted by maximization to be the point where that constraint line touches the highest possible indifference contour. When the reinforcers delivered by each alternative differ in quality (e.g., food versus water), the indifference contours are curved. When the reinforcers delivered by the two alternatives differ only in amount or rate or delay, the indifference contours are straight 45-degree lines. Figure 8-7 shows how two types of constraints interact with two types of indifference contours to determine behavior. The point of maximum value reachable with each constraint is circled in the figure. The circled points represent the predictions by maximization theory of the animal's choice given those constraints.

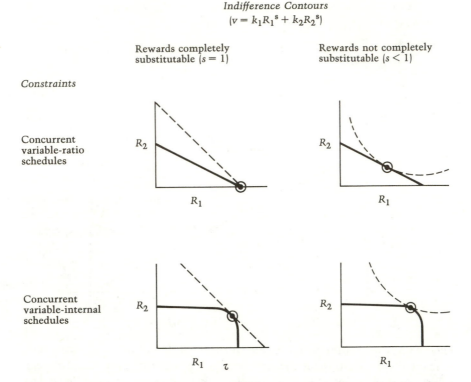

Indifference Contours
$$(v = k_1 R_1{}^s + k_2 R_2{}^s)$$

Rewards completely substitutable ($s = 1$)

Rewards not completely substitutable ($s < 1$)

Constraints

Concurrent variable-ratio schedules

Concurrent variable-internal schedules

Figure 8-7 How two types of concurrent-schedule constraints (solid lines) interact with two types of indifference contours (dotted lines) to determine choice (circled points). Each circled point represents the package of good 1 and good 2 with the highest value given the constraints on choice.

Table 8-1 compares the terminology used in economics with the terminology used in operant-choice experiments. The root beer–Tom Collins mix and food–water experiments just described are really demonstrations that the terminology and theoretical tools of micro economics (a field with relatively undeveloped experimental methodology) is naturally related to the experimental methodology of operant choice (a field with relatively undeveloped theoretical tools). The experiments are not designed to show — and do not show —that rats are just like people or that you can treat people as you might treat other animals.

The above experiments illustrate a relationship between symmetrical choice among rewards in operant experiments and symmetrical

Table 8–1 Comparison of Terminology Used in Operant-Choice
Experiments and in Economics

	Operant Choice (Chapter 6)	Economic Choice (Chapter 8)
Objective contingency	Schedule of reinforcement	Constraint
Positive outcomes Negative outcomes	Rewards (reinforcers) Punishers	Goods }Commodities "Bads" }
Symmetrical choice	Concurrent schedules of reinforcement	Allocation of budget between good 1 at price 1 and good 2 at price 2
Asymmetrical choice	Single schedule of reinforcement	Allocation of time between work and leisure
Subjective choice process	Matching	Maximizing

choice among goods in economics. There is also a relationship between *asymmetrical* choice in operant experiments and the allocation of time between work and leisure in economics, a correspondence noted long ago by Skinner (1953), who compared piecework
wages to ratio schedules of reinforcement.

In Chapter 5, in accordance with Premack's (1965) theory of reinforcement, we modified the original value equation to express the
power of a reinforcer to strengthen a specific response. We subtracted the value of the response from the value of the reinforcer to
obtain net reinforcer value. In economic terms, you could think of
the value of a response as a cost of obtaining the reinforcer. Thus, the
value of the reinforcer alone is like gross economic income, and the
value of the reinforcer minus that of the response is like net economic income. The analogy between animal behavior and the economic concepts of benefit and cost has been made in both animal
ecology (the study of natural animal behavior; see Pyke, Pulliam, and
Charnov, 1977) and operant conditioning (the study of learned, ma-

nipulated, or shaped animal behavior; see Allison, 1983; Collier et al., 1986; Hursh, 1984; Lea, 1978). Whatever we have said about net reinforcement may be extended to net economic cost (and vice versa).

However, you can subtract costs directly from benefits only when the two are conceived as completely substitutable for each other (as when they are both money). When there are various degrees of substitutability between a good and its alternatives, the relation of costs to benefits is not so simple. In the example that opened this chapter (Figure 8-1), if you think of your cups of honey as money and of water as a good, you were paying for water with honey. If, counter to fact, water and honey were completely substitutable for each other, all of your trades would have been net losses (since you lost total amount of drinkable fluid) rather than, as we assumed, exactly even trades.

Cost/benefit analyses generally convert every cost and benefit to monetary terms before comparing them. In the world of commerce, perhaps, such conversions are possible. In the world of natural animal behavior, in laboratory studies of animal behavior, and in much of everyday human activity, conversion of activities to money is awkward at best and often impossible. Therefore we have avoided discussion here of costs and benefits and concentrated directly (more primitively) on trade among goods that may or may not be perfectly substitutable for each other.

The economic analogy has no place for the concept of reinforcement as a strengthening process. Instead of conceiving of a food pellet as reinforcing a bar press (or of an apple as reinforcing the act of picking it), economics conceives of an animal as choosing between a package containing a bar press plus food and another package containing no bar press (therefore offering "leisure") but also no food. It would be like choosing between an apple plus the effort of picking it versus no apple plus, for instance, a snooze under the tree. This admittedly more complex conception has the advantage of encompassing situations where the alternatives to operant emission are not completely substitutable for the rewards obtained through operant emission. This chapter's economic view of choice embraces more aspects of the context of choice than does either a strictly monetary cost/benefit approach or the concept of reinforcement as presented in the previous chapters. We now turn back to an experiment discussed previously where the context of reinforcement was explicitly varied.

Recall the contingencies Baum and I imposed on our subjects in the experiment described in Chapter 5 (Rachlin and Baum, 1972). In that experiment, free food (obtained in the form of a variable-time schedule) was superimposed upon operant-contingent food (from a variable-interval schedule). The superimposition of free goods upon "earned" goods is common in everyday life where welfare or inherited wealth ("free" goods) is superimposed upon a work contingency. More recent experiments with animals (Green, Kagel, and Battalio, 1982) have explicitly examined this relationship and found behavioral effects much like those predicted by economic theory — a decrease in work (emission of the operant) as free food was increased. Interestingly, when animals were relatively satiated (analogously, relatively wealthy) the suppressive effects of free food (analogous to inherited wealth) on operant emission (analogous to work) were greater than they were when animals were relatively hungry (relatively poor).

Figure 8-8 shows how the addition of free food to a ratio schedule reduces responding as the animal adjusts to the new constraints so as to obtain the highest-valued package of the food reward and leisure.[9] Figure 8-8 takes the variable-ratio feedback function of Figure 6-4 and turns the x-axis around so that it indicates leisure $(1 - t/T)$ rather than the rate of operant emission. As before, t is the time spent emitting the operant and T is the duration of the session. This axis reversal converts the feedback function to a constraint line in which a variable-ratio schedule is conceived as offering a trade between amount of food obtained and amount of leisure taken. The more leisure (less operant emission), the less food; the less leisure (more operant emission), the more food. Constraint line XY represents this variable-ratio schedule. Constraint line $X'Y'$ represents the same variable-ratio schedule but with the addition of free food (a variable-time schedule) of an amount represented by the vertical distance X to X' or Y to Y'. The circled points on the lines are the points of highest value, given Equation 8-1b where R_1 is rate of reinforcement but R_2 is replaced by leisure $(L = 1 - t/T)$; the constants were (arbitrarily) set at the following values: $s = \frac{1}{2}$, $k_1 = 2$, and $k_2 = 1$. Thus,

$$v = 2\sqrt{R_1} + \sqrt{L} \qquad (8\text{-}2)$$

Note that the circled point on line $X'Y'$ is to the right of that on line XY, showing an increase in leisure with the addition of the free

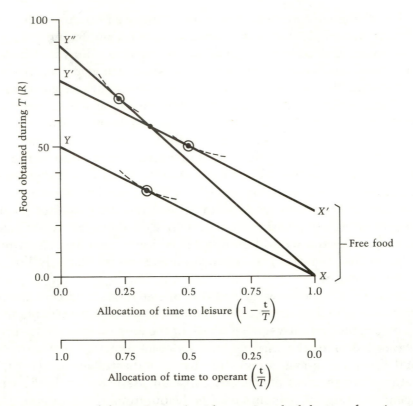

Figure 8-8 Rate of food obtained with a ratio schedule as a function of allocation of time to leisure (line *XY*). The circled point on the line represents the maximum-valued package of food and leisure that can be obtained according to Equation 8-2. Line *X'Y'* represents the addition of free food; line *XY"* represents a ratio schedule (with no free food) that delivers the same rate of food as the original schedule at the optimum rate of response plus the food delivered freely. The uncircled point on line *X'Y'* (where it intersects line *XY"*) is directly above the circled point on line *XY*; it shows the food that would have been obtained had the animal kept emitting operants at the same rate with free food as it did without free food. Line *XY"* through that point is the constraint line of a new ratio schedule that would have delivered the same increment in food as the free food did had the animal kept emitting operants at the original rate. The circled point on line *XY"* is the point of highest value (as determined from Equation 8-2) on that line. Note that this point is to the left of

that on line XY. Thus, not surprisingly, economic theory predicts an increase in operant emission (decreased leisure) when the extra food is made contingent on operant emission, whereas a decrease in operant emission (increased leisure) is predicted when extra food is provided freely. By analogy (and neglecting many other real-world factors, parameters, and value functions that could prevail) an employer who wants a worker to work more hours (to decrease his or her leisure) should raise the worker's hourly salary (going from XY to XY″ and thereby decreasing leisure) rather than give him or her a lump sum bonus (going from XY to X′Y′ and thereby increasing leisure).

The straight lines of Figure 8-8 show (with ratio schedules) the operation of the same economic principles that caused the decrease in responding in my experiment with Baum, in which interval rather than ratio schedules of reinforcement were used. In Figure 5-4 (going from left to right along the x-axis), pigeons obtained extra reinforcers via increases in the maximum rate of reinforcement obtainable with the variable-interval schedule — the extra reinforcers were contingent on their behavior; in Figure 5-5, pigeons obtained extra reinforcers freely, not contingent on their behavior. In the former case, their rate of operant emission increased; in the latter case, it decreased — as you would predict based on an analogy to the ratio schedule example of Figure 8-8.

MAXIMIZATION AND MATCHING

The core of any behavioral choice theory is some subjective process by which the whole organism interacts with the world. The subjective process discussed in Chapter 6 was matching, and in this chapter it is maximizing (see Table 8-1). The relation between these two processes is currently a matter of much debate (Commons et al., 1987). Some say that matching is fundamental — that maximization occurs only when it conforms to matching. Others say that maximization is fundamental — that matching occurs only when it conforms to maximization. The reason that the debate is currently unsettled is because in most cases matching and maximization make the same (correct) predictions of an animal's choices among alternatives.

Consider the simple cases of concurrent interval schedules, illustrated in the lower pair of graphs in Figure 8-7, or concurrent ratio schedules, illustrated in the upper pair of graphs. Suppose R_1 and R_2

are identical reinforcers ($s = 1.0$) differing only in rate. The utility contours (dotted lines) drawn in the left pair of graphs of that figure represent perfectly substitutable alternatives ($v = R_1 + R_2$). With both concurrent ratio schedules (upper graphs) and perfectly substitutable alternatives (left side), the highest reachable contour is at a corner of the constraint line, representing complete allocation to the higher-rate alternative (as in the upper left graph). Thus maximization, like matching (Chapter 6), predicts all-or-none choice of the ratio schedule delivering the higher rate of reinforcement. With concurrent interval schedules, both matching and maximization predict an allocation, not all-or-none, between the alternatives as in the lower left graph. In fact, both theories predict the exact same allocation. Given the general form of the feedback functions (power functions) that we assumed to apply and the general form of the utility equation (also a power function), it can be mathematically shown that any animal that maximizes value will also obey the matching law (Rachlin, 1978).

The exponent of the matching equation (s_R or s_A in Equation 6-7) is the same exponent that measures substitutability (s). Thus, economic theory provides a meaning for the exponent of the generalized matching equation. When the alternative reinforcers are completely substitutable, the matching exponent is 1.0. As the reinforcers grow less substitutable, the matching exponent decreases until, for complements, the matching exponent is negative. With a negative exponent, the higher the rate of reinforcement provided by an alternative, the less that alternative is chosen—a sort of antimatching. Antimatching makes sense for complements. If you were putting bicycles together and you got your frames randomly from one source at a low rate and your pairs of wheels randomly from another source at a high rate, you would have to spend much more time at the lower-rate frame source than at the higher-rate pair-of-wheel source so that you could get an equal number of each. On the other hand, with near substitutes like Coke and Pepsi, you would spend more time at the source that provided the higher reward rate; how much more time would depend on the schedule.

Despite the fact that matching and maximizing predict the same behavior in many situations, the question remains whether there are any situations at all in which matching and maximizing predict different behavior. If so, then those situations could be studied to see which subjective choice process was the true one. One situation, which we have discussed extensively in this chapter, is the choice between nonsubstitutable reinforcers. Matching by itself does not say why the relationship between behavior and value should change so drastically (from matching to antimatching) as the similarity (substitutability) between reinforcers varies. Maximization, however, does explain this shift in terms of a fundamental interaction of the environment and behavior.

If we identify maximization with rationality, then an animal that matches would be (to the extent that matching differs from maximization) behaving less than rationally, or subrationally. In Simon's (1978) terms, the animal would be "satisficing." For instance, people like myself who rarely bother to count their change except by a quick glance are in a sense satisficing. Sometimes we will lose money. However, in another sense our behavior may be rationalized. We rely on people who do count change to keep store clerks honest and we save time and mental effort. Just as satisficing may be rationalized by viewing it as the rational thing to do given limited time and limited information, so matching may be rationalized by a similar tactic. Matching may be seen as a form of maximization given a limited view of the future. As future events are discounted more and more, matching and maximizing converge to a single process. The question of whether matching or maximizing is the fundamental process is thus pragmatically pointless, like the question of whether people behave rationally or not and like William James's question of whether one squirrel chasing another around a tree goes around the other squirrel or not. The answers depend on what you mean by "maximization," "rationality," and "going around." If "maximization" refers to maximization over a wide temporal interval (large T), then animals do not always maximize. (If "rationality" refers to scientific reasoning, then people are rarely rational.) However, if "maximization" means that there will always be some value function and some interval over which that function is maximized, then maximization cannot be wrong (although it may prove to be not as useful as some other method for predicting behavior).

ECONOMICS AND SELF-CONTROL

It takes about five years between the conception and completion of a large commercial building in New York City. Suppose that during the fourth year, when the frame of the building is already up, the costs of completion suddenly escalate and the real estate market collapses. Should the building be abandoned?

During her fourth year of medical school, a student decides that medicine is not for her; she prefers to study Sanskrit. Should she finish medical school?

On a much more immediate level, I am driving around my neighborhood late on a Saturday night looking for a parking space. I drive for 20 minutes, 30 minutes, 45 minutes. Should I give up and park in an expensive garage ($18 overnight)?

All of these problems relate to the economic concept of "sunk costs." You have already invested so much, should you invest more? There are two ways of looking at each of these decisions: from the point of view of the immediate consequences of an act and from the point of view of the project as a whole.

At any moment while parking my car, it is certainly worth going around the block just one more time rather than paying the $18. Then again, given the random nature of parking space openings, I might occasionally have to drive around all night. I cope with this problem by taking the long-term view. I have a general rule that if I do not find a space after two circles around the block, I park in a garage. As a result I park in a garage about three or four times a year. The high cost of the garage is spread (subjectively) across the whole year; it is not confined to one evening. Although, as I write it, my strategy (two times around the block and then into the garage) seems reasonable and obvious, it took me years of anguished searching for a parking place before I adopted it. Even now I find it extremely hard to put into effect. I hate to spend the $18 to park overnight when there might well be a free space just around the corner.

The sunk cost problem is a self-control problem (Northcraft and Wolf, 1984). In businesses, the conflict between the short-term and long-term points of view that causes me so much anguish when I park my car is often personified in a conflict between the comptroller, concerned with this year's cash flow, and the president, concerned with the long-term image of the firm. (A corresponding long-term role might be taken by the medical student's parents.) To abandon a building, no matter how sensible in the short run, might be bad for the firm in the long run. Many businesses keep money-losing "flagship" operations going in a major city for the sake of the firm's image, not valuable in itself but possibly translatable into stability of profits in the long run.

Figure 8-9 shows two alternatives. Let us assume for the moment that choosing either alternative commits you to the illustrated sequence of values for the duration T. Choosing the upper alternative maximizes value over a relatively brief period (t), while choosing the lower alternative maximizes value over the entire interval (T). Either choice would be maximization in some sense, and neither is, on the face of it, the correct choice. Even a laboratory experiment might be terminated prematurely for some reason, and in everyday life natural events of various kinds (death being the most salient) may prematurely terminate a nominally fixed sequence of events. In some circumstances it may be possible to choose the upper branch and then change your mind later and switch to the lower one (like Faust), thus both having your cake and eating it. My driving around and around

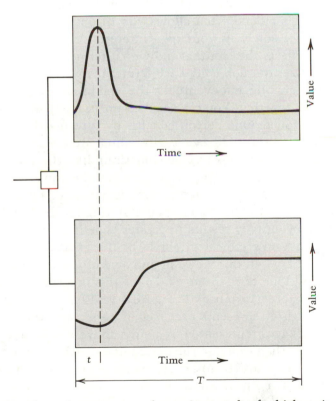

Figure 8-9 Choice between two alternatives, each of which varies in value over time.

the block endlessly looking for a parking space might be seen as a sort of trap induced by my narrow vision of the moment, while my overall rule of going around the block twice and then pulling into a garage might be seen as the product of a wider, more abstract vision that embraces a series of parking episodes.

Social situations often present a related form of self-control problem. The pattern of attained values in the upper part of Figure 8-9 may be viewed as the outcome of a narrow vision of individual choice, while the pattern of values attained in the lower part of the figure is viewed as the outcome of a wider vision of individual choice. If we regard as a problem of self-control any sort of choice between outcomes like those shown in Figure 8-9, then many social interactions are also self-control situations. The sort of social situation that creates such patterns of alternatives has been long known and given many names (including "tragedy of the commons," "prisoner's dilemma," and "social trap"). The general idea is that cooperation with other people often allows you to obtain greater benefits than if you act solely in your own interests. The "tragedy of the commons" reflects the fact that individual farmers tend to let their cattle overgraze common land. Each farmer reaps individual benefits from the overgrazing, but eventually the land becomes barren and all farmers suffer together. You can see the same tragedy in the street in front of my house. One person benefits by littering the street, but when everyone litters, all eventually suffer alike. Overgrazing or littering yields a pattern of value something like the upper one of Figure 8-9, while social cooperation yields the lower one. Here, narrowness or breadth of vision in time is paralleled by narrowness or breadth of vision in the social sphere. Acting for the benefit of the larger group eventually results in greater benefit for the individual.

Jeremy Bentham's ethical principle of the greatest good for the greatest number is, in this view, an outcome of individuals acting in their own best long-term interests. To see this in terms of the principles of this chapter, turn back to Figure 8-1a. Remember, the dotted line in that figure represents packages of honey and water of equal value. All packages represented by points above that dotted line are of higher value than those on the dotted line. Now suppose that two people meet, one with 10 cups of honey (at point A) and one with 10 cups of water (at point H). Both are on the dotted indifference contour (at either end of it). If the people traded with each other, cup for cup, they would move to points along the solid line connecting A and H. All points on the solid line (except A and H) are above the dotted line. Thus, any trade at all (1 cup for 1 cup, 2 for 2, 5 for 5, etc.) would benefit both parties — both would have a package of honey and water worth more to each of them than the package with which they started out. The problem is that any trade takes a certain amount of time. There will be an interval between giving up what you have and getting what you are trading it for. During that brief period it is possible for one party of a trade to keep both shares and the other party to have neither. In our everyday commercial intercourse we bridge that gap many times. In the supermarket we pay our money, get our groceries, and collect our change, perhaps not realizing the degree of trust that such interactions routinely involve.

In an experiment in my laboratory with pigeons, I gave one pigeon complete control of water and another pigeon (in another Skinner box separate from the first) complete control of food. By pecking a key, either pigeon could give up some of its commodity to the other. I hoped that the pigeons would eventually come to trade with each other, but the experiment was, in a sense, a failure. One pigeon would briefly give up a little of its commodity, but the other rarely reciprocated and the trade broke down. This lack of self-control should not have surprised me. Results with people playing a game called the prisoner's dilemma should have led me to suspect that pigeons would do no better.

In the prisoner's dilemma game, two players each have a choice between two responses, A and B. In the most common version, if both players choose A, both get medium rewards. If one chooses A and one chooses B, the player who chooses A is penalized while the one who chooses B is given a high reward. Finally, if both players choose B, both get small rewards. This game presents the players with a dilemma because the optimal strategy for each player individually differs from the optimal strategy for both players as a group.

To be more specific, let us call the players Jason and Melissa. If Jason and Melissa both choose A, each gets $10. If both choose B, each gets $5, but if either chooses B while the other chooses A, the one who chooses B gets $40 while the one who chooses A gets nothing. Now consider the game from Jason's point of view. If Melissa happens to choose A, Jason should choose B because he would then get $40 rather than $10. If, on the other hand, Melissa happens to choose B, Jason should also choose B because he would then get $5 rather than nothing. Either way, it seems, Jason should choose B. Of course, the same considerations govern Melissa's choices as a rational individual. Thus, the rational choice for each individual is B, where each gets $5. Yet considering Jason and Melissa as a group, they should both choose A, where each gets $10.

For the optimal group strategy to work, each player must count on the other to behave for the good of both players. Here is a case where the truly optimal pattern of behavior emerges only when the group is considered as a whole and fails to emerge when the individual is considered.

The prisoner's dilemma gets its name from a negative version of the problem in which there is insufficient evidence to convict either of two prisoners (Christopher and Tiffany) of a major crime (say, drug dealing) but enough to convict them both of a minor crime (say, possession). However, if Christopher confesses to drug dealing and implicates Tiffany and she refuses to confess, he will go free while she will be convicted and probably be given the maximum sentence. The same is true for her. Finally, if both confess, both will get stiff (but not maximum) sentences. With this negative scenario, the best individual strategy is to confess, but the best group strategy (considering Christopher and Tiffany, not society as a whole, as the group) is for both to hold out and not confess.

The moral and political significance of this kind of game is fairly obvious. Individual nations in an arms race are faced with a form of it. Let us agree that the best strategy for the group of nations is multilateral disarmament. The problem is that multilateral disarmament can be accomplished only if each nation engages in unilateral disarmament. But if one nation unilaterally disarms while the others do not, the penalty for that nation may be severe. As a result, no nation disarms. The behavior of people in laboratory studies of the prisoner's dilemma is not much different from the actual behavior of nations. Most people in most versions of the game choose rationally as individuals and consequently fail to adopt the best group strategy.

The outlook for the future of humanity is not, however, completely bleak. When the prisoner's dilemma game is played repeatedly by a pair of players, optimal group behavior sometimes does emerge (Rapoport and Chammah, 1965). In the version played by Jason and Melissa, for instance, the best strategy over a series of games would be alternation, where on every other trial Jason chooses A ($0) while Melissa chooses B ($40) and on alternate trials they reverse. The players would thereby win an average of $20 per trial (instead of $10 if they both chose A or $5 if they both chose B). In experiments with repeated prisoner's dilemma games, optimal patterns sometimes do emerge eventually. However, when the players are told that a fixed number of games will be played, the optimal pattern often breaks up toward the end. Suppose in the very last game it is Jason's turn to choose A and win $0. Since it is the very last game, Jason might defect from the cooperative pattern at that point and choose B, thereby winning $5 in that game instead of $0 (and giving Melissa a mere $5 instead of $40). This in itself would not be disastrous except that if Melissa suspects that Jason might do this, she could defect at the next-to-last game. Similarly, Jason might anticipate Melissa's anticipation of his own defection, and so on back down the line.

Cooperation in the laboratory version of the prisoner's dilemma game is evidently an unstable strategy. One cause of instability might lie in the unspecified framing of the problem, which could lead to a misunderstanding of value (as discussed in Chapter 3). The rewards (usually monetary) specified by the experimenter may not exhaust all possible rewards in the experimental context. For instance, cooperation may emerge if Jason and Melissa each have (or develop) an interest in the other's well-being or an interest in forcing the experimenter to part with as much money as possible regardless of who it goes to. Another possibility is that a cooperative pattern of behavior could be rewarding in itself. The problem is that truly rational behavior does not depend on just knowledge of the rules of the game, but rather on knowledge of psychology — of the behavior of others and of one's own behavior under various circumstances. No matter how clear and straightforward the rules may be, psychology, unfortunately, remains all too murky. Interestingly, the best method of inducing cooperation in people is similar to one that often succeeds with animals. The more the people get to know each other before playing the game, the better the chances are of their cooperating. In the case of animals, the key seems to be prolonged visual contact. Pigeons (Lubinski and MacCorquodale, 1984) and monkeys (Savage-Rumbaugh, Rumbaugh, and Boysen, 1978) will cooperate with each other when they can exchange signals. Lubinski and Mac-Corquodale found that when one pigeon was slow to cooperate (by pecking a key that eventually provided food for both pigeons), the other would begin pecking the glass partition between them, sort of nagging the uncooperative pigeon to get going. Savage-Rumbaugh and colleagues trained one monkey to "ask" another for a tool that the first needed in order to obtain food. Once the food was obtained, the first monkey would reward the second with part of the food. Of course, to say that visual contact seems to be necessary for cooperation is to say that we have not yet analyzed the molecular components of the signals exchanged.

HILL-CLIMBING MECHANISMS

Maximization, however brief the period over which it occurs, is still a program for behavioral observation and prediction rather than a mechanism. A molar behavioral theory need not speculate about how maximization is accomplished. However, mechanisms for maximization have been proposed, and it may be worthwhile to speculate briefly about what they must accomplish. Essentially the job of such mechanisms is to take past events and use them to determine choice among future events. Think of the value space in which indifference contours are drawn as a hill with the highest contours on top of the hill. The animal is conceived of as starting from some point on the hill. If nature has designed the animal's internal choice mechanism wisely, the animal will move up the hill and end up on top—the point of highest attainable value given the constraints on its choices.

The context in which hill-climbing mechanisms have been investigated most thoroughly is that of evolution—how do animals change from generation to generation so as to fit better and better into their ecological niche (Sober, 1984). Here we are concerned with how an animal alters its behavior within its own lifetime so as to obtain the combination of highest possible value.

Perhaps the most obvious of hill-climbing mechanisms would be one that just senses the slope of the hill at the very point where the animal is, moves the animal upward on the hill, and stops where the slope is zero. But an animal possessing such a mechanism would fall into the most blatant of social traps. An animal climbing a real hill by using such a mechanism would stop on the top of the first bump or the first rock it encountered. It would be unable to go down even the slightest amount in order to go up further. To press a lever and get a reward immediately afterward, a rat must "trust" the world for at least a few fractions of a second—between the time that it begins the sequence of muscular movements that lead to a lever press and the time that the reward occurs. Similarly, you have to trust the supermarket clerk between the time you hand him the $20 bill and the time he gives you your groceries and change (if any). No actual hill-climbing mechanism could be so narrowly focused. Even the mechanisms of respondent and operant conditioning initially proposed by Pavlov and Thorndike and developed by Skinner, molecular as they are, can bridge small gaps.

Since a mechanism that senses the slope of the hill at a point is too molecular to be practical, let us consider two hill-climbing mechanisms that sense slope over intervals of time wider than an instant. The two mechanisms are just more molecular versions of the molar processes of maximization and matching. A molecular version of maximization simply shrinks the period T over which maximization is said to occur. Initially the animal would just vary its behavior along any dimension that instinct or resemblance to previous situations might suggest. In evolution the principles of variation are given by genetics. Over an individual's lifetime, the principles of variation might be biologically programmed (instinctive) or socially determined. As behavior varied, value might vary. Patterns of behavior of higher value would be retained, while those of lower value would drop out. The critical element here is the period T over which value would be calculated. As T grows larger and larger, more complex patterns might emerge and higher values might be attained.

In a symmetrical choice situation (such as that imposed by a pair of concurrent schedules of reinforcement), the value of the two alternatives together with the value of the implied third alternative — doing nothing, or leisure — are added over T and behavior is adjusted. If the adjustment results in a greater total value during T, the behavior pattern is further adjusted along the same dimension until total value stops increasing. That is the top of the hill. An animal's ability to avoid traps (being stranded on top of a mere bump) depends on the magnitude of temporal integration (T). For speculation about the nature of such mechanisms, see Houston and McFarland (1980), Sibly and McFarland (1976), and Staddon (1980).

Another kind of hill-climbing mechanism that has been proposed is essentially a molecular version of matching. This mechanism, called *melioration* (Herrnstein and Vaughan, 1980), assumes that on the basis of instinct or past experience, an animal initially divides a situation into a series of choice alternatives and allocates some proportion of time and effort to each alternative during a period T. Then the animal calculates the value of each alternative separately and chooses the highest one. The difference between melioration and molecular maximizing lies in the separateness of the alternatives. In a symmetrical choice situation, a meliorating animal experimentally allocates time (fractions of T) to the two alternatives (plus the third implicit one) as it does in molecular maximization. However, instead of being added, each value is assigned to the activity during which it was obtained; the animal calculates v_1/t_1, v_2/t_2, and v_3/t_3, and then allocates its time during the next interval so that $v_1/t_1 = v_2/t_2 = v_3/t_3$. Ignoring leisure, this implies matching during T: that is, $t_1/t_2 = v_1/v_2$. As with maximization, an animal's ability to avoid traps depends on T, the duration over which values are first integrated and then compared.[11]

Melioration (molecular matching) and molecular maximization, like their molar versions, are both flexible enough to explain all of the available data. Melioration is simpler in the sense that behavioral allocations are outcomes of a more immediate process. An animal that meliorates need worry only about the value of what it is doing now versus the value of what it might do. Melioration allows value to be integrated into a behavioral pattern over periods smaller than T while still (usually) avoiding bumps in the hill narrower than T. For instance, a monkey choosing between climbing one tree or another to get bananas might find it simpler to meliorate than maximize because it could easily identify the trees and climb the better (more fruitful?) one.

On the other hand, maximization is simpler in the sense that the animal need not worry about which reward goes with which particular alternative. This is a great advantage when (as is usual in new situations) the alternatives are not clearly defined. For instance, a cow grazing in a new pasture might find it simpler to maximize than meliorate because it would be difficult to divide the pasture into discrete areas each with its own value. The cow might more easily evolve a pattern of grazing that it liked best.

Experimental tests of melioration (molecular matching) versus molecular maximization are difficult (perhaps impossible) to devise because, as with the molar versions of these views of choice, both frequently predict the same patterns. Where they differ and one seems to be supported, the other may explain the results by redefining the effective alternatives, recalculating value, or reestimating T. The essential test between the two views is more likely to come from their relative usefulness when applied to real-world human problems (from "behavioral engineering") than from any single crucial experiment.[12]

N O T E S

1. The worth of money considered in Chapter 4 may be thought of in relative terms as the worth of money (and what money can buy) versus everything else — all the goods that money cannot buy. As you get more and more money, additional purchasable goods are worth less and less relative to goods not attainable by money.

2. If purchasable goods were completely substitutable for free goods, the exponent s of the value function (Equation 4-1) of Chapter 4 would have been 1.0. The fact that this exponent is often found to be much less than 1.0 (usually around 0.5) confirms the notion (usually considered a romantic one) that there are some things money just can't buy.

3. This assumes that probabilities and delays are equal across alternatives. When the probability or delay of one alternative differs from that of another, the differing parameter must be taken into account, along with amount, when predicting choice. As we will see later in this chapter, the matching law, which takes delay into account in a simple way, is consistent with Equation 8-1. Therefore, delay is easily accounted for. As we will see in Chapter 10, probability may be accounted for when delay is accounted for.

4. However, changes in the price of both goods together could leave the constraint's slope constant and change just its height. For instance, starting with constraint XY, if the price of honey was doubled to $2 per cup while the price of water was doubled to 50¢ per cup and your budget remained at $5, the constraint would move to X'Y', exactly as if the prices had remained the same and your budget had been halved. Thus, for economists, a real price change is a relative price change (one that alters the slope of the constraint). A proportionate change in all prices together is not a price change at all but a budget change.

5. The same must have been true for the Greek language. As Plato put it (*Protagoras*, 358c): "No one ever willingly goes to meet evil."

6. According to Stigler and Becker (1977), the opposite set of circumstances — an elastic demand (many available substitutes) and sensitization (a decrease in price with more and more consumption) — can create another kind of addiction that they call a "positive"

addiction (as opposed to the "negative" addictions discussed in the text). For instance, the demand for the aesthetic pleasure of listening to music may be elastic (in the sense that there are many available substitutes for that particular pleasure), and at the same time the more you listen to a certain kind of music, the more you appreciate it — so a given amount of pleasure is attained from less and less time spent listening. That is, the real price of pleasure from music decreases with consumption. The combination of cheaper real price and elastic demand causes more and more consumption. However, positive addictions are not harmful because if consumption is extrinsically curtailed, demand is reduced, whereas just the opposite happens with negative addictions.

7.   The success of such organizations as Alcoholics Anonymous may be due to the substitution of social rewards for the addictive substance in satisfying this basic need. Presumably satisfaction derived from the more natural social rewards does not habituate, or at least it habituates more slowly than that from the addictive substance. Biological differences in the tendency to become an addict of a particular kind (say, an alcoholic) may thus rest on biological differences in habituation (or sensitization) to the addictive substance.

8.   The utility function for complements is written as $1 - k_1(A_1)^s - k_2(A_2)^s$ because of the negative exponent. (Economists have more sophisticated ways of expressing the exponent and coefficients so that the equation does not have to be changed for analyzing complements.)

9.   Here, instead of subtracting the value of work (the operant) from the value of the reinforcer (as we did in Chapter 5), the value of leisure (the inverse of work) is added to that of the reinforcer. A complete description of behavior would take into account the values of all three activities: (1) consuming the reinforcer, (2) emitting the operant, and (3) leisure (not emitting the operant). We cannot consider such complex cases here.

10.   Since the publication of the epoch-making book of von Neumann and Morgenstern (1944), interest in the mathematical and logical properties of games such as the prisoner's dilemma (and many others) has blossomed. Although this sort of understanding is necessary, it has developed separately from psychological understanding. As a result, after almost half a century, we still await successful application of the theory of games to important human problems.

11. Melioration assumes that an animal somehow calculates an overall value for each alternative by integrating delays between a series of individual choices and reinforcers. A still more molecular theory would be necessary to explain how this is done. In a molecular cognitive theory proposed by Gibbon (1977), called scalar expectancy theory or SET, each experienced delay (between choice and reinforcement) is represented internally not as an individual interval but as a statistical distribution of intervals with a mean equal to the experienced interval and a variance proportional to the mean. In making a choice, SET assumes, the animal selects an interval randomly from each alternative distribution and chooses the smallest one (the shortest delay). Thus an animal's choices depend on the degree of overlap of the distributions corresponding to each alternative. SET has been successful in explaining choices between concurrent schedules of fixed and variable intervals, but less so in distinguishing between behavior with various contingencies of reinforcement. Integration of SET with melioration (not yet accomplished) promises both to explain choices among fixed and variable schedules (which melioration does not currently do) as well as to account for the different molar effects of various contingencies (which SET does not currently do).

12. This chapter restricts itself to a discussion of demand theory economics and choice. For comprehensive treatment of the relationship of economics as a whole to psychology as a whole, see Lea, Tarpy, and Webley (1987).

RATIONAL THOUGHT

AT THE VERY BEGINNING of Chapter 1, rationality was used as an example of a concept that raises questions for theories of judgment, decision, and choice (How do we know when something said or done is rational?). Now we again take up the concept of rationality, not to answer the questions it raises but to discover what sort of answers are possible.

As we have seen, the concept of rational thought is varied and complex. We cannot discuss it without first reviewing its history. Therefore, this chapter reconsiders the historical and philosophical material of Chapter 1 in light of the material presented so far. The intervening chapters presented current research from the perspective of its history; this chapter presents history from the perspective of current research.

ACTIONS AND PASSIONS

Descartes's concept of actions and passions of the soul originated in Aristotle's conception of actions and passions as two categories of movement. According to Aristotle, actions are governed by the rational aspect of the soul and are therefore unique to humans. The process of actions is as follows. In the world, an object, consisting of a certain substance in a certain form, transmits its form through the air or another medium (making an impression much as a signet ring makes an impression of its form on wax) to one or more of a person's sense organs. The form of the object combines in the person's imagination with other forms from memory. The combined images are reflected upon by thought and the person engages in thoughtful (i.e., rational) behavior. Figure 9-1a diagrams the process.

Aristotle's mechanism for action may be understood as a kind of decision theory with "Imagination" and "Memory" standing for representation while "Rational thought" stands for the decision mechanism. When Aristotle developed the laws of deductive logic, he believed that he was merely describing rational thought. So when Gestalt psychologists claimed that the laws of logic are the laws of thought, they were (as they knew) echoing Aristotle.

Aristotle believed that animals other than humans are not capable of rational thought. However, because all animals (including humans) have sensitive souls, all are capable of a different kind of movement — passions. Aristotle's concept of passions differed from modern notions in the sense that passions, for him, are movements — they cannot boil up inside. For him, a man cannot just feel passionate, he has to be passionate. Nevertheless, Aristotle's concept of passions is like the modern concept in the sense that he thought passionate movement to be out of rational control.

The bottom of Figure 9-1 shows how Aristotle supposed passionate movement to work. Again an object in the world transfers its form through a medium to a sense organ and into a person's body. When the form of an object enters the body, it interacts with the soul. Aristotle conceived of the soul as a kind of organization; therefore we can say that the form of the object comes into contact with the body's organization (not the more complex organization of the rational soul possessed only by humans, but a subcategory of that organization, the sensible soul, possessed by all animals).

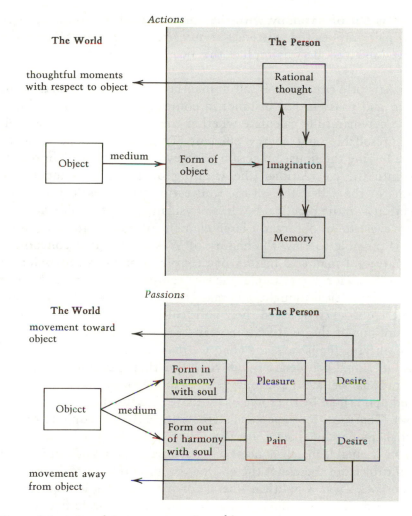

Figure 9-1 Aristotle's two categories of human movement.

At that point the form of the object can be in harmony with the form of the soul or out of harmony with the form of the soul (much as a square peg is in harmony with a square hole and a round peg with a round hole): If its form is in harmony with an animal's soul, the object causes pleasure. Pleasure in turn implies the existence of a desire to move towards the object, and the desire implies the occurrence of the movement itself. If, on the other hand, the form of the object is out of harmony with the animal's soul, the object causes pain; pain implies the existence of a desire to move away from the object, and the desire implies the occurrence of the movement itself.[1]

As Aristotle conceived it, all human behavior is some mixture of action and passion. For instance, a contemporary family buying a house may carefully calculate whether the house is affordable, well built, resellable, and energy efficient. These calculations seem to make buying the house an action. However, the information that is put into the calculations (the wording of an advertisement, the claims of the seller, the off-the-wall estimates of resale value, the rejection of more practical but less physically attractive alternatives) may reveal to an observer a large element of passionate behavior.

It is possible to view the history of Western thought concerning the nature of man as a history of the role of action and passion in human behavior. For example, the two seminal figures in the history of British political thought, Thomas Hobbes (1588–1679) and John Locke (1632–1704), based their political theories on two opposing conceptions of the relative importance of actions and passions.

Simplifying the issue somewhat, we may say that Hobbes believed that individual people are ruled wholly by their passions. Therefore any rational behavior (actions) they exhibit would have to be imposed upon them by the force of the state (presumably for their own good). That position was consistent with Hobbes's support of the English monarchy. Locke, on the other hand, believed that every person is capable of self-control (i.e., rational action) and not in need of control from the state, the church, or any other outside agency. Thus, Locke was a political liberal for his time; his ideas strongly influenced Thomas Jefferson and the other founding fathers of the United States.

Locke, like Hobbes, was an empiricist; both believed that all our ideas arise from individual experience—from our contact, through life, with objects in our environment. They differed, however, in their conceptions of how that experience is processed. For Hobbes, ideas are connected in our minds by random environmental coincidences, and behavior is ruled by immediate pleasures and pains (unless overcome by the state). For Locke, ideas are processed logically and behavior controlled by rational thought (unless overcome by random environmental coincidences).

Both modern cognitive decision theory and modern behavioral choice theory recognize that behavior is a mixture of action (or whatever in the theory corresponds to action) and passion (or whatever in the theory corresponds to passion).[2]

DECISION THEORIES

In the middle of the seventeenth century, the French mathematicians Blaise Pascal (1623 – 1662) and Pierre de Fermat (1601 – 1665) began a correspondence over the analysis of gambling problems that was to develop into the foundations for the calculus of probability. The two mathematicians were first interested in how to divide the stakes of a gamble fairly when it was not certain who would win but when one player was more likely to win than another. For instance, suppose a coin is being flipped; one player gets a point each time the coin comes up heads, the other player gets a point each time the coin comes up tails. The first player to get 3 points wins. But the game is suddenly stopped (a police raid?) at a point when the first player has gotten 2 points and the other has gotten 1 point. How should the stakes (64 pistoles in this case) be divided? Pascal solved the problem by first calculating each player's probability of winning all the stakes and then dividing them proportionately, 48 pistoles for the player with 2 points and 16 pistoles for the player with 1 point (who would need to get tails twice in a row, $p = \frac{1}{4}$, to win).

Pascal and Fermat's probabilities could be (and are) used by gaming establishments to decide among various possible courses of action: What odds should a casino pay for a given bet at roulette or craps or blackjack to be certain of making a profit in the long run? How much cash does a casino of a certain size need to keep on hand? Should there be a limit on bets and if so, what should it be? Such questions are normative ones. They deal with how people (casino owners in this case) should make decisions given certain long-term goals, not how they actually do make decisions.

Because gamblers found normative decision theories so useful and reliable, corresponding normative theoretical principles soon began to be applied to decisions not so obviously related to gambling — decisions of businesses and of nations as well as of individual people in their everyday lives.

This last branch of decision theory, its application to decisions of people in their daily lives, brought it into contact with psychology. However, as soon as you begin to examine how people make decisions in their everyday lives, one fact becomes obvious: We do not always (in fact, we rarely) make the best possible decisions given our long-term goals (or at least given what we claim our long-term goals to be). Businesses and governments, with all their information-gathering resources, their economists, and their computers, apparently do not do such a good job either.

In recent years, businessmen, economists, and politicians — as well as psychologists — have come to believe that an adequate normative theory of decision making (How should people make decisions?) must be preceded or at least accompanied by an adequate descriptive theory of decision making (How do people actually make decisions?). Cognitive decision theories are attempts to answer this latter question.

Let us now review some of the basic assumptions underlying cognitive decision theories. These assumptions are the same as those of cognitive psychology in general, but we will discuss them in the context of decision theory, which comprises only a part of modern cognitive psychology (some other parts are memory, imagery, problem solving, perception, and thinking).

According to modern cognitive decision theory, a decision involves the following process. First, there exists in the world a situation in which choices can be made. This situation is conceived as very complex, containing a set of choice alternatives (at least two and possibly more), each of which involves a set of outcomes (gains or losses of various kinds and degrees). The choice alternatives, in turn, are imbedded in a context or frame. The context may be conceived in very broad terms (the amount of money a person has in the bank, the laws of the state in which the decision is made, the weather) or relatively narrow terms (the words in which a decision problem is couched, the tone of voice in which it is presented, the response required).

Second, a person is faced with the situation. As we have seen, the interior of the person is the locus of the decision theorist's interest, since that is where the decision process is supposed to occur. A good decision theory is one that adequately explains this internal process. Different theories have different conceptions of what the process entails and how it works, but the following elements are common to all cognitive decision theories. Initially the person perceives the situation. The product of this perception is an internal representation. At this stage, objective properties of the situation (let us call them objective presentations) are converted to subjective properties of the person (subjective representations). For instance, there is an objective prize in a lottery (a million dollars, say) and an objective probability of winning (given by the mathematics of probability). One decision theory might say that the person converts the prize (influenced by its context) into a subjective prize value and the probability (influenced by its context) into a subjective probability. The two together constitute internal representations of the presented lottery alternatives (to bet or not to bet). Another decision theory might say that the lottery is perceived as a unit that cannot be analyzed into subjective probability and subjective prize value. In either case, the initial object of a decision theory is to explain how a person converts an objective, external presentation to a subjective, internal representation.

The third part of the decision process is the decision itself. Here the representations of the alternatives are compared. Different decision theories differ on the nature of the decision mechanism — how many subelements it contains, how each works, how they interact. A decision theory may assert that the decision mechanism operates according to perfectly normative principles, like a computer programmed with a set of logical rules. According to such theories, people actually make bad (nonnormative) decisions because of differences between objective presentations and subjective representations of the alternatives, not because of a faulty decision mechanism. It has been argued that people's decision processes work exactly according to the principles of deductive logic. (The other side of the coin is that logical principles are nothing but reflections of ordinary thought.) The logical errors that people often make may be wholly due to misrepresentation of the problems. Indeed, when logical problems are presented in a geometrical form (for instance, as Venn diagrams rather than in verbal form) — a new presentation leading to a new representation — people's decisions conform much better to the laws of deductive logic than they do with the verbal problems. Another example is the finding by Allais (1953) that people's decisions are inconsistent with fundamental axioms of a normative theory (game theory) when problems are presented verbally and Savage's (1954) presentation of the same problems in a tabular form, which apparently facilitates more consistent decisions.

Conceiving of internal processes as a complex perception followed by a perfectly logical, perfectly rational, or even perfectly moral cognitive mechanism is a characteristic of Gestalt psychology.[3] Gestalt psychology was a German movement that greatly influenced American psychology in the 1940s, when several of its leaders came to the United States as refugees. For them, all mental life, even morality, is understood through perception. A person who commits immoral acts is not seen as being possessed of an immoral soul (an internal mechanism that makes immoral judgments); rather, such a person has a moral soul (an internal mechanism that makes perfectly moral judgments) together with a distorted perception. As a result, this person has a representation of the world different from that of people who behave morally. For instance, according to the Gestalt psychologists, the difference between a murderer and a hero lies not in their moral capacities but in their perceptions of the situation in which they kill another person. The situations in which the murderer and hero find themselves may differ vastly but their internal representations (as if one or both of them were wearing distorting glasses) are, for the Gestalt psychologists, the same. Each sees the situation as a demand (an extraordinary demand) to kill another person.

Recall Koffka's (1931) example of the spider and the fly, where a spider that normally kills flies caught on its web runs away from a live fly that had been put into its nest. Recall also Koffka's comment: "The spider's stupidity consists, not in running away from a frail victim, but in mistaking its victim for a formidable foe" (p. 117). This issue—how to characterize the apparent stupidity of spiders and people—is, as we have seen, a crucial issue in modern cognitive decision theory as well as modern behavioral choice theory.

The fourth and final stage of the decision process is the conversion of a decision into a choice. The decision is made internally, but the choice is actual behavior that can be directly observed. A man may decide to buy a coat but not actually buy it until later, or he may never buy it if intervening events make him change his mind. On one hand cognitive decision theory is uninterested in this last stage of the decision process; all cognitive theories are united in seeing choice behavior as mere expression of a more fundamental internal decision process. On the other hand, since a theorist cannot see directly into the mind of another person, that person's actual choice behavior in a given situation constitutes a clue, and sometimes the only clue, to what the person's decision processes might be.

The main practical advantage of decision theories is that because the decision mechanism is supposed to be inside a person, it moves with the person from situation to situation. Therefore a decision theory can be used in the following way:

1. A person's choices are observed in several situations.

2. From those choices an internal decision process is inferred. That is, a decision theory is constructed (or modified) to explain the person's choices in those situations.

3. The theory is used to predict the person's behavior in a new situation.

The better a decision theory is, the more situations it will apply to. To the extent that a decision theory is applied to only one situation or to slight variations of that situation, the great advantage of the theory is lost.

Let us say that in a given case of theorizing, steps 1, 2, and 3 all work. That is, the decision theorist observes a person's choice behavior in one or several situations, infers from those observations the existence of a certain decision process inside the person, and uses that hypothetical process to successfully predict the person's choices in other situations. That theorist may then be said to have discovered the person's actual decision process. (The theory would be descriptive rather than normative, since it predicts and explains actual rather than ideal behavior.)

Once a particular decision process is discovered, the theorist does not have to worry about how such a process originated. It could be an innate process. It could have been acquired through experience. It could have developed through an interaction between innate predispositions and a particular experience. However, once it is there, it is there. The theorist needs to infer only the person's current process. How that process came into being does not in the least affect the theorist's predictions. In general, cognitive theorists need not concern themselves with a person's genetics, learning, or development. (This is not to say that cognitive decision theorists are uninterested in these subjects; rather, as cognitive decision theorists, they need not take them into account.)

CONSCIOUSNESS

In our everyday understanding, consciousness has two roles. In one role, it stands between an incoming stimulus and an outgoing response. It is like a central control room—the place where decisions are actually made. It is the place where a person's willpower resides. If consciousness did play this central role, each person would be the best judge of his own choices because only the person within whom a given conscious process resides has direct access to it. Such a role for consciousness precludes any scientific understanding of decision and choice, whether cognitive or behavioral. Since the object of decision and choice theories is to explain and predict decisions and choices better than the person himself could do without the aid of such theories, those theories must deny individual consciousness a central role.

It was Sigmund Freud (1900) who emphasized most strongly the role of nonconscious processes in everyday life. For Freud, individuals are often least capable of predicting or explaining their own decisions and choices. In this respect, modern theories of decision and choice agree with Freud (while disagreeing about the nature of the processes involved).

A decision theory may nevertheless identify a certain process or group of processes, defined in their own terms, as underlying consciousness. The reasoning behind such theories is similar to that used by a physician who identifies the appendix as the diseased organ causing a patient pain in a given area of the stomach. Certain decision theories actually do see consciousness as playing such a role. For those theories consciousness serves as the pain does for the physician — as an indication or symptom of the underlying process. If those theories were true, people could reveal their conscious processes to an observer by internally reflecting on them (introspecting) and then reporting to the observer what they see. The reader may note that while some decision theories view a person's consciousness as an indication of fundamental mental processes, no modern decision or choice theory views consciousness as an essential part of that underlying process.

We turn now to the differences between behavioral choice theories and cognitive decision theories regarding what goes on inside a person making a choice. Here the difference between decision and choice theories reflects a more general difference between cognitive and behavioral psychology.

CHOICE THEORIES

A behavioral choice theorist, interested in the operation of a person as a whole (much as a driver is interested in the operation of a car as a whole), focuses on behavior (choice behavior) of the whole person as a function of input from the environment (as the driver focuses on the performance of a car as a whole as a function of steering, pressure on the gas pedal, shifting gears, etc.). For the behaviorist, the inputs to the choice process are inputs to the person as a whole. Correspondingly, the outputs of the choice process are outputs of the person as a whole (the person's choices themselves).

B. F. Skinner (b. 1904), the most eminent living behaviorist, entitled his first book *Behavior of Organisms*, because he meant to emphasize his belief that individual organisms could be studied as whole units. For Skinner, the study of how parts of animals (organs) behave is the job of biology and physiology, whereas the study of how animals (organisms, including people) behave is the job of psychology.

This perspective of human behavior is, of course, different from that taken by decision theories. Decision theories exist at what the contemporary philosopher Daniel Dennett (1978) calls "the sub-personal level." That is, they are theories about the interactions of the parts of a person, not of organs as in biology but of conceptual divisions of the nervous system with different functions in the decision process (conceptual mechanisms). Thus, while the behavioral theorist considers the choice process by looking at its operation as a whole (as a driver might view a car), the cognitive theorist considers the decision process by looking at its parts and their interactions, (as a mechanic might view a car). Just as the driver's and the mechanic's views of a single car must be compatible with each other, so too must be the behaviorist's and cognitivist's views of a person's choices. In other words, cognitive decision theories and behavioral choice theories are complementary (or at least not contradictory) explanations of the same choice behavior.

To illustrate how this complementarity might work, let us take up two cases from before: how each theory deals with what seem to be (1) perfectly rational (or logical) decisions or choices and (2) perfectly irrational ones.

Consider the following seemingly rational choice. A man buying a new car considers aesthetics, what he can afford, what he needs, what he wants, what else the money could be spent on, and what *Consumer Reports* says about the car's performance and repair records. He then makes a deliberate choice taking all of these factors into account. As an example of a seemingly irrational choice, let us say the man walks by a showroom, sees an appealing car in the window, goes in, and buys it — disregarding all of the above factors except aesthetics. (Even on this issue he takes into account only immediate appeal rather than how the car will look to him after a few months.) How would decision and choice theories explain these two cases?

A normative decision theory will attribute the first choice to a veridical perceptual mechanism and a smoothly functioning logical mechanism that considers all inputs and emits a decision that takes into account all factors, each with its proper weight. Nevertheless, such a choice may ultimately turn out to be unfortunate. If so, it will be because the man, despite his best efforts, had incomplete or erroneous information. He acted on the basis of probabilities, not certainties, and each of those probabilities was appropriately fed into the final calculation. Thus the decision was correct even if the man was unlucky. Over the long term, decisions made with this sort of calculation will be correct. If the car ends up to be a lemon, the man can console himself with the thought that even batting champions sometimes strike out.

A nonnormative decision theory, such as prospect theory, says that the man tends not to behave in such apparently rational ways. If he does actually make rational choices, the nonnormative decision theory would say that the man adjusted either his perceptions (compensating for illusions) or his decision mechanism (compensating for natural biases) or both. A person may adjust the operation of an internal perceptual mechanism by the use of instruments (as when *Consumer Reports* measures acceleration rather than relying on a seat-of-the-pants feeling) and may adjust decision mechanisms by applying the calculus of probability.

Cognitive decision theory would explain the "perfectly irrational" choice in terms of a particular perception (the man saw the car as a good buy) or a particular decision mechanism (the man weighed appearance very highly in making his decision). It is not hard to imagine cases where apparently irrational choices make a good deal of common sense. For instance, suppose the man buying the car is a busy surgeon. He has no time to read *Consumer Reports* or shop around. He is wealthy and a mistake would be relatively uncostly. He knows that the combination of various laws and the buying power of more careful shoppers will make it unlikely that the car manufacturer and dealer are completely unscrupulous. Therefore he spends a minimum amount of time making a car-buying decision.

As mentioned previously, such behavior has been labeled "satisficing" by the cognitive theorist Herbert Simon (1978). Satisficing entails making a reasonable decision, allowing for time and circumstances, even if it may not be the best one possible. It is up to the particular cognitive decision theory to discover the mechanism responsible for satisficing.

In summary, whether choices seem to be perfectly rational, perfectly irrational, or somewhere in between (satisficing), the cognitive decision theorist always explains them as the result of the current (adjusted) action of an internal decision-making process.

The behavioral choice theorist has only a single internal process to work with. If a single process could explain seemingly rational behavior, how could it also explain seemingly irrational behavior? The answer lies not in the internal process at all but in the interaction between the person and the world — in the concept of reinforcement (or value). The behaviorist looks at the world not as a source of stimuli but as a series of functional relationships. The reliable, efficient, cheap, yet attractive car is one such functional relationship. The flashy car is another one. The former provides lasting value, or repeated reinforcement, in return for the behavior of buying it in the first place, and then driving it, servicing it, and finally perhaps selling it. Buying the car is seen as a function of the value (reinforcers and punishers) that the car provides, just as the obtained value is a function of buying the car. Behavioral choice theories are about the nature of these two functions and how they interact. The difference between buying a reliable, efficient, cheap, yet attractive car and buying a flashy car, according to behavioral choice theories, is a difference in the effect of reinforcement on behavior. In the former case, choice is a function of delayed reinforcement — rewards that may not appear until years after the initial purchase. In the latter case, choice is a function of immediate reinforcement — rewards that are available in the showroom and on the drive home.

Consumer Reports, pocket calculators, and books of resale prices are seen by the behavioral theorist as tools that the man may use to guide buying choices, much as red and green lights, roadside signs, and lines on the road serve to guide driving choices. The guides a person (or other animal) follows in making choices and how the person (or other animal) follows them are, as we have seen, of much concern in behavioral choice theory.

The surgeon's choice of the flashy car can be seen as a function of reinforcers still further away in time than those governing the choice of the person who buys the reliable, cheap, yet attractive car — perhaps a greater income, ultimately, or perhaps higher professional recognition or service to humanity. Pursuing these same lines of reasoning still further, it is possible to imagine that our man is a surgeon who is also a very particular car buyer, a car aficionado perhaps, who is a better surgeon because he has arranged his life so as to provide a mixture of relatively immediate and relatively distant rewards. He might buy the flashy car because such cars have provided him with immediate rewards as well as delayed ones (some became collector's items) in the past.

So for the behavioral theorist, the difference between the person who buys the flashy car and the person who buys the reliable, efficient, cheap, yet attractive car is always explained in terms of the interaction of two functions: the function relating choice to reinforcement in the environment and the function relating reinforcement to choice in the person.

The critical difference between cognitive decision theories and behavioral choice theories lies in their answer to the question "Why, in the same immediate situation, should person A choose one alternative and person B another?" Why should person A choose the flashy car and person B the sensible car? To answer this question, both theories must make inferences from current behavior. The cognitive decision theorist infers differences in parameters and mechanisms of the internal processes of person A and person B. The behavioral choice theorist infers differences in the past experience of these two people — what Skinner calls their "reinforcement history." Thus, the choice theorist sees buying the flashy car not as an event isolated in time but as part of a pattern of events in the person's life. Just as the cognitive decision theorist does not actually see the internal process and has to infer its existence, so the behavioral choice theorist does not actually see the rest of the behavioral pattern and has to infer its existence. To put it another way, in explaining a given act, the cognitive theorist points to somewhere in space that he cannot see (to the interior of the person), while the behavioral choice theorist points to somewhere in time that he cannot see (to the person's reinforcement history).

To underline this point, consider another example. Suppose a woman first states the logical premises

1. All men are mortal.

2. Socrates is a man.

She then states the classically correct conclusion:

3. Socrates is mortal.

One might point to a smoothly functioning internal logical mechanism, as the British empiricist philosopher John Locke did. Or one might point to the woman's experience with men and death, as a later (and still more empirical) British empiricist philosopher, John Stuart Mill, did. In the former case, the conclusion is the product of *deductive* logic. In the latter case, as Mill (1874) showed, the conclusion is the product of *inductive* logic. "Socrates is mortal," for Mill, is simply another case belonging to the same class of events as "Joe is mortal," "Pete is mortal," "Sam is mortal," and so on. The woman, according to Mill, is reasoning inductively in the same way as she does when she says, "The sun rose yesterday, the day before yesterday, the day before that, and so on." Therefore, the sun will rise tomorrow."

Mill was not a behaviorist. The major premise in one case, "All men are mortal," and the implied major premise in the other, "The sun rises every day," were, for Mill, the products of "mental chemistry," a kind of chemical combination of individual instances in the mind. The properties of the compound (as in chemistry) may differ from those of its elements. However, the operation of inductive logic does not depend on mental chemistry; it depends on the relation between the woman's current behavior and the woman's previous experience. (A behaviorist may thus accept Mill's empiricism without adopting his mentalism.)

The main practical advantage of choice theories (which point to past experience) is the same as that of decision theories (which point to current mechanisms)—they can be used to predict a person's behavior from one situation to the next. In the case of choice theories:

1. A person's (or other animal's) choices are observed in several situations.

2. From those choices, the person's values are inferred. That is, a choice theory is constructed (or modified) to explain the person's choices in those situations.

3. The theory is used to predict the person's behavior in another situation.

Like decision theories, choice theories stand or fall on their ability to apply widely across situations. (Choice theories have historically been applied to a much wider range of animal species than have decision theories, but there is no intrinsic reason to limit decision theories to human behavior.)

ACTIONS AND PASSIONS IN BEHAVIORAL THEORY

For the behavioral choice theorist, the difference between actions and passions lies in the relation of each kind of movement to its consequences. In the case of actions, consequences are delayed and movements themselves are extended in time. For instance, reinforcement of a student's studying is often delayed. Some students may enjoy studying for its own sake (in which case some reinforcement is not delayed); usually, however, the consequences of studying (approval from teachers and high grades) are delayed by days or weeks, and ultimate reinforcers (being an educated person and getting a better job) by years. Rarely is an individual instance of studying rewarded, even by a delayed reward. Rather, to the perpetual frustration of students, the relation of an individual episode of studying (say of an hour's duration) to its relatively near and distant rewards is rather vague. Certainly, if the course is meaningful, there exists a general correlation — the more studying, the better, up to a point. However, a student torn between studying and going to the movies on a particular evening will (almost) always be rewarded immediately by the choice of the movie and only distantly and vaguely by the choice to study. Suppose the student chooses to study. The behaviorist can explain such a choice only by viewing studying as part of a wider pattern of behavior. For the behaviorist, the cause of this pattern is not (as it is for the cognitivist) an internal mechanism, but the relationship that exists in the environment between studying and reward.

In general, "thoughtful movement" as conceived by Aristotle and diagrammed in Figure 9-1 is seen by the behaviorist as a relationship at the borderline (of the person and the world) between a given behavior and reinforcement. An action is a vague relationship between current events of long duration and reinforcers far in the future; a passion is a fixed relationship between current events of short duration and immediate reinforcers. There are obviously many behavior–environment relationships between these extremes. (If studying lies at one extreme and going to the movies lies at the other, a third alternative, like writing a letter, might fall somewhere in between.)

This behavioral way of characterizing actions and passions is (again simplifying somewhat) perhaps more like Plato's characterization of behavior than Aristotle's. Plato's main concern in his philosophy was how to live a good life. The most important choices in life, he believed, are between immediate and distant consequences. The consequences of the former acts (later called "passions" by Aristotle) he called "pleasures." The consequences of the later acts (later called "actions" by Aristotle) he called "intelligence." Plato and Aristotle both, in conformance with the Greek ideal of balance or harmony in nature, believed that the best life (true happiness) could be achieved only through a judicious mixture of the two extremes. For Aristotle this mixture was the "golden mean." For Plato, it was a mixture like a mixture between water and honey. As we have seen, behavioral theories focus on how people and other animals actually do go about making such mixtures.

It is important to note that just as few cognitive psychologists deny the existence of a person's reinforcement history that could ultimately be responsible for the person's choices, few behavioral psychologists deny the existence of current internal events that could mediate between earlier experience and current choices. The difference is that the behaviorist constructs a functional model based on inferred past experience to explain (and predict) current behavior, while the cognitivist constructs a structural model based on inferred internal mechanisms.

It should be obvious to the reader that although both cognitive decision and behavioral choice theories attempt to explain and predict the same events, they do it in different ways. The cognitivist and behaviorist may both be right in their inferences of the causes of a given act, or they may both be wrong, or one right and the other wrong (as measured by explanation and prediction). The important thing to note is that the rightness or wrongness of one kind of theory has no bearing on the rightness or wrongness of the other. The reader who can keep this in mind will be saved from a lot of the pointless disputation that has been prevalent recently in modern psychology and philosophy.

NOTES

1. In this figure and its discussion, Aristotle's conceptions of actions and passions are described with a combination of cognitive and behavioral terms. In the figure, outputs of internal mechanisms (the existence of which are inferred from behavior) are efficient causes of the outputs of other mechanisms. It is possible, however, to view Aristotle's conceptions of actions and passions in strictly behavioristic terms by replacing efficient causes with formal causes working in the opposite direction. For instance, movement towards an object may be seen as a form of desire, desire as a form of pleasure, pleasure as a form of harmony. The chain of explanations may be just a way of classifying movements and need not refer to the existence anywhere else of entities that efficiently cause them. This strictly behavioristic interpretation, in keeping with the tenor of Aristotle's thought, was perhaps taken by Randall (1960, p. 31), who said, "In modern terms he [Aristotle] can be viewed as a behaviorist." It was certainly taken by Kantor (1963), who placed Aristotle at the pinnacle of behavioristic thought (far above Skinner). For our purposes, however, the more easily diagrammable (to us) cognitive–behavioral view suffices.

2. Within decision theory, processes have been proposed that combine the two influences in various degrees. Actions and passions may be in harmony or in conflict. It is well known, for instance, that a person asked to judge even something so simple as which of two lines is longer, will be biased if the experimenter seems (even to the slightest degree) to approve of one answer (a form of pleasure?) or disapprove of the other (a form of pain?). Being biased does not necessarily imply being a liar but just that rational judgments may conflict with passions.

3. See note 4 of Chapter 3.

DECISION AND CHOICE RECONCILED

IN THE PREVIOUS CHAPTERS we distinguished between cognitive and behavioral viewpoints; here we will try to integrate them into a single, more global (and, we hope, more powerful) viewpoint.

Consider the following three differences between human decisions and animal choices: (1) Human beings are capable of introspection about their cognitive processes; (2) human beings are capable of understanding, obeying, and formulating verbal rules; and (3) human beings both understand and express numerical probabilities. Nonhuman animals, lacking a formal language, are incapable of performing all these activities. Do these differences create such a wide gulf between human decisions and animal choices as to make them incomparable? Let us consider the three differences one by one.

INTROSPECTION

The science of psychology as practiced by Wundt in Germany and his student Titchner in the United States began as a science of introspection. It was loosely based on the British empiricist philosophers' view of the mind, which was illustrated in Figure 1-4. The box labeled "Reflection" in that figure represents the introspective way of knowing the mind. If, as the British empiricist philosophers said, nothing gets into the mind except through the senses, every idea, no matter how complex, must be composed of sensory elements. In the first psychology laboratories, graduate students were trained to analyze ideas into sensory elements; as a scientific endeavor, this project failed dismally.

Both behaviorism and Gestalt psychology arose as protests against Wundt's conception of psychology. The Gestalt psychologists, whose approach to the study of the mind was rooted in philosophy, particularly the philosophy of Kant, objected to the notion that ideas were nothing but collections of simple sensory elements. The behaviorists, whose approach was based on biology, objected to the method of introspection itself. Watson (1913) and other behaviorists argued that the information you gain by observing objects in the world is true knowledge only if you can use it and communicate it to other people so that they can use it; what you gain by introspection is not true knowledge because it can neither be used nor communicated to others.

Consider the most fundamental sensory level. You know (through optics and physiology) that the world is represented upside down on your retina. Yet no amount of introspection will enable you to see that world upside down. You cannot tap into your own visual process at the retinal level and reflect upon its state. As your nervous system processes information beyond the retina, is there a representation at any level or stage at all upon which you can reflect?

Let us consider the other extreme by jumping to a higher, perhaps the highest, level of mental activity, the creation of a work of art. Recently I saw a movie called *Mystery of Picasso*. At the beginning of the movie the narrator says that the object of the movie is to explore the mind of a great artist (Picasso was then alive). The movie begins. Picasso sits on one side of a translucent screen. The camera is focused on the other side. I, in the audience, see only what is drawn on the screen, not Picasso himself. Colored lines appear. More and more lines are added. I see figures and objects emerge. I see ideas emerge. The drawing seems to be finished, but it is not. A black wash begins to cover certain areas. I want to jump up and shout, "No! Don't mess it up!" But instead of becoming messed up, the picture becomes stronger, more vivid. It is much better now than before.

After several of these translucent plate drawings (each a revelation of another aspect of Picasso's mind), the great painter speaks his first words. He tells the director that he wants to let the audience see him work as he really does. So the camera is turned around and focused on an opaque canvas. Picasso paints a little and the camera takes a picture of the canvas; he paints some more and another picture is taken; this process continues. What I see in the movie is a picture taking shape before my eyes. Unlike the translucent screen, the canvas allows Picasso to paint over any parts he wants to. From a few bold lines on the canvas the picture develops. He paints it over and over and over. It's different, it's better, it's worse. A fish becomes a chicken. A bird becomes a woman. He keeps on working. What actually takes a week is compressed into a few minutes on the screen. At last Picasso speaks again: "Now I know what I was trying to do." He virtually begins again from the beginning. Not only have I been seeing Picasso's mind, but he himself has been seeing it. He does not introspect, decide what he wants to do, and then paint. He paints first. Only then does he know his own mind.

The word *reflection* applies to this process only if we can see Picasso as a whole as a sort of mirror reflecting all of his experience onto the canvas. Perhaps an even better metaphor would be Brunswik's (1952) metaphor of refraction, as when a lens brings a scene into focus on a screen. Picasso, as a whole person, corresponds to the lens. Introspection would be invalid, in this metaphor, because there is no image within a lens. The focal point is outside, not inside. The image Picasso sees is not an internal image, an internal representation. In objective terms, Picasso sees exactly what I see—the image on the canvas. It's just that he sees the image in the light of his ability and experience, while I see it in the light of my own. This and only this is the extent to which Picasso's view of his own mind is superior to mine (or so the movie implies). By implication, if Picasso were to see the painting of an ordinary painter as I have just seen the painting of Picasso, the great painter's view of the mind of ordinary painter would be better (truer in some sense) than the ordinary painter's view of (that part of) his own mind. By further implication, a trained observer of human behavior (an experienced therapist) can know a person's mind better than the person himself can. Metaphorically, a therapist would see life as Picasso sees painting—as a pattern. A therapist is (or should be) to a patient as a trained artist is to an art student. If therapy succeeds, the patient's patterns of interaction with the world will become more harmonious than they were before. Furthermore, just as conceptions of beauty change in art, so must conceptions of happiness change in life. (Freud's psychology, however meaningful it was in turn-of-the-century Vienna, may well have become outmoded for most of us today.)

"All very well and good," you might be thinking, "the author was obviously impressed with this movie." But what has all this got to do with the essential question: Is there some level of representation between the image on an animal's retina and the image on a painter's canvas that is accessible to introspection? This question was addressed in a thorough review of the literature on cognition by Nisbett and Wilson (1977). Following is the abstract that (in oddly molecular, stimulus–response terms) summarizes their findings:

Evidence is reviewed which suggests that there may be little or no direct introspective access to higher order cognitive processes. Subjects are sometimes (a) unaware of the existence of a stimulus that importantly influenced a response, (b) unaware of the existence of the response, and (c) unaware that the stimulus has affected the response. It is proposed that when people attempt to report on their cognitive processes, that is, on the processes mediating the effects of a stimulus on a response, they do not do so on the basis of any true introspection. Instead, their reports are based on a priori, implicit causal theories, or judgments about the extent to which a particular stimulus is a plausible cause of a given response. This suggests that though people may not be able to observe directly their cognitive processes, they will sometimes be able to report accurately about them. Accurate reports will occur when influential stimuli are salient and are plausible causes of the responses they produce, and will not occur when stimuli are not salient or are not plausible causes. (p. 231)

In other words, people's introspections match what the best available cognitive theory says is going on in their minds only where and when their own theory of mind (learned, as language is learned, in society) happens to coincide with the cognitive theory. Such coincidences, Nisbett and Wilson discovered, are surprisingly rare.

Of their many examples, perhaps the one most relevant to the topic of this book is from two studies by Nisbett and Wilson (1977) themselves in a real-world situation—a store where shoppers were asked to evaluate products. Here is the description in the words of the authors:

> In both studies, conducted in commercial establishments under the guise of a consumer survey, passersby were invited to evaluate articles of clothing—four different nightgowns in one study (378 subjects) and four identical pairs of nylon stockings in the other (52 subjects). Subjects were asked to say which article of clothing was the best quality and, when they announced a choice, were asked why they had chosen the article they had. There was a pronounced left-to-right position effect, such that the right-most object in the array was heavily over-chosen. For the stockings, the effect was quite large, with the right-most stockings being preferred over the left-most by a factor of almost four to one. When asked about the reasons for their choices, no subject ever mentioned spontaneously the position of the article in the array. And, when asked directly about a possible effect of position of the article, virtually all subjects denied it, usually with a worried glance at the interviewer suggesting that they felt either that they had misunderstood the question or were dealing with a madman. (pp. 243–244)

Obviously, the position of the article had a strong effect on most of the people's choices, but the process by which position influences choice was unavailable to their introspection.

It would have been possible for Nisbett and Wilson to have argued in exactly the reverse direction. They could have said that people's introspections are valid by definition and that if they disagree with cognitive theory, so much the worse for cognitive theory. However, to have taken that tack would have been to abandon not only cognitive theory but also psychology, and thus to abandon any hope of understanding people's minds.

The reader may feel that, in this section at least, I have lost my objectivity and am not giving introspection a fair hearing. I may be guilty of this charge (although not consciously so). If introspection is a valid indicator of the mind, then animal choice is fundamentally different from human decision and the synthesis attempted by this book is pointless. However, if a person's verbal report about the state of his or her own mind has no more a priori validity than an observer's report about the state of that person's mind, then however different the minds of humans may be from the minds of nonhuman animals (and the differences are undoubtedly vast), a psychologist can observe both and make valid (i.e., potentially confirmable and useful) statements about both.

The fact that introspections are invalid as such does not mean that they are uninteresting. What people say while they are doing a task of any kind may indicate something important about that task. The "protocol analysis" of Ericsson and Simon (1984) examines the verbal reports of people performing various tasks and infers the parameters of the cognitive process underlying the task. Ericsson and Simon are careful not to substitute the content of the report for the cognitive process itself. The report needs to be carefully analyzed and interpreted (in the light of Ericsson and Simon's theory about the fundamental nature of the underlying cognitive process) before the specific parameters of that process are derived from it. According to this theory, only events in short-term memory can be reported upon. However, none of the subjects say anything about short-term memory in their reports; rather, the existence and functioning of short-term memory as well as other cognitive structures are inferred from the reports. In this sense, Ericsson and Simon's analysis involves no more reliance on introspection than does any cognitive analysis.

Ericsson and Simon focus their observation on tasks where performance is unaffected by whether or not subjects are telling the experimenters what they are thinking. To explain the lack of difference in performance on the task with or without an overt verbal report, the authors conclude that the subjects are either already saying things to themselves (covertly) or emitting some other equivalent covert behavior. For instance, if you recite the recipe to yourself (or perhaps picture each step in your mind) whenever you bake an apple pie, the quality of the pie will be unaffected, according to Ericsson and Simon, if you simultaneously say aloud what you are thinking. On the other hand, if you ordinarily bake the pie automatically without taking to yourself, the quality of the pie might well suffer when you have to put into words what you are doing at any moment. What a person says overtly and its effect on performing a task thus indicates what is going on in that person's mind (in particular, his or her short-term memory). Of course, there are many assumptions behind this method (see Hayes, 1986, for a behavioral analysis). The point here is that the method does not rely on introspection; it relies on a cognitive analysis of a verbal report, which is quite a different thing.

If the introspections that seem to report the functioning of our internal cognitive processes are not really direct reports about any internal process at all, what are they? What is their function? All current answers to these questions are just speculations. Here is one:

Introspection is a prediction of the introspectionist's own overt behavior, and introspections are wrong when they predict behavior incorrectly. So when I say that I hate junk food and yet eat a lot of junk food, my wife is correct when she says, "No you don't, you love junk food." We believe so strongly that our introspections are true because we do not want to believe that other people can predict our own behavior better than we can (as my wife often predicts mine).

According to Plato, a person's very happiness is best judged not by the person himself but by people who are familiar with his everyday behavior. The statement "I am happy," for Plato, does not reflect a mood or any other internal state but is a description and a prediction of a molar pattern of behavior — of choices.

RULE-GOVERNED VERSUS CONTINGENCY-GOVERNED BEHAVIOR

Skinner (1969, in press) distinguishes between behavior governed by rules and behavior governed by contingencies. The distinction makes intuitive sense. You may have never been to jail or even gotten a traffic ticket — the contingencies — yet you (generally) obey the law. In learning to drive a car, rule-governed and contingency-governed behavior blend into each other. At first, your behavior is largely rule-governed. You do what the instructor tells you. However, as soon as you get the feel of the road, your behavior becomes contingency-governed and driving becomes second nature. Driving, like most of your activities, ultimately becomes a mixture of rule-governed and contingency-governed behavior just as you follow maps, signs, and instructions on the one hand and conform to the contingencies you have experienced on the other.

Once it is recognized that behavior may be governed by a rule, the difference between cognitive and behavioral interpretations of that rule becomes virtually negligible. For instance, let us assume that my stopping at red lights is governed by the rule "Stop at red lights and go at green lights," with a host of other driving rules serving as context. Let us further assume that I have never been in an accident or gotten a ticket; consequently, my behavior could not be controlled directly by contingencies.

Both cognitivist and behaviorist must infer the existence of an invisible process that actually governs my stopping and going. Figure 10-1 (a more general version of Figure 2-2) shows these two infer-

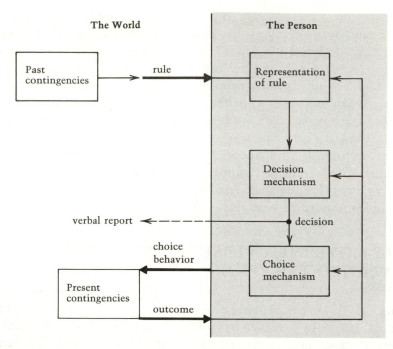

Figure 10-1 A rule as a representation of past external contingencies (behavioral inference) and as a current internal representation (cognitive inference).

ences as the upper right and left boxes. The cognitivist infers the current existence of an internal representation of the rule. The behaviorist infers the past existence of a set of external contingencies that the rule itself represents. The behaviorist says that for people a verbally expressed rule represents past contingencies so that both rules and contingencies are fundamentally contingencies; the cognitivist says that people represent even current contingencies internally as rules so that both rules and contingencies are fundamentally rules.

The behaviorist expresses the rule, however complicated it is, in terms of contingencies: situations, reinforcers, punishers. The rule represents those past events (in a poorly understood way) as a sort of higher-level discriminative stimulus. (Pavlov called such rules "the second signal system.") The red light itself is a discriminative stimulus that tells me to stop. It represents a contingency by which the consequences of stopping are valued higher than those of going.

The green light is a discriminative stimulus that tells me to go for the opposite reason. The rule "Stop at red lights and go at green lights" is a more complex contingency in which the two subcontingencies are components. Abstract rules about love, friendship, justice, and the like are reducible to contingencies and may be expressed in the language of contingencies, according to the behaviorist.

The cognitivist, on the other hand, describes the action of contingencies in terms of equally complex (and equally vaguely understood) internal rules. The cognitivist's language is usually that of computer science — the representations are (or are reducible to) propositions, which in turn are reducible to logical states (Lacey and Rachlin, 1978).

The cognitivist objects to using the behaviorist language (the language of contingencies) to describe rules because the cognitivist believes that rules are learned by processes that may be different from those by which current discriminative stimuli influence behavior. The behaviorist objects to using the cognitivist language (the language of computer science) to describe rules because the behaviorist believes that learning (even of rules) is always functional (related to value) and is "logical" only when logic subserves function. However, if rules and contingencies are mutually translatable, it really makes no difference whether rules or contingencies are held to be fundamental.

Laboratory experiments in decision and choice may be understood in terms of Figure 10-1. In an experiment on human judgment or decision, people are presented with a verbal problem — a rule — and emit a verbal report about their judgment or decision. In an animal choice experiment, subjects are presented with a set of current contingencies and emit choices. Figure 10-1 allows you to see these two experimental procedures as completely separate; human decision is apparently restricted to the upper part — the "higher" processes (ending in a verbal report); animal choice is apparently restricted to the lower part — the "lower" processes (beginning with present contingencies). However, this would be a false view from both cognitive and behavioral standpoints. The upper and lower parts of Figure 10-1 interact strongly with each other.

Recently experimenters have begun to study interaction of rule-governed and contingency-governed behavior by varying the instructions given to human subjects as they emit operants with various current schedules of reinforcement and punishment (see Baron and Galizio, 1983, for a review). A recent experiment by Hayes and others (1986), diagrammed in Figure 10-2, exemplifies these experiments.

The operant contingencies of the experiment by Hayes and his colleagues were as follows. The subjects (undergraduates) pressed two buttons to move the illumination of a light from the upper left corner of a matrix of lights to the lower right corner. One button moved the light to the right; the other moved it down. When the light reached the lower right corner, the subjects got points that they could exchange for money. The contingency manipulated by the experimenters was the relationship between button pressing and the movement of the light. In addition, there were two alternating signals, A and B (actually other lights). In the first phase of the experi-

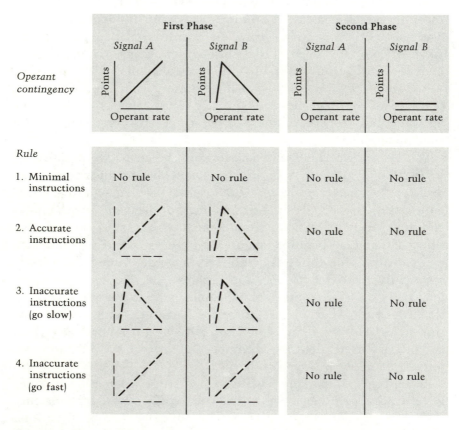

Figure 10-2 Operant contingencies and implied rules in the experiment by Hayes and colleagues (1986).

ment, when signal A was on, the schedule in effect (a fixed-ratio schedule) moved the matrix light in direct proportion to the speed of button pressing: The faster the buttons were pressed, the faster the light moved and the more points the subject got. However, when signal B was on, the schedule in effect (called a differential-reinforcement-of-low-rates schedule) moved the light in inverse proportion to the speed of button pressing; the slower the buttons were pressed, the faster the light moved and the more points the subjects got (but if the rate of button pressing got too low, no points were earned).

All subjects in the experiment were faced with these operant contingencies. However, the different groups of subjects were given different instructions. One group was given minimal instructions. They were told only that they should try to get as many points as possible and that doing so involved the buttons and the lights. A second group was given accurate instructions. They were told that they would get more points by pressing the buttons fast during signal A and slow during signal B. A third and fourth group were given inaccurate instructions. The third group was told that pressing the buttons slowly would yield more points, while the fourth group was told that pressing the buttons rapidly would yield more.

The critical aspect of the subjects' behavior observed by the experiments was the efficiency of pressing—whether they pressed fast during signal A and slow during signal B. As you might expect, the accurate-instructions group did best (almost all of them pressed efficiently), the minimal-instructions group did next best (about a third pressed efficiently), and the inaccurate-instructions groups did worst (a little less than a third of each group pressed efficiently). On the basis of these results alone, you could not distinguish between a subject in the accurate-instructions group and one of the minority (about a third) of subjects in the other three groups who responded efficiently.

The crucial part of the experiment, however, was the second phase. With no further instructions given, the buttons were disconnected from the light for all subjects and button pressing had no effect on light movement (extinction contingency). In other words, during the second phase, the rule remained unchanged while the contingencies changed for all subjects. The question that concerned the experimenters was how soon the subjects would catch on and stop (or slow down) pressing the buttons. In the accurate group, remember, almost all of the subjects had pressed efficiently during the first phase. However, when extinction was instituted, only about half of these subjects slowed their button pressing. On the other hand, of the approximately third of the subjects in the other three groups (groups 1, 3, and 4) who were pressing efficiently during the first phase, a high proportion (88 percent) stopped or slowed down during extinction.

The experimenters interpret these results as indicating that the efficient button pressing of the accurate group during the first phase tended to be rule-governed. When the rule remained unchanged in the second phase, their behavior generally remained unchanged, even though the contingencies had not. Correspondingly, those subjects in the other three groups whose button pressing had been efficient in the first phase must have been contingency-governed. When the contingency changed, their behavior changed even though the rule remained unchanged. In mentalistic terms, this is an experiment on "belief." The accurate-instructions subjects had been rewarded for believing the instructions, and most of them continued in their belief even when it was no longer correct. The inaccurate-instructions subjects were rewarded for disbelieving the instructions, and the skepticism that they had learned paid off when conditions were changed.

This study, in which rule-governed and contingency-governed behaviors were separated, may be related to studies of "set" in humans, where rules learned to solve one problem are carried forward to another problem for which they may be less appropriate. A classic case is the Luchins water jar experiment (Luchins, 1942). In that experiment people were first given a problem that could be solved only by following a complex rule. Afterwards they were given a problem that could be solved by the complex rule or a much simpler rule. Often subjects continued to apply the complex rule.

The study by Hayes and others may also be related to studies of "transfer" in animals, where behavior under one set of contingencies persists when contingencies are changed. A classic case is the failure of extinction of avoidance (Solomon and Wynne, 1954). In that study dogs were trained to jump over a hurdle to avoid shock (following the contingency that faster jumping entails less shock). Their jumps persisted when the contingency was changed to extinction (no shock regardless of jumping). In the human set studies, the initial rule may be interpreted behavioristically as a past contingency opposing the present contingency. In the animal transfer studies, the initial contingency may be regarded cognitively as a past rule opposing a current rule. Alternatively, both set and transfer studies may be viewed in terms of the interaction of a past rule and a present contingency. It does not matter much which view you take as long as you define rules and contingencies consistently.

THE AMBIGUITY OF PROBABILITY

If, as Chapter 2 says, a probability is best interpreted as a guide to behavior, then a probability is a kind of rule. In Chapters 2 and 3, we said that a probability as a rule can refer to two sorts of events: a base rate and an immediate expectancy. The Blue–Green taxicab problem nicely illustrates an instance when the two kinds of probability come into conflict. Here is the problem again (from Tversky and Kahneman, 1982, p. 156):

> A cab was involved in a hit and run accident at night. Two cab companies,the Green and the Blue, operate in the city. You are given the following data:
> (a) 85% of the cabs in the city are Green and 15% are Blue.
> (b) a witness identified the cab as Blue. The court tested the reliability of the witness under the same circumstances that existed on the night of the accident and concluded that the witness correctly identified each one of the two colors 80% of the time and failed 20% of the time.
> What is the probability that the cab involved in the accident was Blue rather than Green?

The base rates are 85:15 in favor of Green, but the witness's testimony (the immediate expectancy) is 80:20 in favor of Blue. Although Bayes' rule provides a way of combining the two into an overall probability, people given this problem do not obey Bayes' rule. A large majority of subjects simply ignore the base rates and make their judgments in terms of the immediate expectancy.

Chapter 4 discussed the cognitive question "How is a probability internally represented?" Here we consider the corresponding behavioral question "What external events does a probability represent?" Furthermore, when probabilities come into conflict, as in the Blue–Green taxicab problem, why do people resolve the conflict as they do? The answer we will arrive at is that the base rate of gains or losses represents an overall rate of reward or punishment, while an immediate expectancy of a gain or a loss represents the delay between a choice and a single outcome, a reinforcer or punisher. People react to the base rates in a verbal problem much as animals do to the overall rate of reward or punishment; people react to immediate expectancy in a verbal problem much as animals react to delay of a reinforcer or punisher; people react to conflicts between base rates and immediate expectancies in verbal problems much as animals react to conflicts between the overall rate of reward or punishment and the delay between choice and a single reinforcer or punisher.

The analogy between base rates of outcomes in verbal problems and overall rates of reward and punishment is obvious; the very word *rates* makes it so. Imagine a person in one room flipping a coin every 10 minutes $(t = 10)$ on the average. The coin has a probability of .5 $(p = .5)$ of turning up heads. Suppose each time the coin turns up heads, the coin flipper delivers a dollar $(A = \$1)$ through a trapdoor to another person in a room next door. The receiver sees nothing of the process by which the dollars are produced. All the receiver knows is that a dollar bill arrives through the trapdoor every 20 $(t/p = 10/.5 = 20)$ minutes on the average. Expressed a rate, the receiver would be getting $\frac{1}{20}$ of a dollar, or 5¢ per minute, on the average.

The rate R is given by

$$R = \frac{pA}{t} \tag{10-1}$$

The ratio of two rates with equivalent amounts $(A's)$ and times $(t's)$ would be the ratio of their probabilities. In the Blue–Green cab problem, the statement that 85 percent of the cabs in the city are Green and 15 percent Blue implies (or is intended to imply) that if you stood on the corner, the rate at which Green cabs came by (Green cabs per day) would be 5.67 $(^{85}/_{15})$ times the rate at which Blue cabs came by (Blue cabs per day). In this obvious sense, probabilities may be equivalent to rates.

The relation of probability to delay is less obvious. Cognitive psychologists have recognized the equivalence by supposing that verbally expressed delays are internally represented as probabilities (Rotter, 1954) — the greater the verbally expressed delay, the lower the subjective probability. For instance, if you tell a child that you are going to give him or her a candy bar immediately, the child may be certain of getting the candy bar. However, if you tell a child that he or she will get a candy bar next week, the child's experience with such promises may well be with uncertain delivery — the more delay, the less likely the delivery. Mischel and Grusec (1967) found that with promised rewards, long delays and low probabilities were equally mistrusted. Children sharply discounted both delayed and improbable rewards.

As Chapter 7 indicated, sharp discounting of delayed rewards is equivalent to a lack of self-control. The fact that one person has more self-control than another (an adult more than a child, for instance) may be due to different experience with the probability of receiving promised rewards and punishments. It makes little difference whether delays are fundamentally conceived to be probabilities or vice versa. The important point is that one can be translated into the other.

Again, consider the two people on either side of the trapdoor. Suppose the one who receives the dollars signals the other by knocking at the door, say, and at that point the coin flipper immediately flips the coin and continues to flip it every 10 minutes $(t = 10)$ on the average until it comes up heads. The coin flipper then passes a dollar through the trapdoor to the receiver. Again, the receiver sees nothing of the process by which the dollar is delivered. All the receiver knows is that there is a delay between the act (the knock) and the reinforcer (the dollar). The average value of this delay is related to the probability of the flipper's coin turning up heads:

$$D = \frac{t}{p} - t \qquad (10\text{-}2)$$

If the coin had two heads $(p = 1)$, the delay would be zero; the receiver would get the dollar immediately after the knock. If the coin had two tails $(p = 0)$, the delay would be infinite and the receiver would never get the dollar. The implicit delay (Equation 10-2) conveyed by a probability is the inverse of the implicit rate (Equation 10-1) except that t is subtracted from the delay because we assume that the coin flipper flips immediately after the knock. Actually there would be a slight delay equal to the time taken to flip the coin and pass the dollar through the trapdoor. Assuming that minimum time to be equal to c minutes, Equation 10-2 may be modified as follows:

$$D = \frac{t + c}{p} - t \qquad (10\text{-}2a)$$

An overall rate, objectively, is nothing but a series of delays. If the receiver of the dollar bills knocked once on the partition and the coin flipper started to flip the coin and kept flipping indefinitely, then the overall rate of dollar deliveries would be nothing but the overlap of delays — the delay from the knock to the first dollar, the delay from the knock to the second dollar, and so on. Subjectively, however, that first delay (between the knock and the first dollar) assumes a vast importance — that is, it has a disproportionately strong effect on choice.

In an experiment performed at Stony Brook (Logue, Smith, and Rachlin, 1985), pigeons chose between pecking a red and a green illuminated disk (key). If a pigeon pecked the red key, it got a small reward almost immediately; if it pecked the green key, it got a larger reward (three times larger) that was delayed for 6 seconds from the peck. Considering only those single rewards, the pigeons all preferred the more immediate but smaller to the more delayed but larger reward; in other words, they lacked self-control. Our experiment superimposed upon this basic choice a constant intertrial interval; if a pigeon chose the immediate reward, it would have to wait longer after the reward to get the next choice. The results were that the pigeons continued to choose the immediate small reward despite the fact that their choice reduced their overall rate of reward to a third of what it would have been otherwise. In human terms, the choice is like the boss asking you every Monday whether you want your weekly paycheck right away or the next day, with the proviso that if you wait until Tuesday, you will be paid three times as much. If you had the mind of a pigeon, you would repeatedly choose the smaller Monday paycheck and receive an overall rate of pay one-third as much as if you waited until Tuesday each week.

It is not as if pigeons are unable to tell the difference between a high rate and a low rate of reward. At the end of the experiment, the pigeons were offered a choice between two rewards (the "first" rewards) exactly equivalent in both delay and amount. The only difference was that if they pecked the red key, they would get the opportunity to choose a second reward sooner; if they chose the green key, they would get the opportunity to choose a second reward later. When the first rewards were exactly balanced in this way, all the pigeons consistently chose the sooner second reward. In other words, when immediate expectancies (of the first reward) were balanced, the pigeons chose the higher overall rate of reward (first and second rewards considered together). When the immediate expectancies were unbalanced, it was as if the temptation (the smaller, more immediate reward) temporarily blinded the pigeons to the higher overall rate. People's judgments in the Blue – Green taxicab problem have been interpreted in a similar fashion (Nisbett et al., 1976). You could say that immediate expectancy, as given by the witnesses' testimony, blinds people to the difference in base rates. When immediate expectancies are removed from the taxicab problem (when the witness is eliminated), people are capable of judging by base rates just as pigeons are capable of choosing a higher overall rate of reward.

Why do immediate expectancies blind us to the overall rates? Let us go back to the example of your hypothetical choice between a smaller paycheck on Monday and a larger one on Tuesday. Why might you choose the smaller Monday paycheck? Several scenarios are possible. First, you might believe that your boss was planning to abscond with the firm's cash on Monday night. A delay, even of one day, might be equivalent to a probability of less than one-third. Your decision to take what you could get on Monday would then be perfectly rational and only seem impulsive. A second reason to take the money Monday might be a temporarily high value for money. You might have a sure tip on a horse running in a race Monday afternoon and paying 10:1. If you were utterly confident of the tip, you would have more money the next day by betting your Monday salary on the horse than by waiting for Tuesday's larger paycheck. Another possibility is that you could be extremely rich; you work only because you enjoy your job. Thus the marginal value of your paycheck is very small in either case (Monday or Tuesday), but you might be temporarily short of pocket money and thus opt for the Monday paycheck.

Finally, to take a more negative possibility, you might be starving and need the money on Monday to buy food. The pain you would suffer between Monday and Tuesday might not be worth the extra money — even if it were three times as much. If the food you could buy on Monday lasted only until the next Sunday (and there was no way to get credit for a day), you might be hungry enough each week to accept the smaller immediate check and thus permanently obtain one-third the salary you could get by merely waiting one day. The pigeons in our experiment were in just such a fix. Their steep discount of rewards delayed by just a few seconds and their consequent lack of self-control need not be regarded as particularly stupid or irrational, however harmful it proved to be in the long run.

A probability, out of context, could stand for a base rate or an immediate expectancy. It may be ambiguous in both cognitive terms (how it is represented) and behavioral terms (what it represents). If a stated probability is a rule and a rule, in turn, represents a contingency, then probabilities as stated in judgment and decision problems may represent either rates or delays of outcomes. Consider again the preference reversal effect discussed in Chapter 4. People choosing between a pair of alternatives varying in probability and amount that are presented together tend to overweight probability and underweight amount, while people judging the value of those alternatives presented separately tend to overweight amount and underweight probability. Thus a person may separately judge alternative X as less valuable than alternative Y but choose alternative Y when presented together with alternative X.

One conceivable explanation for this effect (and it is merely conceivable — an illustration of the ambiguity of probability, not a serious theory) is that when a person is asked to judge the value of an alternative of amount A and probability p, the person interprets p as representing a base rate — an overall rate of reward determined by an infinitely long series of coin flips or dice throws or wheel spins, or as the outcome of any probabilistic process in the real world. That is, the person may interpret the request to evaluate a hypothetical reward (not actually an object of choice) in an objective, relatively dispassionate way, discounting amounts by probabilities in exact proportion to the probabilities. However, when asked to choose between two alternatives, the same subject may interpret probability as an immediate expectancy — not coolly in terms of overall reward but impulsively—in terms of the delay to the very next expected reward. These two interpretations differ. Assuming amounts (A's) and time (t's) to be equal and the constant (c) to be negligible, an interpretation of probabilities in terms of overall rates (via Equation 10-1) gives the following ratio of values:

$$\frac{v_1}{v_2} = \frac{R_1}{R_2} = \frac{p_1}{p_2} \qquad (10\text{-}3)$$

whereas an interpretation of values in terms of immediate expectancies (via Equation 10-2) gives the following ratio of values:

$$\frac{v_1}{v_2} = \frac{D_2}{D_1} = \frac{p_1}{p_2} \times \frac{1 - p_2}{1 - p_1} \qquad (10\text{-}4)$$

(the t's cancel out in both ratios). In the case where $p_1 + p_2 = 1$ (as in the Blue–Green cab problem),

$$\frac{v_1}{v_2} = \left(\frac{p_1}{p_2}\right)^2 \qquad (10\text{-}4a)$$

An interpretation of probabilities in terms of delays thus tends to overweight probabilities. The relative value of $p_1 = .4$ and $p_2 = .6$, interpreted as rates, is .67 (.4/.6), whereas the relative value interpreted as delays is .44 ([.4/.6]^2). The latter ratio represents an overweighting of probability in the sense that it is further from 1, which represents no weighting (see the discussion of bias in Chapter 6). In the preference reversal experiment, people asked to judge the value of two alternatives separately may tend to see probabilities as representing base rates and thus evaluate the alternatives proportionally to probabilities (as Equation 10-3 dictates), while people asked to choose between two current alternatives may see probabilities as representing delays and thus evaluate the alternatives proportional to the probabilities squared (as Equation 10-4a dictates). Thus people would tend to weight probabilities more when making choices than when making judgments — as they indeed do. This extra weight may be the factor that produces preference reversal.

If a probability may be interpreted as a delay, probabilities and delays should be interchangeable in human choices. Several experimental and observational tests of probability/delay interchangeability have been made. In the Mischel–Grusec (1967) study of self-control, children equivalently discounted large delayed rewards and large improbable rewards relative to small rewards that were both immediate and certain.

In another experiment recently performed in the psychology laboratory at Stony Brook (Rachlin, Castrogiovanni, and Cross, 1987), subjects (Stony Brook undergraduates) faced a probabilistic equivalent of the commitment paradigm of Figure 7-2. Recall that choice Y was between a small immediate and a large delayed reward. Figure 10-3 translates the commitment paradigm to probabilistic terms. The probabilistic equivalent of choice Y is between a small (relatively) certain and a large uncertain reward. Just as pigeons prefer small immediate to large delayed rewards, our human subjects preferred small certain to large uncertain rewards (decision theorists call this commonly found preference "conservatism"). However, just as the pigeons tended to commit themselves to the large delayed reward at choice X, so our subjects tended to commit themselves to a large improbable reward at a probabilistic equivalent of choice X. This was a choice between a pair of almost equally improbable outcomes: One outcome of choice X was another choice (choice Y) between a small certain and a large uncertain reward, and the other was a single option only (choice Z), which was a large uncertain reward.

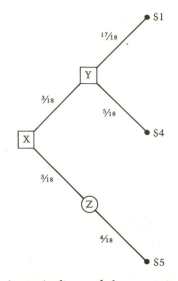

Figure 10-3 Probabilistic equivalents of the commitment paradigm of Figure 7-2.

In our experiment the subjects gambled poker chips (which we gave them) for real monetary rewards. The probabilities were realized as spinners with winning and losing sectors. The probabilities at choice X were $3/18$ for advancing to each alternative. The probabilities at choice Y were a $5/18$ chance to win $4 versus a $17/18$ change to win $1. At point Z subjects had only a $4/18$ chance to win $5. At choice X our subjects tended to choose the alternative leading to Z — the larger, more improbable reward — more frequently than the alternative leading to Y. However, when they were at point Y, they strongly preferred the smaller, more certain reward. Thus, their choice at X may be seen as a commitment to the larger but less probable reward, just as a pigeon's choices at X are seen as a commitment to the larger but more delayed reward.[1]

ONE-SHOT PROBABILITIES

In everyday life, many decisions are one-shot decisions. A businessman, for instance, may have only one opportunity to build a factory or merge with another company. In laboratory situations, however, the number of repetitions and the time between repetitions of a gamble are often left ambiguous.

In deriving Equation 10-4a, we assumed that the constant c of Equation 10-2a was negligible relative to the constant t. In other words, we assumed that the time between repetitions of a gamble was much greater than the duration of the gamble itself. As a result, we predicted a strong aversion to risky gambles (gambles with low probabilities of winning). The truer this assumption is (the longer the interval between gambles relative to the duration of the gamble itself), the more risk aversion Equation 10-2a predicts. When a decision is clearly stated as a one-shot decision, the assumption that t is long relative to c is most nearly true—t would be infinite for a one-shot gamble. Therefore, people should be more risk averse with clearly stated one-shot decisions than with repeated gambles.

Keren and Wagenaar (1987) found exactly this result. Subjects choosing between gambles that they knew they would play just once were more risk averse than subjects choosing between the same set of gambles that they knew would be repeated several times.

FRAMING

The importance of framing on choice may be most vividly underscored in ethology in the small-bird-in-winter problem analyzed by McNamara and Houston (1982). The ultimate objective of the bird's feeding patterns must be to survive from day to day. Under favorable conditions and at the beginning of the day, when there is plenty of time to forage, the bird maximizes overall value by being risk averse, choosing high-probability rewards even of low amount. However, if a bird reaches evening in a relatively deprived state, it will not survive the night unless it eats a sufficient amount to balance its overnight loss of energy. At this point, the frame shifts from one of gains to one of losses; the bird's only chance is to take risks—to choose low-probability, high-amount alternatives. Like the farmer in Chapter 4 who will lose his farm unless he takes an offered gamble, the bird must become risk seeking. McNamara and Houston provide evidence that birds actually do reverse their foraging strategies in the predicted manner.[2]

Figure 10-4 compares large, delayed gains and losses with small, immediate gains and losses. The thin lines *BE* and *CF* indicate a discounting of both gains and losses in the present. The figure as-

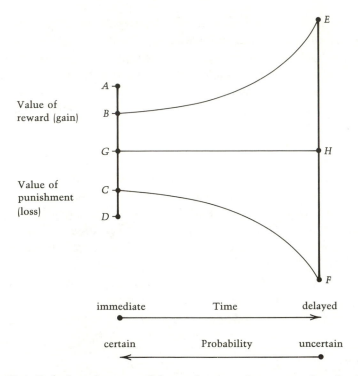

Figure 10-4 Relations between delay and uncertainty, reward and gain, and punishment and loss.

sumes that the discount of both the gain and the loss are such that the small, immediate gain (*GA*) is greater than the present value of the large, delayed gain (*GB*) and that the small, immediate loss (*GD*) is greater than the present value of the large, delayed loss (*GC*). The rank order of the present values of the four outcomes (*A* > *B* > *C* > *D*) implies choice of the small, immediate (or certain) gain over the large, delayed (or uncertain) gain and a corresponding choice of the large, delayed (or uncertain) loss over the small, immediate (or certain one. The figure is illustrative only, showing how uncertainties of gains and losses in a gamble are analogous to delays of reinforcers and punishers. The outcome of a given alternative may consist of one or more large or small reinforcers or punishers in various combinations of delay/immediacy or certainty/uncertainty. The figure does not show how those outcomes might be combined and evaluated.

A gambler at a racetrack or a casino has a menu of degrees of risk from which to choose. At the racetrack there are favorites and long shots. Similarly, at the roulette table, you can bet on red versus black (about even odds) or on a particular number (with much lower odds but a higher payoff). If the values of the outcomes were actually as depicted in Figure 10-4 and if you wanted to maximize (subjective) gains, you would tend to play favorites because GA (the present value of the small payoff) is larger than GB (the present value of the large payoff). However, if you wanted to minimize (subjective) losses, you would play long shots because GC (the present value of the large loss) is less than GD (the present value of the small loss).

Of course, there are many assumptions behind these speculations. A major one is that players do not view each loss as a loss but add up losses over a series of individual gambles until a win occurs (so that long shots involve large delayed losses as well as large delayed wins). Given that this assumption and other assumptions underlying Figure 10-4 are valid, this analysis predicts that gamblers who have long experience with losses (which includes most veteran gamblers at casinos and racetracks) will behave (unconsciously or consciously) so as to minimize losses and thus tend to bet on long shots. In contrast, naive gamblers, who have limited experience with losses, will behave so as to maximize wins and thus tend to bet on favorites.

For purely illustrative purposes, it may be worth discussing an experiment currently under way at Stony Brook designed to test out another implication of the analogy illustrated in Figure 10-4. The experiment involves the game of blackjack. That game is especially interesting because there exists a set of normative rules (called "basic") by which the game should be played.[3] Basic tells the blackjack player whether to "hit" (to draw another card) or "stand" (not to draw another card) for each possible set of conditions in the game. Ignoring the rules of the game itself, it is sufficient to know that by following basic, the average amount of the game is almost (but not quite) equal to the amount bet. That is, a player who follows basic strictly will lose only a very slight percentage of the amount bet over the long run (the appendix to this chapter contains the rules of blackjack and the rules of basic from Keren and Wagenaar, 1985). Violations of basic are costly because they reduce the expected amount of the game. Although basic is somewhat complicated, it is by no means impossible to memorize; most experienced blackjack players are familiar with it. Nevertheless, not many players consistently follow basic.

There are two ways in which basic may be violated — hitting when basic says stand and standing when basic says hit. It is important to realize that both of these violations reduce the odds of winning. However, if you hit when basic says stand, you will know sooner about the outcome. Either you will "bust" (the total value of your cards will be over 21) and you will lose immediately, or you will improve your hand and be more certain of winning. If you hit when you should stand, therefore, you buy immediacy of outcome for decreased odds of winning. If, on the other hand, you stand when you should hit, you buy delay of outcome for decreased odds of winning. By standing you will not find out whether you win or lose until the end of the game, after the dealer's hand is dealt.

According to Figure 10-4, a player can maximize the subjective present value of gains by choosing a smaller, more immediate win over a larger, more delayed win; a player can minimize the subjective present value of losses by choosing a larger, more delayed loss over a smaller, more immediate one. Thus, a blackjack player focusing on gains will tend to hit (even when basic says stand) because hitting increases the immediacy of the outcome. On the other hand, a blackjack player focusing on losses will tend to stand (even when basic says hit) because standing delays the outcome.

Keren and Wagenaar (1985) studied thousands of hit/stand decisions of blackjack players (mostly experienced) at a casino in Amsterdam and found that they very strongly tended to stand even when basic says hit. In terms of our analysis here, the Amsterdam players were more concerned about minimizing subjective losses than maximizing subjective winnings. By standing they were delaying the moment when they would lose.

Our own observations of blackjack players at a series of "Las Vegas nights" on Long Island confirmed that casino players do indeed have a strong tendency to stand when basic says hit. However, when we observed younger, less experienced players (Stony Brook undergraduates) at a series of blackjack sessions in the laboratory, we found just the opposite. These players tended to hit when basic would have told them to stand.

There were two fundamental differences between our laboratory players and casino ("Las Vegas night") players. First, the laboratory players were younger and less experienced than the casino players; second, the laboratory players were playing with money that we gave them while the casino players were playing with their own money. We do not yet know which of these two factors (or for sure whether either of them) was responsible for the strong difference between casino and laboratory gambling. Either factor could have caused laboratory players to value the maximization of subjective winnings over the minimization of subjective losses (hence preferring immediacy to delay, hence hitting when they should have stood) and the casino players to value the minimization of subjective losses to the maximization of subjective winnings (hence, preferring delay to immediacy, hence standing when they should have hit).

This experiment illustrates the major point of this book — that judgments, decisions, and choices of humans (and other animals as well) can be understood best as a single complex process in a broad context. Behaviorists and cognitivists are not studying two different things but the same thing from two different viewpoints.

FREEDOM AND PREDICTION OF BEHAVIOR

The issue of free will in a deterministic world cannot be treated adequately here; it deserves a book of its own. However, consider the following tentative conception of freedom: You are free to the extent that you can predict your own behavior better than other people can predict it. The prison warden can usually predict the prisoner's eating, sleeping, and recreation better than the prisoner can himself. To the extent that the warden is able to predict his own behavior — including his treatment of prisoners — the warden is free and the prisoner is not.

A person may gain freedom, as defined here, through self-knowledge. The prisoner will never be free with regard to the details of everyday life. However, in a higher sense — a sense acknowledged by philosophers from Plato's time to the present day — even a prisoner may be free. More abstract, more molar aspects of the prisoner's behavior may not be predictable by anyone but himself.

In a deterministic world, all behavior is controlled in some sense, and control can be measured only in terms of prediction. If one person controls the behavior of a second person and you want to predict the second person's behavior, you would have to observe the first person, not the second. Similarly, to predict the way a horse will go (to the extent that the rider controls the horse), you would have to observe or ask the rider, not the horse. When a government becomes despotic, the behavior of its citizens may be predicted (to the extent that the government exerts control) by observing the laws and regulations of the government or the actions and statements of the rulers. Accordingly, as a parent relinquishes control of a child's behavior, it becomes less and less possible to predict the child's choices by observing or asking the parent and more and more possible to predict the child's choices by observing or asking the child. At some point the child becomes better able to predict his or her behavior than any observer, whether a parent or not. At that point, the child may be said to be free.

Some people, suffering under the yoke of control by others, may seek freedom by behaving randomly, but at best randomness makes their behavior equally unpredictable to everyone. Random behavior would be a poor kind of freedom, a freedom based on *equality of ignorance.* The successful study of choice would result in a much greater degree of individual freedom—one based on *inequality of knowledge;* this would be freedom for people who know themselves. A society of independent people, all highly knowledgeable about human choice and each most familiar with his or her own history (therefore with the personal rules that guide their own choices), would be a "free society" in the best sense of that term.

NOTES

1. In both the delay experiment with pigeons and the probability experiment with human subjects, we varied the distance between X and the outcome (either Y or Z). In both cases, decreases of this distance led to a highly significant tendency to choose Y over Z. In the probability experiment, when the (probabilistic) distance between X and its outcome was reduced from $3/18$ (improbable) to $15/18$ (highly probable), the average preference for Z, the commitment alternative, shifted from .53 (a slight preference) to .18 (a strong aversion). Whether the probability–delay correspondence is merely an analogy between two different variables or whether the correspondence signifies some fundamental, underlying identity is still a matter of debate.

2. In this case past experience of the species as it interacted with its environment—rather than past experience of an individual animal—determines behavior.

3. We ignore an additional set of rules for counting cards that have been played. Card counting (estimating the good and bad cards left in the deck after each deal) is used mostly to adjust betting decisions. Here we are not interested in betting decisions; we assume that, for

whatever reasons, a player has already chosen to play blackjack, has already made a bet, and is now concerned with only one choice: the subsidiary decision of whether to "hit" or "stand."

APPENDIX: RULES OF BLACKJACK
(from Keren and Wagenaar, 1985)

A blackjack game has a dealer (representing the house) and from one to 7 players. Four ordinary 52-card decks are shuffled together and placed in a card-holding device called a shoe. A plastic card is inserted approximately three-quarters of the way through the shoe (i.e., after approximately three packs, or 156 cards). Whenever the plastic card is reached, all the cards are reshuffled before the game continues.

The players place all bets except "insurance" (discussed later) before any cards are dealt. Each casino establishes a minimum and maximum bet per box (each player has a box in which bets are placed). After bets have been placed, the dealer deals two cards to each player and a single card to the dealer (called the dealer's "up-card"), all cards being face up. The numerical value of each card is simply its face value except for the picture cards, all of which have a value of 10. The player can choose either 1 or 11 as the value of an ace. A hand containing an ace that can be counted as 11 without the total of the hand exceeding 21 is termed a "soft" hand (e.g., an ace and a six is called a "soft 17"). All other hands are termed hard hands.

The object of each player is to obtain a total greater than that of the dealer but not exceeding 21. If the first two cards dealt to either the player or the dealer consist of an ace and a 10-value card, they constitute a "blackjack" or "natural"; this is the best hand possible and beats any other hand, including any other combination of 21. The player who gets a blackjack wins 1.5 times his or her original bet unless the dealer also gets blackjack, in which case the game is considered a draw and no money changes hands.

After the initial cards have been dealt, the players have an opportunity to draw additional cards. Proceeding clockwise, each player in turn may either "stand" (draw no additional cards) or "hit" (request additional cards from the dealer). These extra cards are dealt face up, one at a time. If the player "busts," that is, if the total value of his or her hand exceeds 21, the bet is lost to the dealer, who then proceeds to the next player.

After all players have finished drawing cards, the dealer deals cards to the dealer's hand. As long as the dealer's total is 16 or less an additional card must be dealt. If the dealer's total is 17 or more, the dealer must stand. If the dealer busts (exceeds 21), all remaining players (those who did not bust) win an amount equal to their original bet. If neither dealer nor player busts, the dealer collects the bet of any player whose total is less than the dealer's total and pays an amount equal to the original bet to any player whose total exceeds the dealer's total. In a tie between dealer and player, no money changes hands.

Under certain circumstances, a player has three additional options:

Splitting pairs. If the first two cards dealt to a player are of the same denomination (e.g., two sixes or two queens), the player may split the pair, place the value of the original bet on each of the two new hands, and then proceed as usual, playing each hand separately.

Doubling. If the first two cards dealt to a player total 9, 10, or 11, the player has the option to "double down," in which case the initial bet is doubled and just one additional card is drawn.

Insurance. If the dealer's upcard (first card) is an ace, each player may place an additional side bet (not more than half the original bet) that the dealer will end up with a blackjack, that is, receive a 10 as second card. If the dealer does indeed receive a blackjack, the player wins twice the amount of the side bet. Otherwise, the side bet is lost to the dealer.

REFERENCES

Ainslie, G. 1975. Specious reward: A behavioral theory of impulse control. *Psychological Bulletin* 82: 463–496.

Allais, M. 1953. Le comportement de l'homme rationnel devant le risque: Critique des postulats et axiomes de l'école américaine. *Econometrica* 21: 503–546.

Allison, J. 1983. *Behavioral economics.* New York: Praeger.

Anderson, G., and Brown, R. I. F. 1984. Real and laboratory gambling, sensation seeking and arousal. *British Journal of Psychology* 75: 401–410.

Bar-Hillel, M. 1979. The role of sample size in sample evaluation. *Organizational Behavior and Human Performance* 24: 245–257.

Baron, A., and Galizio, M. 1983. Instructional control of human operant behavior. *Psychological Record* 33: 495–520.

Baum, W. M., and Rachlin, H. 1969. Choice as time allocation. *Journal of the Experimental Analysis of Behavior* 12: 861–874.

Beach, L. R., and Mitchell, T. R. 1978. A contingency model for the selection of decision strategies. *Academy of Management Review* 3: 439–449.

Becker, G. S. 1976. *The economic approach to human behavior.* Chicago: University of Chicago Press.

Bridgman, P. W. 1927. *The logic of modern physics.* New York: Macmillan.

Bruner, J. S.; Goodnow, J. J.; and Austin, G. A. 1956. *A study of thinking.* New York: Wiley.

Brunswik, E. 1943. Organismic achievement and environmental probability. *Psychological Review* 50: 255–272.

Brunswik, E. 1952. The conceptual framework of psychology. In *International Encyclopedia of Unified Science.* Vol. 1, no. 10. Chicago: University of Chicago Press.

Calvino, I. 1988. *Six memos for the next millenium.* Cambridge, Mass.: Harvard University Press.

Catania, A. C., and Reynolds, G. S. 1968. A quantitative analysis of the responding maintained by interval schedules of reinforcement. *Journal of the Experimental Analysis of Behavior* 11: 327–383.

Cohen, L. J. 1981. Can human irrationality be experimentally demonstrated? *The Behavioral and Brain Sciences* 4: 317–370.

Collier, G. H.; Johnson, D. F.; Hill, W. L.; and Kaufman, L. W. 1986. The economics of the law of effect. *Journal of the Experimental Analysis of Behavior* 46: 113–136.

Commons, M. L.; Mazur, J. E.; Nevin, J. A.; and Rachlin, H. 1987. *Quantitative analysis of behavior. Vol. 5, The effects of delay.* Cambridge, Mass.: Ballinger.

Cotton, J. W. 1953. Running time as a function of amount of food deprivation. *Journal of Experimental Psychology* 46: 188–198.

Davison, M. 1988. Concurrent schedules: Interaction of reinforcer frequency and reinforcer duration. *Journal of the Experimental Analysis of Behavior* 49: 339–350.

Dennett, D. 1978. *Brainstorms.* Montgomery, Vt.: Bradford Books.

de Villiers, P. 1977. Choice in concurrent schedules and a quantitative formulation of the law of effect. In W. K. Honig and J. E. R. Staddon (Eds.), *Handbook of operant behavior.* Englewood Cliffs, N.J.: Prentice-Hall.

Duncan, B., and Fantino, E. 1970. Choice for periodic schedules of reinforcement. *Journal of the Experimental Analysis of Behavior* 14: 73–86.

Ebbesen, E. B., and Konečni, J. J. 1975. Decision making and information integration in the courts: The settling of bail. *Journal of Personality and Social Psychology* 32: 805–821.

Ebbeson, E. B., and Konečni, V. J. 1980. On the external validity of decision-making research: What do we know about decisions in the real world? In T. S. Wallsten (Ed.), *Cognitive processes in choice and decision behavior.* Hillsdale, N.J.: Erlbaum.

Eddy, D. M. 1982. Probabilistic reasoning in clinical medicine: Problems and opportunities. In D. Kahneman, P. Slovic, and A. Tversky (Eds.), *Judgment under uncertainty: heuristics and biases.* New York: Cambridge University Press.

Einhorn, H. J. 1980. Learning from experience and suboptimal rules in decision making. In T. S. Wallsten (Ed.), *Cognitive processes in choice and decision behavior.* Hillsdale, N.J.: Erlbaum.

Ericsson, A. K., and Simon, H. A. 1984. *Protocol analysis: Verbal reports as data.* Cambridge, Mass.: MIT Press.

Fantino, E., and Abarca, N. 1985. Choice, optimal foraging, and the delay-reduction hypothesis. *The Behavioral and Brain Sciences* 8: 315–329.

Fantino, E. and Davison, M. 1983. Choice: Some quantitative relations. *Journal of the Experimental Analysis of Behavior* 40: 1–13.

Freud, S. [1900] 1960. *The psychopathology of everyday life.* Vol. 6, Standard edition. London: Hogarth.

Gibbon, J. 1977. Scalar expectancy and Weber's law in animal timing. *Psychological Review* 84: 279–325.

Gilbert, T. F. 1958. The fundamental dimensional properties of the operant. *Psychological Review* 65: 272–285.

Ginossar, Z., and Trope, Y. 1987. Problem solving in judgment under uncertainty. *Journal of Personality and Social Psychology* 52: 464–474.

Gleick, J. 1987. *Chaos: making a new science.* New York: Viking.

Green, L.; Kagel, J. H.; and Battalio, R. C. 1982. Ratio schedules of reinforcement and their relationship to economic theories of labor supply. In M. Commons, R. J. Herrnstein, and H. Rachlin (Eds.), *Quantitative analysis of behavior.* Vol. 2. Cambridge, Mass.: Ballinger.

Grether, D. M., and Plott, C. R. 1979. Economic theory of choice and the preference reversal phenomenon. *American Economic Review* 69: 623–638.

Grosch, J., and Neuringer, A. 1981. Self-control in pigeons under the Mischel paradigm. *Journal of the Experimental Analysis of Behavior* 35: 3–22.

Hawkins, R. D., and Kandell, E. R. 1984. Is there a cell-biological alphabet for simple forms of learning? *Psychological Review* 91: 375–391.

Hayes, S. C. 1986. The case of the silent dog—verbal reports and the analysis of rules: A review of Ericsson and Simon's *Protocol analysis: verbal reports as data. Journal of the Experimental Analysis of Behavior* 45: 351–363.

Hayes, S. C.; Brownstein, A. J.; Haar, J. R.; and Greenway, D. E. 1986. Instructions, multiple schedules, and extinction: Distinguishing rule-governed from schedule-controlled behavior. *Journal of the Experimental Analysis of Behavior* 46: 137–148.

Helson, H. 1958. The theory of adaptation level. In D. C. Beardslee and M. Wertheimer (Eds.), *Readings in perception.* New York: Van Nostrand.

Herrnstein, R. J. 1961. Relative and absolute strength of response as a function of frequency of reinforcement. *Journal of the Experimental Analysis of Behavior* 4: 267–272.

Herrnstein, R. J. 1970. On the law of effect. *Journal of the Experimental Analysis of Behavior* 13: 243–266.

Herrnstein, R. J., and Boring, G. G., eds. 1965. *A source book in the history of psychology.* Cambridge, Mass.: Harvard University Press.

Herrnstein, R. J., and Loveland, D. H. 1975. Maximizing and matching on concurrent ratio schedules. *Journal of the Experimental Analysis of Behavior* 24: 107–116.

Herrnstein, R. J., and Vaughan, W., Jr. 1980. Melioration and behavioral allocation. In J. E. R. Staddon (Ed.), *Limits to action: the allocation of individual behavior.* New York: Academic Press.

Houston, A. I., and McFarland, D. J. 1980. Behavioral resilience and its relation to demand functions. In J. E. R. Staddon (Ed.), *Limits to action: the allocation of individual behavior*. New York: Academic Press.

Hull, C. L. 1943. *Principles of behavior: an introduction to behavior theory*. New York: Appleton-Century-Crofts.

Hursh, S. R. 1984. Behavioral economics. *Journal of the Experimental Analysis of Behavior* 42: 435–452.

Johnson-Laird, P. N.; Legrenzi, P.; and Sonino-Legrenzi, M. 1972. Reasoning and a sense of reality. *British Journal of Psychology* 63: 395–400.

Kahneman, D., and Tversky, A. 1972. Subjective probability: A judgment of representativeness. *Cognitive Psychology* 3: 430–454.

Kahneman, D., and Tversky, A. 1973. On the psychology of prediction. *Psychological Review* 80: 237–251.

Kahneman, D., and Tversky, A. 1979. Prospect theory: An analysis of decisions under risk. *Econometrica* 47: 263–291.

Kantor, J. R. 1963. *The scientific evolution of psychology*. Vol. 1. Chicago: Principia Press.

Keren, G., and Wagenaar, W. A. 1985. On the psychology of playing blackjack: Normative and descriptive considerations with implications for decision theory. *Journal of Experimental Psychology: General* 114: 133–158.

Keren, G., and Wagenaar, W. A. 1987. Violation of utility theory in unique and repeated gambles. *Journal of Experimental Psychology: Learning, Memory and Cognition* 13: 387–391.

Koffka, K. 1931. *The growth of the mind*. New York: Harcourt, Brace.

Lacey, H. M., and Rachlin, H. 1978. Behavior, cognition and theories of choice. *Behaviorism* 6: 177–202.

Lambert, J. V.; Bersch, P. J.; Hineline, P. M.; and Smith, G. D. 1973. Avoidance conditioning with shock contigent upon the avoidance response. *Journal of the Experimental Analysis of Behavior* 19: 361–367.

Lea, S. E. G. 1978. The psychology and economics of demand. *Psychological Bulletin* 85: 441–466.

Lea, S. E. G., Tarpy, R. M. and Webley, P. 1987. *The individual in the economy*. Cambridge: Cambridge University Press.

Lichtenstein, S., and Slovic, P. 1971. Reversals of preference between bids and choices in gambling decisions. *Journal of Experimental Psychology* 89: 46–55.

Logue, A. W.; Rodriguez, M. L.; Peña-Correal, T.; and Mauro, B. 1984. Choice in a self-control paradigm: Quantification of experience-based differences. *Journal of the Experimental Analysis of Behavior* 41: 53–69.

Logue, A. W.; Smith, M. E.; and Rachlin, H. 1985. Sensitivity of pigeons to prereinforcer and postreinforcer delay. *Animal Learning and Behavior* 13: 181–186.

Lubinski, D., and MacCorquodale, K. 1984- "Symbolic communication" between two pigeons without unconditioned reinforcement. *Journal of Comparative Psychology* 98: 372–380.

Lucas, J. R. 1970. *The concept of probability.* Oxford: Clarendon Press.

Luce, R. D. 1959. *Individual choice behavior.* New York: Wiley.

Luchins, A. S. 1942. Mechanization in problem solving: The effect of Einstellung. *Psychological Monographs* 54 no. 248.

Machina, M. 1987. Decision-making in the presence of risk. *Science* 236: 537–542.

McNamara, J. M. and Houston, A. I. 1982. Short-term behavior and lifetime fitness. In D. J. McFarland (Ed.), *Functional ontogeny.* London: Pitman.

Mazur, J. E. 1986. Choice between single and multiple delayed reinforcers. *Journal of the Experimental Analysis of Behavior* 46: 67–78.

Mazur, J. E., and Logue, A. W. 1978. Choice in a "self-control" paradigm: Effects of a fading procedure. *Journal of the Experimental Analysis of Behavior* 30: 11–18.

Milgram, S. 1963. Behavioral study of obedience. *Journal of Abnormal and Social Psychology* 67: 371–378.

Mill, J. S. 1874. *A system of logic, ratiocinative and inductive, being a connected view of the principles of evidence, and the methods of scientific investigation.* 8th ed. New York: Harper & Row.

Miller, A. G.; Gillen, B.; Schenker, C.; and Redlove, S. 1973. Perception of obedience to authority. *Proceedings of the 81st Annual Convention of the American Psychological Association* 8: 127–128.

Mischel, W. 1984. Convergences and challenges in the search for consistency. *American Psychologist* 39: 351–364.

Mischel, W., and Baker, N. 1975. Cognitive transformations of reward objects through instructions. *Journal of Personality and Social Psychology* 31: 254–261.

Mischel, W., and Grusec, J. 1967. Waiting for rewards and punishments: Effects of time and probability on choice. *Journal of Personality and Social Psychology* 5: 24–31.

Neuringer, A. 1986. Can people behave "randomly"?: The role of feedback. *Journal of Experimental Psychology: General* 115: 62–75.

Nevin, J. A., and Baum, W. M. 1980. Feedback functions for variable-interval reinforcement. *Journal of the Experimental Analysis of Behavior* 34: 207–218.

Nisbett, R. E.; Borgida, E.; Crandall, R.; and Reed, H. 1976. Popular induction: Information is not necessarily informative. In J. S. Carrol and J. W. Payne (Eds.), *Cognition and social behavior.* Hillsdale, N.J.: Erlbaum.

Nisbett, R. E., and Wilson, T. D. 1977. Telling more than we can know: Verbal reports on mental processes. *Psychological Review* 84: 231–259.

Northcraft, G. B., and Wolf, G. 1984. Dollars, sense, and sunk costs: A life cycle model of resource allocation decisions. *Academy of Management Review* 9: 225–234.

Pavlov, I. P. 1927. *Conditioned reflexes.* Translated by G. V. Anrep. London: Oxford University Press.

Payne, J. W. 1980. Information processing theory: Some concepts and methods applied to decision research. In T. S. Wallsten (Ed.), *Cognitive processes in choice and decision behavior.* Hillsdale, N.J.: Erlbaum.

Pettigrew, J. 1979. The ultimate attribution theory: Extending Allport's cognitive analysis of prejudice. *Personality and Social Psychology Bulletin* 5: 461–476.

Pitz, G. F. 1977. Decision making and cognition. In H. Jungerman and G. deZeeuw (Eds.), *Decision making and change in human affairs.* Dordrecht, Holland: Reidel.

Plato 1961. *The collected dialogues.* Edited by E. Hamilton & H. Cairnes. Princeton, N.J.: Princeton University Press.

Premack, D. 1965. Reinforcement theory. In D. Levine (Ed.), *Nebraska symposium on motivation: 1965.* Lincoln: University of Nebraska Press.

Premack, D. 1971. Catching up with common sense or two sides of a generalization: Reinforcement and punishment. In R. Glaser (Ed.), *The nature of reinforcement.* New York: Academic Press.

Pyke, G. H.; Pulliam, H. R.; and Charnov, E. L. 1977. Optimal foraging: A selective review of theory and tests. *Quarterly Review of Biology* 52: 137–154.

Rachlin, H. 1978. A molar theory of reinforcement schedules. *Journal of the Experimental Analysis of Behavior* 30: 345–360.

Rachlin, H. 1985. Maximization theory and Plato's concept of the Good. *Behaviorism* 13: 3–20.

Rachlin, H. C., and Baum, W. 1972. Effects of alternative reinforcement: Does the source matter? *Journal of the Experimental Analysis of Behavior* 18: 231–241.

Rachlin, H., and Burkhard, B. 1978. The temporal triangle: Response substitution in instrumental conditioning. *Psychological Review* 85: 22–48.

Rachlin, H.; Castrogiovanni, A.; and Cross, D. V. 1987. Probability and delay in commitment. *Journal of the Experimental Analysis of Behavior* 48: 347–354.

Rachlin, H., and Green, L. 1972. Commitment, choice and self-control. *Journal of the Experimental Analysis of Behavior* 17: 15–22.

Rachlin, H.; Green, L.; Kagel, J. H.; and Battalio, R. C. 1976. Economic demand theory and psychological studies of choice. In G. Bower (Ed.), *The Psychology of Learning and Motivation.* Vol. 10. New York: Academic Press.

Rapoport, A., and Chammah, A. M. 1965. *Prisoner's dilemma.* Ann Arbor: University of Michigan Press.

Rescorla, R. 1967. Pavlovian conditioning and its proper control procedures. *Psychological Review* 74: 71–80.

Rotter, J. B. 1954. *Social learning and clinical psychology.* Englewood Cliffs, N.J.: Prentice-Hall.

Russo, J. E., and Rosen, L. D. 1975. An eye fixation analysis of multialternative choice. *Memory and Cognition* 3: 267–276.

Ryle, G. 1949. *The concept of mind.* London: Hutchinson House.

Samuelson, P. A. 1973. *Economics: An introductory analysis.* 9th ed. New York: McGraw-Hill.

Savage, L. J. 1954. *The foundations of statistics.* New York: Wiley.

Savage-Rumbaugh, S.; Rumbaugh, D. M.; and Boysen, S. Linguistically mediated tool use and exchange by chimpanzees. *The Behavioral and Brain Sciences* 1: 539–554.

Silby, R., and McFarland, D. 1976. On the fitness of behavior sequences. *American Naturalist* 110: 601–617.

Simon, H. A. 1978. Information-processing theory of human problem solving. In W. K. Estes (Ed.), *Handbook of learning and cognitive processes.* Vol. 5. Hillsdale, N.J.: Erlbaum.

Skinner, B. F. 1938. *The behavior of organisms: An experimental analysis.* New York: Appleton-Century-Crofts.

Skinner, B. F. 1975. *Verbal behavior.* New York: Appleton-Century-Crofts.

Skinner, B. F. In press. Rules and behavior. In S. C. Hayes (Ed.), *Rule-governed behavior: Cognition, contingencies, and instructional control.* New York: Plenum Press.

Slovic, P., and Tversky, A. 1974. Who accepts Savage's axiom? *Behavioral Science* 19: 368–373.

Sober, E. 1984. *The nature of selection: Evolutionary theory in philosophical focus.* Cambridge, Mass.: MIT Press.

Solomon, R. L., and Wynne L. C. 1954. Traumatic avoidance learning: The principles of anxiety conservation and partial irreversibility. *Psychological Review* 61: 353–385.

Staddon, J. E. R. 1980. Optimality analyses of operant behavior and their relation to optimal foraging. In J. E. R. Staddon (Ed.), *Limits to action: The allocation of individual behavior.* New York: Academic Press.

Staddon, J. E. R., and Simmelhag, V. L. 1971. The "superstition" experiment: A reexamination of its implications for the principles of adaptive behavior. *Psychological Review* 78: 16–43.

Stevens, S. S. 1957. On the psychophysical law. *Psychological Review* 64: 153–181.

Stigler, G. J., and Becker, G. S. 1977. De gustibus non est disputandum. *The American Economic Review* 67: 76–90.

Thorndike, E. L. 1911. *Animal intelligence.* New York: Macmillan.

Thorndike, E. L., and Woodworth, R. S. 1901. The influence of improvement in one mental function upon the efficiency of other functions. *Psychological Review* 8: 247–261.

Tinklepaugh, O. L. 1928. An experimental study of representative factors in monkeys. *Journal of Comparative Psychology* 8: 197–236.

Tolman, E. C. 1938. The determiners of behavior at a choice point. *Psychological Review* 45: 1–41.

Tversky, A. 1972. Elimination by aspects: A theory of choice. *Psychological Review* 79: 281–299.

Tversky, A. 1977. Features of similarity. *Psychological Review* 84: 327–352.

Tversky, A., and Kahneman, D. 1974. Judgment under uncertainty: Heuristics and biases. *Science* 185: 1124–1131.

Tversky, A., and Kahneman, D. 1981. The framing of decisions and the rationality of choice. *Science* 211: 453–458.

Tversky, A., and Kahneman, D. 1982. Evidential impact of base rates. In D. Kahneman, P. Slovic, and A. Tversky (Eds.), *Judgment under uncertainty: Heuristics and biases.* New York: Cambridge University Press.

Tversky, A., Sattath, S., and Slovic, P. 1988. Contingent weighting in judgment and choice. *Psychological Review* 95: 371–384.

von Neumann, J., and Morgenstern, O. 1944. *Theory of games and economic behavior.* Princeton, N.J.: Princeton University Press.

Wason, P. C. 1966. Reasoning. In B. Foss (Ed.), *New horizons in psychology.* Middlesex, England: Penguin.

Watson, J. B. 1913. Psychology as a behaviorist views it. *Psychological Review* 20: 158–177.

Wittgenstein, L. 1958. *Philosophical investigations:* 3rd ed. New York: Macmillan.

Yourgrau, W., and Mandelstam, S. 1968. *Variational principles in dynamics and quantum theory.* New York: Dover.

INDEX